Re-Thinking Reason

SUNY Series, Teacher Empowerment and School Reform

Henry A. Giroux and Peter L. McLaren, Editors

Re-Thinking Reason

New Perspectives in Critical Thinking

Edited by
Kerry S. Walters

State University of New York Press

Published by
State University of New York Press, Albany

For information, address State University of New York Press,
State University Plaza, Albany, N.Y. 12246

Production by M. R. Mulholland
Marketing by Fran Keneston

Library of Congress Cataloging–in–Publication Data

Re-thinking reason : new perspectives in critical thinking / edited by
    Kerry S. Walters.
        p.   cm. — (SUNY series, teacher empowerment and school
    reform)
        Includes bibliographical references and index.
        ISBN 0-7914-2095-7 (alk. paper). — ISBN 0-7914-2096-5 (pbk. :
    alk. paper)
        1. Critical thinking—Study and teaching (Higher)   2. Reasoning—
    Study and teaching (Higher)   I. Walters, Kerry S.   II. Series:
    Teacher empowerment and school reform.
    LB2390.35.R4   1994
    378.1'7—dc20   93-42902
                                                                                CIP

10 9 8 7 6 5 4 3 2 1

For June, Ike, and Patt
and for Jonah Isaac,
who truly brings me peace and laughter

Contents

Foreword:
Critical Thinking as a Political Project

The present volume assembled and introduced by Kerry S. Walters marks an important moment in the debates surrounding critical thinking. As someone who approaches critical thinking from the standpoint of epistemology of critical pedagogy (i.e., an epistemology that locates the construction of meaning historically within competing discourses that occupy relations inscribed by race, class, and gender interests), I admire Kerry Walters' attempt to give voice to what he calls a "second wave" in critical thinking research and pedagogy. In an examplary introduction, Walters criticizes the logistically reductive ploy by "first wave" critical thinkers of collapsing critical thinking into propositional expression or the heady calculus of formal, objective argumentation that all too often functions as a trompe d'oeil whereby creativity and the imagination are construed as antithetical to good thinking. Kerry essentially locates the problem of "first wave" mainstream analyses of critical thinking and the pedagogical applications often fashioned there (Edward Glaser, Robert Ennis, and Harvey Siegel are singled out as major culprits) as consisting of an unjustifiable and at times dangerous veneration of rationality and the normative methodological standards of universality, objectivity, and abstraction. This can only lead, notes Kerry, to totalization, desubjectification, and decontextualiztion.

The sanctification of inferential procedures rules out the more creative modes of intelligibility, empathy, visceral or bodily knowledge (my own preferred term is "enfleshment"), and an understanding of and tolerance for contingency and ambiguity. But Kerry does not simply recognize that critical thinking is more than the inexorable workings of deterministic and impersonal formulae or an ensemble of instituted procedures. While recognizing that unpredictability is always already a characteristic of epistemology, a characteristic that models the ontological openness of physical systems, he is intent on establishing the important fact that thinking is intrinsically unisolatable. In other words, thinking is not detachable from the contexts in which such activity occurs. At the same time that the first wave critical thinkers strive to institutionalize their closed system of discourse, they unwittingly remake the relations of power that result from the erroneous assumption that knowledge is impartial, neutral and, apolitical.

In a bold but conceptionally inevitable move, Kerry seeks to give impetus to nonanalytic, imaginative, and contextual ways of thinking, ways of thinking that take into account the ideological situatedness of the thinker herself. Foregrounding the politics of location from which all thinkers (wittingly or unwittingly) enunciate their ideas is a move gaining legitimacy in more progressive stands of postmodern social theory where the need for metadiscursive and contextual styles of discourse has been recognized along with a respect for the specificity and particularity of the object under investigation. All thinking takes place somewhere, and second wave critical thinkers explode the myth that meaning can be understood in antiseptic isolation from larger discourses of power and privilege. All sign systems that serve as vehicles (or perhaps even 'performances') of meaning are populated by prior meanings. Linguistic systems and discourse themselves are, after all, the product of historical struggles over signs and could in fact be described as the outcomes of wars of intellectual and material position. This does not mean, of course, that all second wave theorists identified by Walters constitute a unitary and homogenous movement since, Mark Weinstein has so presciently pointed out, critical thinking (even among some second wave proponents), still "assumes procedures and prin-ciples of reasoning and logic that transcend the particularity of forms of discourse" (1993, p. 101). Weinstein rightly notes that such an oversight leaves out advances made by feminists, social constructionists, and postmodernists.

While critical thinking and critical pedagogy both share a common adjective, their differences are apparent upon consideration of their historical trajectories, conceptual traditions and ethical and political underpinnings. Both educational projects invite tireless confusion with each other as they are more frequently than not discussed conjointly as synonymous or at least close relatives. With its roots in critical social theory and its emphasis on intellectual labor in the service of race, gender, and class equality, critical pedagogy has produced a generation of critical thinkers who have found it difficult to enter into a sustained dialogue with advocates of critical thinking whom they claim fail to take seriously key criticalist assumptions: that knowledge is not preonto-logically stored in nature's archive waiting to be discovered by the thinker with the right formulae but rather is fundamentally mediated by the language of analysis adopted by the thinker; that all theoretical and philosophical discourses are constituted within relations of power, which are informed by history and culture; that logical facts can never be isolated from the domain of values or removed from forms of ideological inscription; that the relationship between object and concept and object and signifier and signified is never stable or fixed and is often mediated by the social relations of capitalist production and consumption; that language is central to the formation of subjectivity (conscious and unconscious awareness); that certain groups in any society are privileged over others and while the reasons for the privileging may vary widely, the subordination and superordination that characterizes contemporary societies is most forcefully reproduced when subordinates accept their social status as natural, necessary, or inevitable; that oppression has many faces and that focusing on only one at the expense of others (e.g., class oppression vs. racism) often eludes the interconnection among them; and that mainstream research and teaching and thinking practices are generally, although most often unwittingly, implicated in the reproduction of systems of class, race, and gender oppression (Kincheloe and McLaren, in press).

In short, all forms and types of thinking represent social practices and therefore all thinking has the power to both influence and inform social, cultural, and political formations. What types of ideological and political affiliations are associated with certain strands of critical thinking? Given that critical pedagogy is directed at disrupting the hegemony of white supremacist and capitalist cultures, in particular, our own; and given that critical pedagogy fundamentally requires a transdisciplinary mode of inquiry, it is not surprising that criticalists have often found the first wave of critical thinkers to be unwitting agents in the reproduction of existing relations of power, regardless of the "good intentions" such agents may express.

Many criticalists reject the concept of experience as either transparently reflective of social life or as always already given through socially constructed signs and systems of representation. Rather, experience mediates between what we see and how our perceptions have been disciplined for us through social, cultural, political, and institutional determinations. Individuals have shifting determinations. While on the one hand individuals are more than the capricious effects of discourse (as some poststructuralists maintain) preconstructed by the discourse of consumer capitalism, they cannot, on the other hand, simply be reduced to autoconstitutive subjects of the unitary, rational, Cartesian subject. Rather, subjects are situated in discursive formations that select, integrate, and position enunciative fields in ways that are

historically and socially specific (Thibault, 1991). According to expo-
nents of critical pedagogy, critical thinking must take into serious consideration how human agency and the capacity to affect social change
can be realized in a world of material and discursive constraints (Giroux
and McLaren, 1993). Critical pedagogy implicates historical agency in
discursive will formation. In other words, critical thinking is involved in
both forms of self-fashioning and the transformation of the oppressive
social conditions in which human desire is produced. Critical pedagogy
does not, for instance, simply want to enlist critical thinking into the
service of transnational corporations and the logic of consumption and
the exploitation of economic and political conditions among less
developed nations. Rather, critical pedagogy attempts to link critical
thinking to both local and global projects of social transformation and
social justice.

From the perspective of critical pedagogy, mainstream forms of
critical thinking as part of the educative process have traditionally
attempted to prepare individuals for deliberation and debate in public
spheres, such as schools, churches, and government institutions. But
what happens when changes occur within these public spheres? What
happens when new modalities of social integration appear within the
context of our postmodern condition such that individuals and groups
are constructed through technocratic and consumer society mechanisms
leading to patterns of nonreciprocal recognition? Certainly critical
thinking takes place within such a milieu, and it is not surprising to learn
that first wave thinkers have derisively dismissed the criticalists who
argue that all theoretical traditions must be held accountable for their
role in the struggle for social justice.

It is to Kerry Walters' credit that *Re-thinking Reason* builds a formid-
able bridge that joins the fields of critical pedagogy and critical thinking.
I want to make clear that this bridge is not a one-way thoroughfare. It is
not just critical pedagogy that will be transported across the bridge to
enhance the field of critical thinking. Much in the realm of critical
thinking will be concomitantly used to deepen and add refinement to the
project of critical pedagogy.

Within Walters' "second wave" of critical thinkers I believe there
exist what might be called potentialities that point to what could tenta-
tively be referred to as a "third wave." These third wave potentialities
speak to critical pedagogy's concern with reasoning as a sociopolitical
practice (see Giroux, Warren in this volume). I believe there is a difference between the second wave liberal humanist assertion that critical
thinking be understood contextually (a position that does not sufficiently

situate critical thinkers in relationship to their own complicity in relations of domination and oppression) and the criticalist assertion that
one's intellectual labor must be understood ethicopolitically in the
context of a particular political project. Third wave thinkers assume
such a criticalist position.

This nascent "third wave" does not presume to reflexively know
what understanding is but attempts to move beyond both the linguistic
idealism of and functional totality propagated by analytical philosophy
and its emplacing logics. In so doing, third wave critical thinkers link
meaning to an understanding not simply of propositional logic but of the
role that language itself plays in the construction of meaning and
subjectivity. This is a decidedly "postmodern" wave. To view such
antifoundationalism as a hasty adoption of untenable assumptions
about thinking (a perspective that I'm sure reflects the position of most
first wave and some second wave thinkers) would be a mistake because
the third wave postmodern critique of representation uncovers the
political function of philosophical rhetoric and asserts that representations are constitutive of the truth that they supposedly reflect.
Contingency in the form of symbolization and metaphor and paradox
deforms the literal character of everday necessity (Laclau and Mouffe,
1985, p. 114).

Critical thinkers need to address the role of contingency in the
politics of theory as well as recognize that there is no thinking outside of
a politics of representation. We cannot call thinking 'critical' and then
ignore the terms and conditions of its discursive, ethical, and textual
address. This is a point that *Re-thinking Reason* makes eminently clear.
This is not to say that critical thinkers need to be indifferent to questions
of logical consistency or verifiability but that they must effectively
undermine the logic of identity so central to the entrenchment of
logocentric reasoning. Critical thinking needs to develop itself to the
point at which it is able to contest the epistemological closure of the so-
called "objectivity" and "scientificity" of mainstream approaches to
thinking and pedagogy. In doing so, it will be able to move from the
politically and ethically sterile preoccupation with explanation to a
concern with understanding in the context of developing a pedagogy
and politics of social justice. As *Re-thinking Reason* reminds us, this is not
a position that vitiates the objectivity of knowledge but rather
underscores its insinuation in human interest and social power. Here,
the emphasis is not on the procedural characteristics of the thinking
process but on the social effects that follow from such thinking. In light
of such an emphasis, critical thinkers need to strengthen the link

between thinking as a project of empowerment and a reorganization of human will and desire not only in the service of self-knowledge and new forms of self-scrutiny and self-fashioning but also in the struggle for social transformation.

Since all forms of critical thinking are attached to certain social, political, and institutional conventions, approaches to critical thinking will never be exhaustive. We will never be able to fully override the social forces that help shape the direction of our desire—regardless of the approach to critical reasoning that we engage—but that should not provide us with an excuse to ignore how such forces are implicated in the magnificent array of discursive resistances to such forces that we witness in the lives of progressive students and their teachers, as well as artists, social activists, revolutionaires, and other cultural workers whom Gramsci called "organic intellectuals." We need to expand our criteria of what counts as critical in critical thinking and this means not giving up the concept of truth as regulative ideal. But it does suggest that there should be more than one such ideal.

Re-thinking Reason is committed to expanding the parameters of the debate over critical thinking. It is a book that also undeniably enhances and refines the central categories of this debate. The critique that *Re-thinking Reason* mounts against a unitary or single approach to critical thinking and its principled commitment to the necessity of heterogeneity expands the dimensions of the conflicts within the politics of reason, increases our awareness of what is morally and politically at stake in the debate over critical reasoning, and deepens the significance of the history of thinking about thinking in educational contexts. The results are not only timely and illuminating but also urgently important if we are to take seriously our commitment as educators to explore the productive possibilities of reasoning in the context of a struggle for social and cultural justice.

Peter L. McLaren
University of California, Los Angeles

References

Giroux, Henry , and McLaren, Peter (Eds.). (1993). *Between Borders*. New York and London: Routledge.

Kincheloe, Joe, and McLaren, Peter. (in press). "You can't get to the emerald city from here: Rethinking critical theory and qualitative research." In Norman K. Denzin and Yvonna S. Lincoln (Eds.) *Handbook of Qualitative Research.* Newbury Park, Calif.: Sage Publications.

Laclau, Ernesto, and Mouffe, Chantal. (1985). *Hegemony and Socialist Strategy: Towards a Radical Democratic Politics.* London: Verso.

McLaren, Peter. (1993). *Life in Schools: An Introduction to Critical Pedagogy in the Social Foundations of Education.* 2nd edition. New York: Longman.

McLaren, Peter and Lankshear, Colin (Eds.). (1993). *Politics of Liberation: Paths from Freire.* London and New York: Routledge.

McLaren, Peter and Leonard, Peter (Eds.). (1993). *Paulo Freire: A Critical Encounter.* London and New York: Routledge.

Thibault, Paul J. (1991). *Social Semiotics as Praxis.* Minneapolis: University of Minnesota Press.

Weinstein, Mark. (1993). "Critical thinking: The great debate." *Educational Theory* 43:1, 99–117.

Acknowledgments

Peter Elbow, "Teaching Two Kinds of Thinking by Teaching Writing," from *Change: The Magazine of Higher Learning* 15 (1983): 37–40. Reprinted with permission of publisher.

Blythe McVicker Clinchy, "On Critical Thinking and Connected Knowing," from *Liberal Education* 75 (1989): 14–19. Reprinted with permission of publisher.

Delores Gallo, "Educating for Empathy, Reason, and Imagination," from *Journal of Creative Behavior* 23 (1989): 98–115. Reprinted with permission of publisher.

Kerry S. Walters, "Critical Thinking, Rationality, and the Vulcanization of Students," from *Journal of Higher Education* 61 (1990): 448–67. Reprinted with permission of publisher.

Anne M. Phelan and James W. Garrison, "Toward a Gender-Sensitive Ideal of Critical Thinking: A Feminist Poetic," from *Curriculum Inquiry*, 24 (1994). Reprinted with permission of publisher.

John E. McPeck, "Critical Thinking and the 'Trivial Pursuit' Theory of Knowledge," from *Teaching Philosophy* 8 (1985): 295–308. Reprinted with permission of publisher.

Connie Missimer, "Why Two Heads Are Better Than One: Philosophical and Pedagogical Implications of a Social View of Critical Thinking," from *Philosophy of Education. Proceedings* (1988): 288–302. Reprinted with permission of publisher.

Karl Hostetler, "Community and Neutrality in Critical Thought: A Non-objectivist view on the Conduct and Teaching of Critical Thinking," from *Educational Theory* 41 (1991): 1–12. Reprinted with permission of publisher.

Karen J. Warren, "Critical Thinking and Feminism," from *Informal Logic* 10 (1988): 31–44. Reprinted with permission of publisher.

Richard W. Paul, "Teaching Critical Thinking in the Strong Sense: A Focus on Self-Deception, World Views, and a Dialectical Mode of Analysis," Revised Version. Original appeared in *Informal Logic* 4 (1982): 2–7. Reprinted with permission of author and publisher.

Henry A. Giroux, "Toward a Pedagogy of Critical Thinking," from *Teachers as Intellectuals: Toward a Critical Pedagogy of Learning*. Bergin & Garvey, 1988, pp. 60–65. Reprinted with permission of publisher.

Laura Duhan Kaplan, "Teaching Intellectual Autonomy: The Failure of the Critical Thinking Movement," from *Educational Theory* 41 (1991): 361–70. Reprinted with permission of publisher.

Thomas H. Warren, "Critical Thinking Beyond Reasoning: Restoring Virtue to Thought," from *Philosophy of Education. Proceedings* (1988): 201–9. Reprinted with permission of publisher.

Lenore Langsdorf, "Is Critical Thinking a Technique, or a Means of Enlightenment?" from *Informal Logic* 8 (1986): 1–17. Reprinted with permission of the publisher.

Introduction:
Beyond Logicism in Critical Thinking

Kerry S. Walters

What does it mean to think well? What's the most effective way to teach students the basics of "good thinking"?[1] These two questions are important ones that have especially preoccupied the academy for the last two decades. But they are even more pressing today, because conventionally accepted answers to them are now being called into question by dissenting voices from philosophy, psychology, education, feminist theory, and critical pedagogy. As a consequence of this multidisciplinary challenge, received ways of envisioning "critical thinking," as the theory and pedagogy of thinking skills are generally called, are evolving in new and promising directions. The essays collected in this volume, written by scholars from education, the humanities, and the social sciences, defend perspectives on the cutting edge of this transition. They represent a "second wave" in critical thinking research and pedagogy that should be of interest to present and future teachers, from any discipline and at any instructional level, who worry about how best to encourage thinking skills in students. Although the essays are primarily concerned to examine, challenge, and reformulate conventional theoretical accounts of the foundations and nature of critical thinking, they do not sacrifice pedagogy for theory. Almost all of them either explicitly discuss concrete pedagogical applications of second wave critical thinking or suggest directions in which such a pedagogy might go.

Each of the authors here takes exception to what may be described as the "logicistic" bent of the critical thinking model currently ensconced in colleges and universities. By "logicism," I mean *the unwarranted assumption that good thinking is reducible to logical thinking*. A logicistic approach to critical thinking conveys the message to students that thinking is legitimate only when it conforms to the procedures of informal (and, to a lesser extent, formal) logic and that the good thinker necessarily aims for styles of examination and appraisal that are analytical, abstract, universal, and objective. This model of thinking has become so entrenched in conventional academic wisdom that many educators accept it as canon.

In contrast to the logicistic model, the second wave of thinking skills research and pedagogy defended by this volume's authors argues that good thinking includes but is not exhaustively defined in terms of logical operations and that critical thinking instruction is therefore not straighforwardly reducible to conventional training in logical analysis. Logical skills are essential functions of good thinking, but so are non-analytic ones such as imagination and intuition, and the good thinker knows how to utilize both types. Similarly, while some styles of thinking call for the manipulation of formal operations that are abstract, this does not necessarily mean they are universally applicable. Other legitimate styles adopt a contextual approach that focuses more on normative assumptions and worldview presuppositions than upon formal logical propriety. Finally, while fair-mindedness is a desideratum of good thinking in all situations, a dogmatic objectivism that insists upon subject-neutral cogitation is not. The thinker is always present in the act of thinking, and it is precisely her active participation, with all its attendant affective, theoretical, and normative presuppositions, from which any analysis of fair-mindedness must proceed.

The essays comprising this volume explore critical thinking from the standpoint of this emerging reappraisal. Each of them takes as its point of departure the conviction that students are better taught to think well if thinking skills instruction goes beyond the conventional model's near exclusive reliance on traditional logical analysis. Some of the essays focus primarily on theoretical examinations of the nature of thinking that avoid the logicistic bias, while others are more directly concerned with nonlogicistic pedagogical strategies. Some directly examine the epistemic and cognitive foundations of good thinking, others approach the issue of critical thinking from feminist and/or Freirean perspectives, and still others are concerned with styles of critical thinking that can serve as vehicles for emancipation and personal enrichment, not simply analytical techniques. Moreover, the perspectives defended here are not always in unanimous accord. Dialogue between second wave advocates exhibits that degree of open-endedness and occasional disagreement on specific points characteristic of all healthy discussions. But despite the pluralism of their approaches, all of the essays here are directed toward the same goal: a radical reformulation and enrichment of critical thinking theory and pedagogy. Consequently, there is more harmony than cacophony in the chorus of their voices.

The essays speak for themselves, and I have no desire in my introductory remarks to anticipate their arguments in detail. But it will be helpful to set the stage for them by providing an overview of the current thinking skills debate. To that end, I'll discuss here the logicistic orientation of conventional critical thinking and briefly indicate the lines of objections as well as alternatives to it defended by the second wave of thinking skills research.

The Critical Thinking Explosion

In 1983, *A Nation at Risk* voiced an at least decade-long concern shared by both educators and laypersons that instruction in thinking skills should be emphasized in formal courses of study at all rungs of the educational ladder.[2] This conviction was sparked by a growing awareness on the part of educators that their students, ignorant of how to think in a critical and reflective manner, were ill-prepared to master domain-specific material encountered in course work. Declines in national academic performance and SAT scores, plummeting levels of student literacy in mathematics and the sciences, and the difficulty an alarming percentage of students experienced in comprehending or formulating simple arguments, all highlighted the need to reinvigorate the curriculum by complementing "reading, 'riting, and 'rithmetic" with a fourth "R": reasoning.

In addition to concerns about levels of academic achievement, educators, public policy analysts, and others emphasized the need for curricular enhancement of thinking skills because of the need to prepare students for future participation in a pluralistic and democratic society. An individual unschooled in the basics of argument analysis and claim comparison is ill-prepared to enter a world in which he is daily confronted with political ideology, marketing rhetoric, alternative worldviews, and competing value systems. Individual as well as social well-being is predicated upon the ability of citizens to think through personal and public issues for themselves. Reflective and responsible participation in mundane decision-making processes as well as crisis situations presupposes an electorate capable of sound judgment, and an increasing number of persons feared that conventional education failed to encourage the prerequisite habits of critical analysis.

To address these two needs, colleges and universities across the United States incorporated the teaching of critical thinking into their academic packages. Sometimes offered as a specific class (usually taught by members of philosophy departments), sometimes mainstreamed across the disciplines, critical thinking education has become the highly touted goal of hundreds of educational institutions in the last ten years. What once was typically offered (if at all) as an elective or remedial course is now in many instances a graduation requirement.

Reflecting this institutional surge of interest in critical thinking instruction, learned journals representing a number of disciplines run dozens of articles each year that discuss the theory and pedagogy of thinking skills. National and regional workshops geared to train professors and administrators in the latest strategies for teaching critical thinking regularly meet. The publishing industry continues to churn out critical thinking textbooks and manuals. Although the academy's systematic campaign to institutionalize thinking skills instruction initially encountered a degree of scepticism from some of its members, critical thinking is now accepted by most educators as both a pedagogical and even normative necessity. As one of them put it in 1985, instruction in thinking skills "is not an educational option. Students have a moral right to be taught how to think critically."[3]

In short, beginning in the 1970s and continuing to the present, a curricular trend toward thinking skills instruction escalated into what can only be described as a critical thinking explosion. This is not to say that critical thinking as an educational objective is a new idea. As we shall see shortly, the ideal of schooling students in what is now called "critical thinking" was explicitly defended in this century as early as the 1940s.[4] But the decline in student performance, which became distressingly evident in the 1970s and 1980s, as well as the perceived need to better prepare students for responsible citizenship, focused the nation's attention on the need for immediate remedial measures, and critical thinking as a central curricular concern came into its own.

The Received Model of Critical Thinking

The explosion of interest in critical thinking that spread across the academy in the last twenty years, focusing squarely and almost exclusively as it does on the canons of logical analysis, operates from an orientation I earlier characterized as logicistic. As a consequence, standard textbooks and courses in critical thinking typically concentrate on exercises and lectures that drill students in the mechanics of logical argumentation (inductive and deductive reasoning, fallacy recognition, quantitative and statistical calculation, evidence assessment, and problem solving), while ignoring or at best minimally attending to modes of thinking that emphasize imaginative creativity, personal commitment, self-inspection, or a sensitivity to contextual styles of discourse and persuasion. An examination of college and university catalogs reveals, in fact, that many institutions use the terms "critical thinking" and "informal logic" interchangeably in their rosters of course descriptions. As Joanne Kurfiss correctly notes, "teaching 'critical thinking,' at least at the introductory level, has become almost synonymous with the methods of applied informal logic."[5]

The logicistic reduction of critical thinking to logical analysis is, then, the defining feature of the currently received approach to teaching thinking skills. The obvious question to be asked is why critical thinking took this logicistic direction. Four explanations are especially pertinent.

The first is the obvious fact that ability to manipulate the rigorous techniques of logical analysis is a necessary condition for success in academic courses of study. Students are expected to wrestle with competing arguments and claims across the disciplines, and the degree to which they can reflectively adjudicate between them is frequently proportionate to their skill in calling on the basic techniques of informal (and, to a lesser degree, formal) logic. In the face of a student population often unschooled in even the most elementary rules of inference, assessment, and evaluation, it is understandable that critical thinking courses should have addressed the problem by concentrating so heavily on the mechanics of logical analysis. One significant factor in critical thinking's drift toward logicism, then, is the presence of a real need to train students in analytical strategies that will initiate them into the rigorous world of academic/intellectual discourse.

Another explanation for the logicistic orientation of conventional critical thinking—and one, moreover, that's often overlooked—is the fact that most courses in critical thinking typically have been taught by academic philosophers whose professional training included a rigorous and systematic study of logic. In addition, until quite recently most of the standard textbooks in critical thinking were authored by philosophers. The virtual monopoly on undergraduate instruction in thinking skills enjoyed (or sometimes endured) by philosophy departments ensured that most courses in critical thinking would reflect the discipline's high regard for logical analysis. This is not to suggest that academic philosophers are an uninspired breed of logic-choppers (I, after all, am an academic philosopher!), but only that most of them, by virtue of both their intellectual tradition and training, tend to think of courses in thinking skills in terms of courses in elementary logic. Nor, obviously, are they alone in this regard. The very fact that curricular responsibility for critical thinking courses normally has been handed to philosophy departments suggests that colleagues from other disciplines as well as administrators likewise assume that good thinking just is logical thinking, or they at least trust philosophers to define thinking for the academic community.

A third reason for critical thinking's logicistic drift is the simple fact, readily acknowledged by anyone who has taught a course in thinking skills, that it is much more difficult to devise classroom lectures and strategies on imaginative or contextual (etc.) ways of thinking than simply to plan the course around instruction in straightforward logical technique. Notwithstanding the inevitable ambiguity in interpretation and judgment surrounding informal logic (especially, for example, in its treatment of fallacies), it is still relatively simple to teach students the basics of logical analysis. It is a much more complicated enterprise, from both the instructor's and the student's perspective, to teach logical techniques *and* evaluative strategies that fall out of the mainstream approach. In constructing a syllabus that concentrates on logical skills, the instructor has a multitude of resources on which to rely. Interest in nonanalytical ways of thinking, on the other hand, has only recently emerged, and consequently teaching resources are not as available. There are no mainstream textbooks currently on the market that approach thinking skills from other than logicistic perspectives (for an extended defense of this claim, see Laura Duhan Kaplan's essay in this volume). Consequently, instructors who make use of conventional text-books are forced either to ignore alternative strategies and modes of pre-sentation or supplement textbook material with exercises and lectures of their own making. The latter project, given the relative lack of con-venient resource materials, is an onerous task indeed.

There is little doubt that part of the reason for the conventional approach to teaching critical thinking is the relative unavailability of nonlogicistic texts from which instructors can take their cues. But the problem is not simply one of lack of unorthodox texts. More pro-foundly, the fact that it is difficult to locate alternative materials reflects the reality that mainstream *theoretical analyses* of critical thinking, which in turn inform and fashion *pedagogical applications* of it, work from the presumption that good thinking is reducible to logical thinking and that therefore the proper way to teach students how to think well is to concentrate on honing their analytical skills. This theoretical conviction about the nature of thinking is the final and most significant explanation of why conventional instruction in critical thinking operates from a logicistic perspective. Theory does not, of course, always dictate practice. Sometimes the practical tail wags the theoretical dog. But in the context of critical thinking, the influence of theoretical accounts of good thinking on instructional styles is evident as well as pervasive.

Most orthodox theoretical accounts of critical thinking argue that the ultimate function of good thinking (and, by implication, the primary goal of thinking skills instruction) is to distinguish between justified and unjustified claims or beliefs. This is done by applying the rules and techniques of formal and informal logic to propositional expressions in order to determine if their statements are true and their arguments valid or sound. Justified claims and beliefs, then, reduce to those that stand up to the rigorous tests of logical analysis, while unjustified ones, obviously, do not. A good thinker, consequently, is one who is skilled in the manipulation of logical criteria and who willingly abides by the evaluative conclusions it generates.

But why does conventional critical thinking theory accept the logical canon as a necessary and sufficient guide for the ascertainment of justified belief? The standard answer is that logical rules of inference and appraisal guarantee certain methodological principles that supposedly are necessary for distinguishing between legitimate and illegitimate claims. These principles are prescriptive as well as descriptive. Sound thinking *should* invoke them, and justified beliefs, the consequences of sound thinking, *are arrived at* through their invocation. The three primary principles are objectivity, abstraction, and universality. Good thinking demands that the thinker adopt an impersonal, distanced relationship to the object of her investigation, suspending theoretical and normative presuppositions as well as her affective responses to the topic at hand. This *objective* stance ensures fair-mindedness and impartiality, both of which are viewed as sine qua non conditions for clear analysis. Moreover, good thinking requires that the thinker detach the claim or argument under examination from its broader context in order to concentrate exclusively on its logical propriety. Such *abstraction* clears the field of supposedly irrelevant historical or ideological considerations by allowing the thinker to examine the object of inquiry in isolation from "extraneous" factors. Finally, the analytical procedures invoked by good thinking are equally applicable to all knowledge claims because they are formal, in the sense that they are defined by logical rules independent of time, place, or content. Their *universality* thereby ensures that the good thinker can utilize them in any discourse context whatsoever as a means of determining justified belief.

That this idea of what constitutes good thinking is endorsed by most conventional critical thinking theorists is obvious when one focuses on the particular models they defend. To illustrate the point, three of the most representative of them, defended by Edward Glaser, Robert Ennis, and Harvey Siegel, will briefly be examined.

In the 1940s, the psychologist Edward Glaser defended a still influential model of critical thinking that presupposed the reducibility of good to logical thinking. According to Glaser, critical thinking, or that set of cognitive operations that exemplify good thinking, is definable in terms of three functional characteristics: "(1) an attitude of being disposed to consider in a thoughtful way the problems and subjects that come within the range of one's experience, (2) knowledge of the methods of logical inquiry and reasoning, and (3) some skill in applying those methods."[6] It's clear from Glaser's discussion of these three characteristics that what constitutes the "thoughtful" disposition of his first point is a willingness and ability to conform in a dispassionate, objective way to the "methods of logical inquiry and reasoning" he appeals to in his second. That these methods are exclusively analytical is clearly indicated by Glaser's list of critical thinking's primary programmatic concerns: definition, inference, scientific method and attitude, prejudice, propaganda, and values and logic. Moreover, the ability to invoke formal analytical standards in each of these concerns is, Glaser claims, a skill transferable to all forms of disciplinary discourse. It depends neither on the context of investigation nor the psychological, theoretical, or normative predispositions of the individual thinker. Logical skills are properly understood as abstract methodological blueprints which provide sufficient evaluative standards for sound thinking.

A subsequent proponent of the view that good thinking is logical thinking is the philosopher Robert Ennis. In his highly influential "A Concept of Critical Thinking" (1962), Ennis defines critical thinking in a straightforwardly logical way as "the correct assessment of statements."[7] According to Ennis, a critical thinker is characterized by her mastery of analytical operations that enable her to judge relationships between propositions (the "logical" dimension), evaluate the claims of others (the "criterial" dimension), and persuasively defend her own beliefs (the "pragmatic" dimension). Success in the exercise of these skills more specifically entails mastery of twelve operations that are clearly logical in nature. They include examining claims for ambiguity, contradiction, deductive necessity, inductive strength, specificity, and evidence reliability. The obvious implication is that dexterity in the exercise of rationality's three functions (the logical, criterial, and pragmatic dimensions) requires the ability to manipulate the rules and procedures of logic. In later publications,[8] Ennis allows that good thinking includes a willingness as well as the ability to utilize logical techniques, but his acknowledgement of the role dispositional factors play in critical thinking does not affect the logicistic drift of his theoretical model. Within the context of Ennis's paradigm, an attitudinal disposition to think "well" clearly means the willingness to exercise one's logical expertise.

The final representative of conventional critical thinking theory to be considered here is Harvey Siegel, a philosopher who champions what is known as the "reasons conception" of critical thinking.[9] Siegel is one of the leading figures in what has come to be known as the "Informal Logic Movement,"[10] and his model of critical thinking both reflects and encourages logicistic strategies in the classroom.

The reasons conception of critical thinking is described by Siegel in the following manner:

> To be a critical thinker is to be appropriately moved by reasons. To be a rational person is to believe and act on the basis of reasons. There is then a deep conceptual connection, by way of the notion of reasons, between critical thinkers and rational persons. Critical thinking is best conceived, consequently, as the educational cognate of rationality: critical thinking involves bringing to bear all matters relevant to the rationality of belief and action; and education aimed at the promulgation of critical thinking is nothing less than education aimed at the fostering of rationality and the development of rational persons.[11]

The obvious question prompted by this passage is: What does Siegel mean by "rationality"? He answers by saying that rationality is "coextensive with the relevance of reasons" and that to be a rational or critical thinker is to be moved by "the importance, and convicting force, of reasons."[12]

This statement is revealing once one realizes what Siegel intends by the "relevance of reasons." Although he explicitly states that he does not wish to conflate critical thinking and informal logic,[13] what constitutes relevant reasons (or "principles," as he elsewhere refers to them) is determined by the rules and criteria of logical analysis. A claim is relevantly reasoned or justified if it rejects "arbitrariness, inconsistency, and partiality [and] presupposes a recognition of the binding force of standards, taken to be universal and objective."[14] In light of the formal qualities of universality and objectivity he ascribes to these standards, Siegel can only have in mind the methodological and evaluative criteria appropriate to logical analysis. Like the later Ennis, Siegel claims that mere ability without disposition to think "rationally"—i.e., logically—is insufficient. This, in fact, appears to be his primary justification for denying that he identifies critical thinking with informal logic. But, again, like Ennis, Siegel's logicistic reduction of good thinking to logical thinking entails that his disposition to think rationally is nothing more than a thinker's willingness to abide by the formal constraints of logical propriety.

The reductionistic models of Glaser, Ennis, Siegel and other like-minded theorists provide conventional critical thinking with justifications of its logicistic approach. If good thinking in fact is identical to logical thinking, then it follows that the best way to encourage better thinking in students is to train them in logical analysis: this is the conditional defended by received critical thinking theory and exemplified in its pedagogy.

The Second Wave of Critical Thinking

Good thinking necessarily implies the ability to manipulate the analytical procedures of informal and formal logic. Second wave proponents of critical thinking are in unanimous agreement on this point. They are not irrationalists. But they do contend that the logicistic reduction of good thinking to logical thinking legitimizes a theoretical model and pedagogical tone that are both problematic. The former's emphasis on logical operations imposes a paradigm that is conceptually rigid as well as out of touch with the ways in which reasonable people actually think. The latter's emphasis on the mechanics of logical analysis risks giving students the impression that logical thinking is the only cognitive game in town, thereby generating the possibility of transforming prospective good thinkers into mechanical logic-choppers.

More specifically, second wave theorists argue that logicism's normative/methodological standards of universality, objectivity, and abstraction, when examined from a nonlogicistic perspective, in fact reveal themselves to be disguised justifications of *totalization, desubjectification,* and *decontextualization.* An examination of each of these charges goes to the heart of both the second wave's criticism of logicism as well as its own alternative approach.

Universality/Totalization. The logicistic model of critical thinking claims that the rules of inference and appraisal characteristic of logical analysis are (1) sufficient directives for how to think well and (2) sufficient standards for the determination of justified beliefs. Logical thinking, in other words, provides both a methodology and a set of evaluative criteria that are applicable to any legitimate investigation. This claim of universal applicability, of course, is touted by advocates of the received model as one of its virtues. They see it as guaranteeing uniform standards, principles, and techniques by which to guide and discipline thinking.

On a nonlogicistic reading, however, the universality claimed by the conventional model tends toward an unwarranted totalization. To "totalize" a methodology or set of evaluative criteria is to posit them as the only legitimate ones available and, by implication, to discount alternative approaches and standards.[15] The logicistic model is a totalization in the sense that it claims logical thinking is the *only* mode of good thinking and logical technique the *only* method for determining the justifiability of claims. Logical operations and analysis are not viewed simply as necessary conditions for the possibility of good thinking. Instead, they are perceived, along with a "disposition to think logically," as sufficient ones.

The totalization toward which logicism's ideal of universality leans gives rise to three consequences that directly impact on the theory and pedagogy of critical thinking.

In the first place, it tends to disenfranchise any style of thinking or evaluative criterion that is not in the analytic mainstream. For example, cognitive operations such as creative imagination, intuition, or insight, because they do not obviously conform to the inferential procedures associated with logical analysis, are immediately suspect. This is not to say that the conventional model of good thinking completely ignores them, but only that it tends to reduce them to either disguised or opaque inferential processes or, more commonly, to ignore or only minimally treat them in its pedagogy. Yet, as Delores Gallo and Kerry Walters argue in their contributions to this volume, good thinking is predicated upon the exercise of nonanalytical modes of thinking, such as imagination and empathic intuition, as well as the straightforwardly logical ones defended by conventional critical thinking. The good thinker does not simply react to received claims and problems, although the ability to do so is undeniably crucial. She also occasionally goes beyond them by creatively suspending strict rules of inference and evidence in order to envision new possibilities, innovative procedures, and fresh, potentially fecund, problems. Consequently, effective training in thinking skills entails exposure to strategies and exercises that strengthen creative as well as analytic modes.[16]

Second, logicism's tendency to totalization encourages a thinking style that can give rise to an unreasonably aggressive or adversarial spirit. The reduction of good thinking to logical thinking tends to emphasize a cognitive style that Peter Elbow and Richard Paul in their contributions refer to respectively as "the doubting game" and "sophistry." Critical thinkers, working under the logicistic assumption that good thinking entails dissection of every claim they encounter in order to discover its logical weaknesses, assume an a priori scepticism that transforms dialogue into a forensic exercise that has as its only point beating one's opponent by challenging his logic and evidence. Such an attitude is only to be expected if one operates from a model that totalizes logical technique as the sufficient condition for sound thinking.[17]

This adversarial spirit is not, however, maximally conducive to good thinking from the perspective of second wave critical thinking advocates. While it is true that certain contexts call for the critical thinker to challenge the logical soundness of arguments and the evidential backing of beliefs, it is equally true that good thinking requires him at times to suspend his scepticism long enough to relate empathically to perspectives contrary to his own, to accept them in a noncontentious spirit in order to explore their styles as well as content. Elbow refers to this receptive spirit as "the believing game," Blythe Clinchy calls it "connected knowing," and most of the other authors in this volume discuss its functional importance to good thinking. Their willingness to temper the adversarial spirit bred by logicism with empathic, connected styles is predicated on a rejection of the totalized claim that logical analysis is the only way of adequately appraising beliefs.

Finally, conventional critical thinking's totalization of logic gives rise to theoretical frameworks as well as pedagogical attitudes that breed intolerance of thinking styles that embrace ambiguities or unresolved contraries. Given its logicistic drift, the received model views ambiguous statements as prima facie dubious and sets of contraries as unresolved confusions. Thinking, if it is sound, functions in a straight-forwardly inferential fashion in which each step smoothly and transparently prepares the way for the next. Similarly, sound thinking must generate beliefs that are consistent with one another. The good thinker, then, eliminates ambiguities and resolves tensions, contraries, and oppositions. Failure to do so indicates a breakdown in the analysis.

The second wave of critical thinking argues that the urge to resolve ambiguity and standing contraries, while appropriate in some contexts, is misguided in others. Part of what it means to be a good thinker is to recognize a multiplicity of cognitive approaches and styles, ones that very often are not consistent with one another but are nonetheless complementary. Some of these styles properly aim for maximum clarity and resolution, while others accommodate themselves to the presence of ambiguity and even paradox in both process and conclusion. Anne Phelan and James Garrison, for example, defend a style of thinking they call a "feminist poetic"; Walters contrasts what he calls the "pattern of discovery" mode of thinking, which can tolerate a certain degree of ambiguity, and the "calculus of justification" mode, which cannot; and both Clinchy and Elbow argue for a critical thinking that sometimes "embraces" rather than always strives to eliminate contraries. The point is not that these authors deny the virtues of clear, concise, logical thinking. Rather, they argue that some styles of thinking are comfortable with ambiguity, that ambiguity is often inevitable in both process and belief, and that the nonlogicistic critical thinker does not automatically discount ambiguity as mere sloppy thinking.

Because the methodological and evaluative standard of uni-versality espoused by conventional critical thinking tends in both theory and pedagogy toward totalization, logicistic interpretations of good thinking may be viewed as "Procrustean" in spirit. Procrustes, you may recall, was the legendary innkeeper whose perverse sense of profes-sional propriety led him to lob off the limbs of his clients so that they would not overflow his uniformly sized beds. It never seems to have occurred to Procrustes that a more sensible strategy would have been to accommodate his beds to his customers, rather than the other way around. Similarly, logicistic critical thinking's tendency to totalize lobs off styles of thinking and investigation that fail to conform to its paradigm of logical analysis. True, some ways of thinking fit best into logical beds, but others do not, and it is these latter styles to which second wave critical thinking wishes to draw our attention.

Objectivity/Desubjectification.   There is a longstanding although increasingly challenged tradition in the West that has it that objectivity is a necessary condition for good thinking and belief justification. A thinker is objective in this sense when he detaches himself from both the act and object of thinking to ensure that the enterprise is "untainted" by personal convictions, presuppositions, or biases, regardless of whether they are psychological, theoretical, or normative in nature. Such an immaculate approach, tradition has it, is guaranteed by formal analytical techniques that concentrate on the internal logical structure and evi-dential strength of arguments and claims and ignore the thinker's personal (and therefore irrelevant) predilections.

The received model of critical thinking endorses this traditional notion of objectivity. Its logicistic approach is geared toward training students to cultivate "fair-mindedness," an attitude it claims is sustained only by separating personal considerations from claim investigation and argument appraisal. Good thinking, then, is reduced to anonymous thinking.

In contrast, second wave critical thinking argues that the ideal of "desubjectifying" thinking is impossible, and that even if it were not, it would not necessarily lead to maximally good thinking. Thinking is always performed by a subject who is an active participant in the process. Moreover, the involvement of the subject in the process of thinking, far from sullying the outcome, in fact can enrich it.

The traditional assumption that good thinking is desubjectivized (or anonymous) thinking ignores the constructivist dimension of knowing. The knowing subject is not a passive spectator who simply receives information that is anonymously processed in a formalistic black box. Instead, she brings to the act of knowing a complex set of presuppositions and commitments, and this set necessarily informs the type of information she concentrates on as well as the inflections she places on it. There is not, then, a radical separation between the knower and the object of knowing or the knower and the act of knowing. This does not entail that all thinking is irremediably subjective or private. As John Dewey was fond of pointing out, a reflective awareness of the personal commitments and prejudices one brings to the process of thinking is in itself a safeguard against falling into the trap of radical privatism. Although the subject is always an active participant in the process of thinking, she is nonetheless capable of recognizing her own predilections and thereby preventing them from imperialistically absorbing alternative ones. This modified notion of objectivity, unlike the traditional one, does not insist on the impartiality or neutrality supposedly guaranteed by desubjectification. Instead, it argues that awareness of one's constructivist input is sufficient to guard against overweeningly subjective projections. One acknowledges one's participation and commitments without uncritically abandoning oneself to either of them.[18]

In addition, the subject's reflective participation in the act of thinking makes room for a personal response to arguments, claims, and situations disallowed by the logicistic model's endorsement of desubjectification. It recognizes, as Elbow, Clinchy, and Gallo point out, the importance of interpersonal, affective, and empathic elements in reacting to and appraising alternative perspectives. It encourages the thinker to examine her own worldview commitments as well as those of others in a critical yet nonadversarial manner, thereby rescuing her, as Paul argues, from a sterile, uninvolved method of investigation and assessment. Moreover, as Karl Hoestetler, Henry Giroux, and Laura Duhan Kaplan suggest, the thinker's self-aware participation in the act of thinking fine-tunes her appreciation for the necessity to commit herself to certain beliefs and styles of appraisal that enhance community and liberation, rather than impersonally and passively regarding them as phenomena that have no significant impact on her life. The subject, in short, has a personal and frequently normative stake in what she thinks about, and to insist on distancing herself from the act of thinking is to indulge in either self-deception or rationalized indifference. It follows that good thinking need not strive for anonymous thinking. The good thinker recognizes the importance of giving a fair hearing to diverse perspectives but does not suppose that such an ideal demands an artificial neutrality on her part.

Just as conventional critical thinking's tendency toward total-ization bespeaks a Procrustean spirit, so its emphasis on desubjecti-fication points to an unwarranted reification. The ideal of anonymous thinking may suit contrived classroom situations where students are called on to decide between two or more arguments in which they have no personal interest and even less commitment, but it is clearly inap-propriate for "realworld" modes of investigation and appraisal. Human beings are not detached thinking substances. They are embodied, affective, and engaged subjects who approach decision making and claim appraisal from standpoints necessarily informed by their personal perspectives. To ignore the complexity of thinking by adopting a reified model that emphasizes impersonal analysis at the expense of the personal dimension is, perhaps, to ensure that students become adept at the "logical game," but it is also to ill-train them in the art of good thinking.

Abstraction/Decontextualization. The reification engendered by logicistic critical thinking's interpretation of objectivity as desubjecti-fication also emerges in its acceptance of abstraction as both a meth-odological and evaluative criterion. Just as logicistic notions of objectivity hold that the aspiring good thinker must remove himself from the act of thinking, so logicistic notions of abstraction maintain that the object of thought must be detached from its environment. In the former case, the object of the reification is internal, directed at the subject; in the latter case, it is external, directed toward the object.

Abstraction, in the sense advocated by the received model of critical thinking, involves the deliberate effort to focus exclusively on the logical and evidential strengths of a single argument, irrespective of considerations of its origin, ideological inflection, historical setting, or, often, even its relationship to alternative arguments. According to the received view, these factors are as irrelevant to the critical scrutiny of an argument as are the thinking subject's personal presuppositions and commitments. An examination of them admittedly may provide insight into the argument's functional connection to a broader context, but the purpose of logical thinking is first and foremost to inspect and evaluate the argument's internal logical structure. Consequently, the good thinker takes pains to abstract arguments and claims he examines from the contexts in which they arise in order to hone in on their logical strengths and weaknesses.

The logicistic notion of abstraction leads to a decontextualization of thinking that second wave pedagogues claim is as problematic as the tendency toward desubjectification. They contend that just as subjects cannot be separated from the process of thinking, so thinking itself cannot be separated from the context in which it arises. All thinking is performed in concrete situations by concrete individuals, and to abstract from either of these two settings is to risk missing the overall meaning, purpose, and nuances of a claim or argument. Styles of thinking as well as ideas themselves are inextricably connected with broader, more complex environments of discourse, place, time, value, and worldview, and to neglect these environments is to limit the function and range of thinking in an unwarranted way.

In her discussion of feminism and critical thinking, for example, Mary Warren argues that all thinking is conditioned (although not inevitably determined) by what she and others refer to as "conceptual frameworks." These frameworks set the conceptual and methodological tone not only of *what* we think about but also *how* we go about thinking. A patriarchal frame of reference, for instance, establishes certain prescriptive methodological procedures and conceptual blueprints that validate standards of investigation and appraisal quite differently from those endorsed by, say, nonpatriarchal frameworks. Consequently, failure to subject framework assumptions to critical examination hazards an implicit canonization of what in fact may be historically conditioned epistemic and methodological principles. This is a point that logicistic abstraction misses. Its methodological decontextualization focuses on specific arguments within conceptual frameworks without subjecting the frameworks themselves to critical scrutiny. Similarly, as Connie Missimer points out in her contribution, a decontextualized approach to critical thinking (what she calls the "Individual View") neglects to consider alternative arguments or paradigms and even goes so far as to dismiss them if they run counter to conventional wisdom as defined by the received framework. Good thinking, maintains Missimer, is a social artifact, predicated on a community of inquirers, that regularly examines arguments and claims by weighing them against alternative ones. But the logicistic model's emphasis on abstraction often reduces it to an exercise in which an isolated individual focuses on discrete arguments and claims within a single conceptual framework.

A decontextualized approach often leads to a pedagogy of critical thinking that, as both John McPeck and Richard Paul point out in their contributions to this volume, trivializes the meaning of what it is to think well. McPeck contends that the abstraction espoused by the conventional model postulates critical thinking as a "general ability" whose nature in no way depends on the context of discourse or examination to which it's applied. This reification of thinking skills in turn transforms critical thinking instruction into a kind of "trivial pursuit" game in which student players dislocate claims and arguments from their broader contexts in order to manipulate them in accordance with the mechanics of logical analysis. In a similar fashion, Paul argues that critical thinking instruction that focuses on decontextualized arguments schools students in sophistry rather than good thinking. This "weak sense" approach to teaching thinking skills fails to encourage students to reflect on the theoretical and normative worldview commitments that inform discrete beliefs and arguments and directs them instead to the nuts and bolts of "atomistic" analysis, in which mechanical fallacy-spotting is a primary goal.

Abstracting beliefs and arguments from their wider concerns also tends to discourage self-examination and the search for meaning that are necessary for individual well-being and honesty. Since all thinking is informed by conceptual frameworks, the good thinker must examine her own commitments and presuppositions as well as those of others. But to decontextualize thinking is to inhibit this kind of reflection by sundering beliefs from their broader attitudinal and conceptual contexts. It forces the thinker, as Lenore Langsdorf says in her contribution, to focus on techniques of "instrumental reason"—the mechanics, for instance, of problem solving—at the expense of self-reflective "judgment," which explores the relationship between discrete claims and the broader matrices, personal as well as cultural, to which those claims are organically connected. Thomas Warren echoes Langsdorf's concern by arguing that conventional models of critical thinking focus so exclusively on the decontextualized analysis of beliefs that they ignore the central roles of "ponderment" and "wonder" in good thinking. Effective thinking, he contends, is much more than a calculative strategy for assessing detached claims. It is a "quest for meaning," whose success depends on a self-exploration motivated by a disposition similar to Platonic eros. Both Langsdorf and Warren conclude, then, that personal enlightenment is as important a goal for the critical thinker as is the mastery of logical technique. Unfortunately, logicistic strategies of teaching thinking skills tend to avoid discussions of the former and overplay the latter.

There is one more problem with the conventional model's decontextualized approach to thinking skills: it tends to abstract claim assessment and argument evaluation from related questions of intellectual responsibility as well as emancipation from social and political forms of ideology. This is a particularly ironic consequence, given the conventional model's claim that one of its educational aspirations is to prepare students for responsible participation in a pluralistic democracy.

According to second wave advocates such as Laura Duhan Kaplan and Henry Giroux, the good thinker is one who exercises reflective autonomy in her responses to competing ideas from both the intellectual and political marketplaces. But reflective autonomy is predicated upon the ability to weigh particular claims against the background of broader concerns and alternative perspectives. Only after such a contextual analysis is attempted is the critical thinker in a position either to decide between competing positions or to replace both with a third. Conventional thinking skills instruction, given its emphasis on the decontextualized analysis of discrete arguments, ill-prepares students for this broader enterprise. Instead, according to Kaplan, it encourages a "banking" approach to judgment, in which the thinker works strictly within the confines of the status quo options given to him, while at the same time hampering his realization that knowledge claims, as Giroux says, are inseparable from "human interests, norms, and values" and must be evaluated with reference to them. After all, if the primary function of a good thinker is to focus on the logical value of discrete arguments, there's no need to worry about the arguments' social and normative implications. This short-sightedness not only bespeaks a breakdown in effective thinking. It also generates an ethical indifference and social complacency that suggest frightening possibilities.

Second wave critical thinking, then, calls for a theory and pedagogy that corrects logicism's unfortunate tendencies toward totalization, desubjectification, and decontextualization. In place of the received model, it defends an account of good thinking that stresses the primacy of logical analysis and creative modes of thinking, acknowledges the influence of affective, cultural, and normative elements in the appraisal of beliefs, tempers the adversarial nature of logicistic critical thinking with an emphasis on empathic, interpersonal, and connected styles, is sensitive to the contextual matrices that accent both the process and standards of thinking, and takes seriously the emancipatory and enlightening functions of good thinking. It seeks, in short, to provide a model of critical thinking that takes into account the embodied, historical, and multiconnotated nature of human thought and discourse.

The Second Wave Challenge

The second wave challenge to the logicistic model aims for nothing less than a radical rethinking of what it means to be a reasonable, reflective person. As we've seen, this does not mean that the second wave dismisses the functional importance of logical analysis to good thinking. But it does entail that the hitherto conventional identification of critical and logical thinking be reexamined and that the theory and pedagogy of thinking skills progress to a richer, more integrated stage of development. Instruction in critical thinking as a central component of college and university curricula is here to stay. The task facing educators now is to ensure that it weans itself away from its logicistic loyalties to incorporate strategies that better reflect the rich complexity of good thinking. To accomplish this goal, two things are needed: a more inclusive theoretical model of critical thinking that recognizes the multi-functionality, contextuality, and emancipatory nature of good thinking, and a pedagogical approach capable of incorporating second wave insights into existing critical thinking classes.

The essays in this volume do not claim to address either of these needs in a definitive, complete way. Indeed, it is unlikely that the needs can ever be once-and-for-all met. As the second wave contends, thinking is a dialogical, open-ended process, and that obviously includes the enterprise of thinking about thinking itself. But the fourteen perspectives collected here go a long way toward invigorating the ongoing conversation about thinking skills. They chart paths that go beyond logicism and towards a style of thinking that is analytic yet creative, rigorous but not rigid, and critical as well as committed. This new style, the second wave argues, avoids the drift to totalization and reification characteristic of logicism and consequently provides a model of thinking that is grounded in experience as well as open to alternative ways of knowing, evaluating, and appraising. Such a model promises to truly prepare students for initiation into the life of the mind as well as the world of concrete relationships and responsibilities.

Notes

1. Here and throughout this Introduction I prefer to use the phrase "good thinking" in place of the more usual "rationality" because the latter, at least as it's commonly employed, carries with it the implication of the exclusively analytical process of investigation and appraisal. As the second wave of critical thinking suggests, however, this logicistic reading of "rationality" begs the

question of what it means to be a reflective, sound-thinking individual. Perhaps a less laden term such as "reasonableness" should be substituted for "rationality" in all discussions of critical thinking.

2. National Assessment of Education Progress, *A Nation at Risk: The Imperative for Educational Reforms* (Washington, D.C.: U.S. Government Printing Office, 1983). A Gallup survey two years after the publication of *A Nation at Risk* indicated that the improvement of thinking skills in students was considered a top priority of American educators. See A. Gallup, "The Gallup Poll of Teachers' Attitudes Toward the Public Schools," *Phi Delta Kappan* 66 (1985): 327.

3. Stephen P. Norris, "Synthesis of Research on Critical Thinking," *Educational Leadership* 42 (1985): 40–45.

4. Obviously, the ideal of teaching students thinking skills extends back to antiquity. A good case can be made for the claim that Aristotle was the first advocate of critical thinking. His *Prior Analytics* develops the theory of syllogistic inference, the *Posterior Analytics* defends a theory of demonstration, the *Topics* is a manual of inductive reasoning, and his *De Sophisticus Elenchus* examines fallacy types. Moreover, Sophistic eristic as a style of argumentation is another likely locus classicus of critical thinking. My claim here is not that thinking skills instruction was invented de novo in the 1940s, but only that its most recent permutation—logicism—explicitly emerged then.

5. Joanne G. Kurfiss, *Critical Thinking: Theory, Research, Practice, and Possibility* (Washington, D.C.: ASHE-ERIC Higher Education Report, No. 2, 1988), p. 14.

6. Edward M. Glaser, *An Experiment in the Development of Critical Thinking* (New York: Teachers College of Columbia University, Bureau of Publications, 1941). Along with G. Watson, Glaser has also formulated the "Watson-Glaser Critical Thinking Appraisal," a widely used multiple-choice test of reasoning skills at high school and college levels.

7. Robert H. Ennis, "A Concept of Critical Thinking," *Harvard Educational Review* 32 (1962): 81–111. Like Glaser before him, Ennis also coauthored a thinking skills measurement known as the "Cornell Tests of Critical Thinking Ability."

8. See, for example, Robert H. Ennis, "A Conception of Rational Thinking," in J. R. Coombs, ed., *Philosophy of Education 1979: Proceedings of the Thirty-fifth Annual Meeting of the Philosophy of Education Society* (Bloomington, Ill.: Philosophy of Education Society, 1980), pp. 3–30; and "Rational Thinking and Educational Practice," in J. F. Soltis, ed., *Philosophy and Education: Eightieth yearbook of the National Society for the Study of Education, Part 1* (Chicago, Ill.: The National Society for the Study of Education, 1981), pp. 143–83.

9. As Siegel frankly and graciously acknowledges, his "reasons conception" model of critical thinking is heavily indebted to the work of philosopher of education Israel Scheffler. For Scheffler on education and thinking skills, see, for example, his *Conditions of Knowledge* (Chicago, Ill.: Scott Foresman, 1965) and *Reason and Teaching* (New York: Routledge & Kegan Paul, 1973).

10. The "Informal Logic Movement," a leading voice in the popularization of the logicistic model of critical thinking, hosted its first international conference on informal logic and thinking skills in 1978. For the proceedings, see J. Anthony Blair and Ralph H. Johnson, eds., *Informal Logic: The First International Symposium* (Inverness, Calif.: Edgepress, 1980). The collection contains an informative essay on the history of the Movement: J. A. Blair and R. H. Johnson, "The Recent Development of Informal Logic," op. cit., pp. 3–28.

11. Harvey Siegel, *Educating Reason: Rationality, Critical Thinking, and Education* (New York: Routledge, 1988), pp. 32–33.

12. Ibid., p. 33.

13. Ibid., p. 7.

14. Ibid., p. 34.

15. I adapt the term "totalization" from Karl Mannheim's discussion of "total ideologies": those ideological constructs that are closed conceptual frameworks in the sense that they claim to provide necessary and sufficient explanatory and evaluative standards, and hence disenfranchise dissenting perspectives in an a priori way. See K. Mannheim, *Ideology and Utopia: An Introduction to the Sociology of Knowledge*, trans. Louis Wirth and Edward Shils (New York: Harcourt, Brace, 1956). For an extended treatment of ideological totalization in the Mannheimian sense, see Chapter One of my *The Sane Society Ideal in Modern Utopianism* (New York and Toronto: Edwin Mellen Press, 1989). I discuss the problems of closed conceptual frameworks more fully in "On Worldviews, Commitment, and Critical Thinking," *Informal Logic* 11 (1989): 75–89.

16. For discussions of the centrality of imagination and intuition to good thinking as well as effective instruction in thinking skills, two recent works are especially recommended: Kieran Egan and Dan Nadaner, eds. *Imagination and Education* (New York: Teachers College Press, 1988) and Nel Noddings and Paul J. Shore, *Awakening the Inner Eye: Intuition in Education* (New York: Teachers College Press, 1984).

17. For more on the adversarial tendencies of the logicistic model's totalizing propensity, see my "Critical Thinking and the Danger of Intellectual Conformity," *Innovative Higher Education* 11 (1987): 94–102, and "On Bullshitting and Brainstorming," *Teaching Philosophy* 11 (1988): 301–13.

18. In her *Reflections on Gender and Science* (New Haven: Yale University Press, 1985), Evelyn Fox Keller defends a modified concept of objectivity she calls "dynamic objectivity." In contrast to traditional "objectivism," which insists on the anonymity of the thinker, dynamic objectivity makes room for an empathic connection between knower and known that acknowledges the epistemic role of subjective experience without propelling the knower into a radically self-enclosed privatism. See especially Chapter Six, "Dynamic Objectivity: Love, Power, and Knowledge," pp. 115–26.

I.

Toward an Inclusive Model of Thinking

The five essays in Part One seek to enrich the theory and pedagogy of thinking skills by defending models of good thinking that are more inclusive than the one endorsed by mainstream critical thinking. The latter tends to equate *good* thinking with *logical* thinking, and thereby necessarily disenfranchises ways of thinking, strategies for decision making, and dispositions that do not strictly conform to the standards of logical analysis. But good thinkers, the authors in this section argue, are characterized by their ability to think imaginatively, creatively, and empathetically, as well as logically.

Peter Elbow's essay sets the tone by distinguishing between two complementary ways of thinking: "first order" (intuitive and creative) and "second order" (analytical and discursive). The good thinker utilizes both, and Elbow shows how they can be enhanced pedagogically through composition exercises that stress free exploratory writing as well as more traditional discursive essaying.

Blythe Clinchy's essay continues the theme by defending a distinction between "separate thinking" and "connected thinking" (a distinction discussed in some length in her *Women's Ways of Knowing*, coauthored with Mary Belenky, Nancy Goldberger, and Jill Tarule). Separate thinking, the style championed by conventional critical thinking pedagogy, advocates an approach in which the thinker adopts a methodological and dispositional attitude of sceptical detachment. In connected thinking, however, the thinker personally engages with the issue under consideration by empathically relating to it. Both styles of thinking are essential to good thinking, leading Clinchy to conclude that "something goes wrong when we teach *only* critical [i.e., separate] thinking."

Delores Gallo's essay focuses more specifically on the relation of dispositional attitudes such as empathy to critical thinking. She argues, contrary to the received model's insistence that the good thinker is a detached, "objective" thinker, that empathic connections enhance both critical and creative thinking. She concludes her theoretical remarks with concrete strategies for encouraging empathy—and hence reason and imagination—in the classroom.

Kerry Walters further explores the relationship between critical and creative thinking in his contribution by distinguishing between two sets of cognitive functions: the "calculus of justification" and the "pattern of discovery." The first is constituted by analytical skills, the second by nonanalytical faculties such as imagination, intuition, and insight. Irreducible to one another but complementary, the utilization of both functional sets is necessary for good thinking, or "rationality." Unhappily, however, conventional critical thinking emphasizes the calculus of justification at the expense of the pattern of discovery, thereby schooling students in a distorted model of thinking skills.

The contribution of Anne Phelan and James Garrison concludes this section. In it, they argue for a "new" logic—what they call a "feminist poetic"—that methodologically embraces both doubting and believing (what Clincy calls separated and connected knowing) rather than attempting to eliminate one or the other. Phelan and Garrison claim that such an approach appreciates the irreconcilability of certain paradoxes, contradictions, and contraries (such as, for example, doubting and believing), unlike conventional critical thinking, which finds such unresolved contraries repugnant and seeks to eliminate them. But the traditional distaste for paradox and unresolved contraries reveals a gender bias that is unwarrentedly exclusivistic. In offering an alternative to it, Phelan and Garrison appeal to recent feminist critiques (Sarah Ruddick's, Evelyn Fox Keller's, and Mary Belenky's) of "objectivism."

1

Teaching Two Kinds of Thinking
by Teaching Writing

Peter Elbow

When I celebrate freewriting and fast exploratory writing on first drafts—the postponing of vigilance and control during the early stages of writing—it seems to many listeners as though I'm advocating irrationality. Some say, "Yes, good, we all need holidays from thinking." Others say, "Horrors! If we invite people to let down their guard, their vigilance muscles will get flabby and they'll lose their ability to think critically." But I insist that I'm teaching thinking.

Of course freewriting is not the only way I teach thinking through writing. I also teach it by emphasizing careful, conscious, critical-minded revision. Thus I teach two kinds of thinking. I'll call them first order and second order thinking.

First order thinking is intuitive and creative and does not strive for conscious direction or control. We use it when we get hunches or see gestalts, when we sense analogies or ride on metaphors or arrange the pieces in a collage. We use it when we write fast without censoring and let the words lead us to associations and intuitions we had not forseen. Second order thinking is conscious, directed, controlled thinking. We steer; we scrutinize each link in the chain. Second order thinking is committed to accuracy and strives for logic and control: we examine our premises and assess the validity of each inference. Second order thinking is what most people have in mind when they talk about "critical thinking."

Each kind of thinking has its own characteristic strengths and weaknesses. I like to emphasize how first order thinking often brings out people's best and most intelligent thinking. If you want to get people to seem dumber than they are, try asking them a hard question and then saying, "Now think carefully." Thinking carefully means trying to think about thinking while also thinking about something else—and it often leads people to foolishness. This is one of the main reasons why normally shrewd and sensible students often write essays asserting things they do not really believe and defending them with fake reasoning they would never fall for if they were just talking thoughtfully with a friend.

If you want to get people to be remarkably insightful, on the other hand, try asking them the hard question and then saying, "Don't do any careful thinking yet, just write three or four stories or incidents that come to mind in connection with that question and then do some fast exploratory freewriting." It turns out that such unplanned narrative and descriptive exploratory writing (or speaking) will almost invariably lead the person spontaneously to formulate *conceptual* insights that are remarkably shrewd. These are fresh insights that are rooted in experience and thus they usually get around the person's prejudices, stock responses, or desires for mere consistency; they are usually shrewder than the person's long held convictions. In addition (to bring up a writer's concern) these insights are usually expressed in lively, human, and experienced language.

Finally, when someone really gets going in a sustained piece of generative writing and manages to stand out of the way and relinquish planning and control—when someone lets the words and images and ideas choose more words, images, and ideas—often a more elegant shape or organization for the material is found, one more integral than careful outlining or conscious planning can produce. It is not that the rough draft writing will itself be well organized in its totality—though that occasionally happens. What is more common is that the exploratory zigzagging leads finally to a click where the writer suddenly sees, "Yes, that's the right handle for this whole issue, I couldn't find it when I just tried to think and plan."

Yet despite my fascination with the conceptual power of intuitive thinking—of what might seem to some like careless thinking—I have learned to also tell the other side of the story. That is, we are also likely to be fooled by first order thinking. In first order thinking we do not reflect on what we are doing, and hence we are more likely to be steered by our assumptions, unconscious prejudices, and unexamined points of view. And often enough no shape or organization emerges at all—just randomly ordered thoughts. We cannot count on first order thinking to give us something valuable.

Thus the two kinds of thinking have opposite virtues and vices. Second order thinking is a way to check, to be more aware, to steer instead of being steered. In particular, we must not trust the fruits of intuitive and experiential first order thinking unless we have carefully assessed them with second order critical thinking. Yet we probably will not have enough interesting ideas or hypotheses to assess if we use only our assessing muscles: we need first order thinking to generate a rich array of insights. And first order thinking does not just give us more, it is faster too. Our early steps in second order thinking are often slow backwards steps into wrongheadedness. Yet this is no argument against the need for second order thinking. Indeed I suspect that the way we enlarge the penumbra of our tacit knowledge is by searching harder and further with the beam of our focal knowledge.

We are in the habit—in academe, anyway—of assuming that thinking is not thinking unless it is wholly logical or critically aware of itself at every step. But I cannot resist calling first order thinking a bona fide kind of thinking because it is a process of making sense and putting things together. Though not consciously steered or controlled, the first order is nevertheless purposive and skillful.

Enhancing Thinking

There is an obvious link between the writing process and these two kinds of thinking. I link first order creative thinking with freewriting and first draft exploratory writing in which one defers planning, control, organizing, and censoring. I link second order thinking with slow, thoughtful rewriting or revising where one constantly subjects every-thing to critical scrutiny. But I am not content merely to assert a link. The two writing processes enhance the two thinking processes.

It is obvious how careful revising enhances second order thinking. If having any language at all (any "second signaling system") gives us more power over our thinking, it is obvious that a written language vastly increases that power. By writing down our thoughts we can put them aside and come back to them with renewed critical energy and a fresh point of view. We can better criticize because writing helps us achieve the perennially difficult task of standing outside our own thinking. Outlines are more helpful while revising than at the start of the writing process because finally there's something rich and interesting to outline. Revising is when I ask both the writer and the readers to isolate the central core of inference in a paper: What is the assertion and what premises does it rest on? This is the best practice for critical thinking because instead of being a stale exercise unconnected to the student, it is an exercise in assessing and strengthening thinking that is embodied in one's own or someone else's live discourse. Since we are trying for the tricky goal of thinking about our subject and thinking about our thinking about it, putting our thoughts on paper gives us a fighting chance. But notice that what most heightens this critical awareness is not so much the writing down of words in the first place, but the coming back to a text and reseeing it from the outside (in space) instead of just hearing it from the inside (in time).

But does freewriting or uncensored generative writing really enhance creative first order thinking? You might say that speaking is a better way to enhance creative thinking—either through creative brainstorming or through the back and forth of discussion or debate. But that only works if we have other people available, people skilled at enhancing our creative thinking. Free exploratory writing, on the other hand, though we must learn to use it, is always available. And since the goal in creative thinking is to harness intuition—to get the imagination to take the reins in its own hands—solitary writing for no audience is often more productive than speaking. Speaking is almost invariably to an audience that puts pressure on us to make sense and be able to explain inferences.

It may be argued that intuitive thinking is best enhanced by silent musing or going for a walk or sleeping on it or any of a host of other ways to push a question away from focal attention back to the preconscious. But such attempts at nonlinguistic processing often merely postpone thinking instead of being actually productive. Freewriting and exploratory writing, on the other hand, are usually productive because they exploit the autonomous generative powers of language and syntax themselves. Once you manage to get yourself writing in an exploratory but uncensored fashion, the ongoing string of language and syntax itself becomes a lively and surprising force for generations. Words call up words, ideas call up more ideas. A momentum of language and thinking develops and one learns to nurture it by keeping the pen moving. With a bit of practice, you can usually bring yourself to the place where you can stop and say, "Look at that! I've been led by this unrolling string of words to an insight or connection or structure that I could not have proposed if I were just musing or making an outline. I wasn't steering, I was being taken for a ride." In short, by using the writing process in this two-sided way I am fostering opposite extremes: an improved ability to allow ourselves to be taken on rides, yet also an improved ability to assess critically the resulting views.

Practical Consequences

There is no one right way to think or write. We all know too many good thinkers or writers who contradict each other and even themselves in their methods. But this notion of opposite extremes gives a constructive and specific picture of what we are looking for in good thinking and writing. Even though there are many good ways to think and write, it seems clear that excellence must involve finding *some* way to be both abundantly inventive yet toughmindedly critical. Indeed this model of conflicting goals suggests why good writers and thinkers are so varied in their techniques: if they are managing to harness opposites—in particular, opposites that tend to interfere with each other—they are doing something mysterious. Success is liable to take many forms, some of them mysterious or surprising.

As a teacher, it helps me to have these two clear goals in mind when I come across a student about whom I must say, "She clearly is a smart person, but why is she so often wrong?" or, "She clearly thinks hard and carefully, but why is she so characteristically uninteresting or unproductive in her work?" I can ask of any person or performance, "Is there enough rich material to build from?" and "Is there a careful and critical enough assessment of the material?"

If I am careful to acknowledge to my students that there is really no single best way to think or write and that excellence in these realms is a mystery that can be mastered in surprising ways, I can turn around and stress simplicity by harping on two practical rules.

First, since creative and critical thinking are opposite and involve mental states that conflict with each other, it helps most people to learn to work on them separately, moving back and forth between them. If we are trying to think creatively or write generatively, it usually hinders us if we try at the same time to think critically or to revise: it makes us reject what we are thinking before we've really worked it out—or to cross out what we've written before we've finished the sentence or paragraph and allowed something to develop. But if we hold off criticism and revising for a while we can build a safe place for generative thinking or writing. Similarly, if we devote certain times to wholehearted critical thinking, we can be more acute and powerful in our critical assessment.

One of the main things that holds us back from being as creative as we could be is fear of looking silly or being wrong. That worry dissipates when we know we will soon turn to wholehearted criticism and revising and weed out what is foolish. Similarly, one of the main things that keeps us from being as critical as we could be is fear that we'll have to reject everything and be left with nothing at all. But that worry also dissipates when we know we have already generated an extremely rich set of materials to work on.

Secondly, it usually helps to start with creative thinking and exploratory writing and then engage in critical assessment and revising afterwards—after there is already lots to work on. It is not that we should necessarily try to force our writing into two self-contained steps (though I aim for this when all goes smoothly). Often I cannot finish all generating or all first order thinking before I need to do some revising or criticizing. Indeed, sometimes I can force a new burst of generativity with an interlude of criticizing. And it is useful to say that we are never finished with intuitive generating even when we are criticizing and revising.

I used to think that I should try to make my students good at creative generating before I went on to revising and being critical. But I have discovered that some students will not let go and allow themselves to be creative till after we do some hard work on critical thinking and revising. They do not feel safe relaxing their vigilance till I demonstrate that I am also teaching heightened vigilance. Sometimes, early in the semester, I ask students to rethink and revise a paper in order to prove to them that they are not stuck with what they put down in early drafts and that careful critical thinking can make a big difference.

However, the fact remains that it usually hinders people to start by planning, critical thinking, and making outlines. My agenda for the beginning of a semester is always to enforce generating and brainstorming and the deferral of criticism in order to build students' confidence and show them that they can quickly learn to come up with a great quantity of words and ideas. Then gradually we progress to a back and forth movement between generating and criticizing. I find I help my own writing and thinking, and that of my students, by training a class to start with first order thinking and generating and take it on longer and longer rides—holding off longer and longer the transition to criticizing and logic. Back and forth, yes, but moving so that each mentality has more time to flourish before we go to its opposite.

Mutual Reinforcement

The history of our culture is often experienced as a battle between reason and feeling, rationality and irrationality, logic and impulse. Because intuitive first order thinking is indissolubly mixed up with feeling, irrationality, and impulse, we end up in an adversarial situation where disciplined critical thinking and uncensored creative thinking face each other uneasily from entrenched positions. It seems as though logic and reason have just barely and only recently won the battle to be our standard for thinking, and therefore advocates of reason and logic tend to criticize all relaxations of critical vigilance. Similarly, champions of creative first order thinking sometimes feel they must criticize critical thinking, if only to win some legitimacy for themselves. But this is an unfortunate historical and developmental accident. If we would see clearly the truth about thinking and writing we would see that the situation is not either/or, it's both/and: the more first order thinking, the more second order thinking, and vice versa. It's a matter of learning to work on opposites one at a time in a spirit of mutual reinforcement rather than in a spirit of fearful combat.

2

On Critical Thinking and Connected Knowing

Blythe McVicker Clinchy

We hear a great deal about the virtues of critical thinking: how important it is to teach it, how hard it is to teach it, how we might do better at teaching it.

I believe in critical thinking, and I come from an institution that believes in it. We pride ourselves on our high standards, and we work hard to bring our students up to these standards. Often, we fail. At least I do. In the not-so-distant past, when a student failed to reach these high standards, I figured it was either her fault or mine. Maybe she was lazy, preoccupied, or poorly prepared; maybe I needed to improve my teaching techniques.

But lately I have begun to think that when our students fail to meet the standards and become critical thinkers, the fault may not lie so much in them or me but in our standards. It is not that they are bad students or that I am a bad teacher, but that there is something deeply wrong about our enterprise.

There is nothing wrong with trying to teach critical thinking, but something goes wrong when we teach *only* critical thinking. Something goes wrong, at least for women students, when we subject them to an education that emphasizes critical thinking to the virtual exclusion of other modes of thought.

I have come to believe, moreover, that some of the women who succeed in such a system—who become powerful critical thinkers, and, in their terms, "beat the system" by achieving summa cum laude and Phi Beta Kappa—may be as badly damaged as the ones who fail. I want to tell the stories of some of these women and I want to propose that their stories might be happier if our colleges put more emphasis on a form of uncritical thinking we call *connected knowing*.

I draw mainly on two studies: one is a longitudinal study I did at Wellesley with my colleague Claire Zimmerman (1982, 1985a, 1985b) in which we interviewed undergraduates annually throughout their four years at the college; the other is a study I conducted with Mary Belenky, Nancy Goldberger, and Jill Tarule—involving interviews with 135 women of different ages and social and ethnic backgrounds, including undergraduates and alumnae from a variety of educational institutions—which is reported in our book, *Women's Ways of Knowing* (1986). I talk most about women because that's what I know most about. When I use the word "women," rather than "people," I don't mean to exclude men, but in these two studies we interviewed only women.

Epistemological Positions

In *Women's Ways of Knowing* we describe five different perspectives on knowledge that women seem to hold. Like William Perry (1970), we call these perspectives "positions." Our positions owe much to his and are built upon his, but they do differ. Our definitions of the epistemological positions emphasize the source, rather than the nature, of knowledge and truth. Reading an interview we asked ourselves, "How does the woman conceive of herself as a knower?" "Is knowledge seen as originating outside or inside the self?" "Can it be passed down intact from one person to another, or does it well up from within?" "Does knowledge appear effortlessly in the form of intuition or revelation, or is it attained only through an arduous procedure of construction?" And so on.

I need to describe two of these positions to set the stage for talking about critical thinking and connected knowing. They are familiar to all who teach.

Received Knowledge. Some of the women we interviewed take a position we call *received knowledge.* Like Perry's Dualists, they rely on authorities to supply them with the right answers. Truth, for them, is external. They can ingest it but not evaluate it or create it for themselves. Received knowers are the students who sit there, pencils poised, ready to write down every word the teacher says.

Subjectivism. A second mode of knowing we call *subjectivism.* Subjectivists have much in common with Perry's Multiplists. Their conception of knowledge is, in a way, the opposite of the received knowers: subjective knowers look inside themselves for knowledge. They are their own authorities. For them, truth is internal, in the heart or in the gut. As with Perry's Multiplists, truth is personal: You have your truths, and I have mine. The subjectivist relies on the knowledge she has gleaned from personal experience. She carries the residue of that experience in her gut in the form of intuition and trusts her intuitions. She does not trust what she calls the "so-called authorities" who pretend to "know it all" and try to "inflict their ideas" on her.

The subjectivist makes judgments in terms of feelings: an idea is right if it feels right. In the Wellesley study, we asked students how they would choose which was right when competing interpretations of a poem were being discussed. One said, "I usually find that when ideas are being tossed around I'm more akin to one than another. I don't know—my opinions are just sort of there....With me, it's more a matter of liking one more than another. I mean, I happen to agree with one or identify with it more."

Many of our students—especially in the first year—operate from both positions, functioning as received knowers in their academic lives and as subjectivists in what they refer to as their "real" or "personal" lives. Some students make finer discriminations than this and operate differently in different parts of the curriculum: they may adopt a posture of received knowledge as they approach the sciences and move into subjectivism as they approach the gray areas of humanities.

As a developmental psychologist, I have learned to respect received knowledge and subjectivism. Some of the received knowers describe a time in their lives when they were incapable of learning from others, when they could not make sense of words spoken to them. They are thrilled, now, at their capacity to hear these words and store them. And subjectivists spoke movingly of having freed themselves from helpless dependence upon oppressive authorities who used words as weapons, forcing them to accept as truths principles that bore no relation to their own experiences. For these women, it is a genuine achievement to define their own truths based on their own experiences.

But clearly, both positions have limitations. When these women are my students rather than my research informants, the limitations of the positions seem to loom larger than the virtues. When I am teaching Child Development, for example, I do not want students to swallow unthinkingly Piaget's interpretations of his observations, but I do want them to pay close attention to what he has to say. I do not want them simply to spout off their own interpretations and ignore the data. Students who rely exclusively on received or subjective knowledge are in some sense not really thinking. The received knower's ideas come from the authority; the subjectivist's opinions are "just there." Neither has any procedures for developing new ideas or testing their validity. As a teacher, I want to help these students develop systematic, deliberate procedures for understanding and evaluating ideas.

Separate Knowing

We have identified two broad types of procedures for such under-standing. "Separate knowing" we could just as easily call *critical thinking*. Some just call it *thinking*. We used to, too, but now we claim it is only one kind of thinking.

The heart of separate knowing is detachment. The separate knower holds herself aloof from the object she is trying to analyze. She takes an impersonal stance. She follows certain rules or procedures to ensure that her judgments are unbiased. All disciplines and vocations have these impersonal procedures for analyzing things. All fields have impersonal standards for evaluating, criteria that allow one to decide whether a novel is well constructed or an experiment has been properly conducted or a person should be diagnosed as schizophrenic.

We academicians tend to place a high value on impersonality. Some of us, for example, pride ourselves on blind grading: we read and grade a paper without knowing who wrote it, to ensure that our feelings about a person do not affect our evaluation of her product. In separate knowing, you separate the knower from the known. The less you know about the author, the better you can evaluate the work.

When a group of us were planning a series of lectures in a team-taught freshman interdisciplinary course, some of us tried to entice the man who was lecturing on Marxism to tell the students about Marx as a person. The lecturer argued that Marx's biography was irrelevant to his theory and only would lead students astray. He finally grudgingly agreed to, as he put it, "locate Marx" within an intellectual tradition; that was as personal as he was willing to get.

Separate knowing often takes the form of an adversarial pro-ceeding. The separate knower's primary mode of discourse is the argu-ment. One woman we interviewed said, "As soon as someone tells me his point of view, I immediately start arguing in my head the opposite point of view. When someone is saying something, I can't help turning it upside down." Another said, "I never take anything someone says for granted. I just tend to see the contrary. I like playing devil's advocate, arguing the opposite of what somebody's saying, thinking of exceptions to what the person has said or thinking of a different train of logic."

These young women play what Peter Elbow (1973) calls "the doubting game." They look for what is wrong with whatever it is they are examining—a text, a painting, a person, anything. They think up opposing positions. The doubting game is very popular in the groves of academe.

Teachers report, however, that they often have trouble getting their women students to play the doubting game. Michael Gorra, who teaches at Smith College, published a piece in the *New York Times* (1988) entitled "Learning to Hear the Small, Soft Voices." Gorra complained that he has trouble getting a class discussion off the ground because the students refuse to argue, either with him—when he tries to lure them by taking a devil's advocate position—or with each other. He tells about an incident in which two students, one speaking right after the other, offered diametrically opposed readings of an Auden poem. "The second student," Gorra writes, "didn't define her interpretation against her predecessor's, as I think a man would have. She didn't begin by saying, 'I don't agree with that.' She betrayed no awareness that she had disagreed with her classmate, and seemed surprised when I pointed it out."

Gorra has found the feminist poet Adrienne Rich helpful in trying to understand this phenomenon. In her essay "Taking Women Students Seriously," (1979) Rich says that women have been taught since early childhood to speak in "small, soft voices." Gorra confirms: "Our students still suffer, even at a women's college, from the lessons Rich says women are taught about the unfeminity of assertiveness. They are uneasy with the prospect of having to defend their opinions, not only against my own devil's advocacy, but against each other. They would rather not speak if speaking means breaking with their classmates' consensus. Yet that consensus is usually more emotion, a matter of tone, than it is intellectual."

I have had similar experiences, and a few years ago I might have described and analyzed them in much the same way, but our research helps me see them somewhat differently. It is not that I do not sympathize with Gorra; I do, and I value what he is trying to teach. Separate knowing is of great importance. It allows you to criticize your own and other people's thinking. Without it, you couldn't write a second draft of a paper; without it, you are unable to marshall a convincing argument or detect a specious one. Separate knowing is a powerful way of knowing.

Argument, furthermore, is a powerful mode of discourse. We all need to know how to use it. Our interviews confirm Gorra's sense that many young women are reluctant to engage in argument, and I agree— and so would many of the women—that this is a limitation. But argument is not the only form of dialogue, and if women are asked to engage in other types of conversation—to speak in a different voice, to borrow Carol Gilligan's (1982) phrase—they can speak with eloquence and strength.

Gorra may not know about this different voice, as I did not, because, like most of us professors, he does not invite it to speak in his classroom. In his classroom, as in most classrooms run by teachers who pride themselves on encouraging discussion, discussion means disagreement, and the student has two choices: to disagree or remain silent. To get a somewhat different slant, Gorra might want to dip into another of Adrienne Rich's essays, "Toward a Woman-Centered University" (1979), where she says that our educational practice is founded upon a "masculine, adversarial form of discourse," and she defines the problem of silence not as a deficiency in women but as a limitation in our educational institutions.

I agree: Argument is the only style of discourse that has found much favor in the groves of academe. But there *is* a different voice.

Connected Knowing

In our research, we asked undergraduate women to respond to comments made by other undergraduates. We asked them to read the following quotation—"As soon as someone tells me his point of view, I immediately start arguing in my head the opposite point of view"—and tell us what they thought about it. Most said they did not like it much, and they did not do it much.

These women could recognize disagreement, but they did not deal with disagreement by arguing. One said that when she disagreed with someone she did not start arguing in her head but instead started trying to imagine herself into the person's situation: "I sort of fit myself into it in my mind and then I say, 'I see what you mean.' There's this initial point where I kind of go into the story and become like Alice falling down the hole."

It took us a long time to hear what this woman was saying. We thought at the time that she was just revealing her inability to engage in critical thinking. To us, her comment indicated not the presence of a different way of thinking but the absence of any kind of thinking—not a difference but a deficiency. Now we see it as an instance of what we call *connected knowing*, and we see it everywhere. It is clear to us that many women have a proclivity toward connected knowing.

Contrast the comment illustrating connected knowing with the one illustrating separate knowing. When you play devil's advocate, you take a position contrary to the other person's, even when you agree with it, even when it seems intuitively right. The women we interviewed ally themselves with the other person's position even when they disagree with it. Another student illustrates the same point. She said she rarely plays devil's advocate: "I'm usually a bit of a chameleon. I really try to look for pieces of truth in what the person says instead of going contrary to them. Sort of collaborate with them." These women are playing what Elbow (1973) calls the believing game: Instead of looking for what's wrong with the other person's idea, they look for why it makes sense, how it might be right.

Connected knowers are not dispassionate, unbiased observers. They deliberately bias themselves in favor of what they are examining. They try to get inside it and form an intimate attachment to it. The heart of connected knowing is imaginative attachment: trying to get behind the other person's eyes and "look at it from that person's point of view." This is what Elbow means by "believe." You must suspend your belief, put your own views aside, try to see the logic in the idea. You need not ultimately agree with it. But while you are entertaining it you must, as Elbow says, "say yes to it." You must empathize with it, feel with and think with the person who created it. Emotion is not outlawed, as in separate knowing, but reason is also present.

The connected knower believes that in order to understand what a person is saying one must adopt the person's own terms and refrain from judgment. In this sense, connected knowing is uncritical. But it is not unthinking. It is a personal way of thinking that involves feeling. The connected knower takes a personal approach even to an impersonal thing like a philosophical treatise. She treats the text, as one Wellesley student put it, "as if it were a friend." In Martin Buber's (1970) terms, the text is a "thou"—a subject—rather than an "it"—an object of analysis.

While the separate knower takes nothing at face value, then, the connected knower, in a sense, takes everything at face value. Rather than trying to evaluate the perspective she is examining, she tries to understand it. Rather than asking, "Is it right?" she asks, "What does it mean?" When she says, "Why do you think that?" she means, "What in your experience led you to that position?" and not "What evidence do you have to back that up?" She is looking for the story behind the idea. The voice of separate knowing is argument; the voice of connected knowing is narration.

Women spend a lot of time sharing stories of their experience, and it sometimes seems that first-year college students spend most of their time this way. This may help account for the fact that most studies of intellectual development among college students show that the major growth occurs during the first year.

Thinking With Someone

When I say that women have a proclivity toward connected knowing, I am not saying that women will not or cannot think. I am saying that many women would rather think with someone than against someone. I am arguing against an unnecessarily constricted view of thinking as analytic, detached, divorced from feeling.

Similarly, I am not saying that connected knowing is better than separate knowing. I want my students to become proficient in both modes. I want to help them develop a flexible way of knowing that is both connected and separate. Bertrand Russell—no slouch at critical thinking—shares this view. In his *History of Western Philosophy* (1961), he says, "In studying a philosopher, the right attitude is neither reverence nor contempt." You should start reading with a kind of "sympathy," he says, "until it is possible to know what it feels like to believe in his theories." Only when you have achieved this, according to Russell, should you take up a "critical" attitude. Russell continues, "Two things are to be remembered: that a man whose opinions are worth studying may be presumed to have had some intelligence, but that no man is likely to have arrived at complete and final truth on any subject whatever. When an intelligent man expresses a view that seems to us obviously absurd, we should not attempt to prove that it is somehow true, but we should try to understand how it ever came to seem true."

This integrated approach—neither reverent nor contemptuous, both attached and detached, appreciative and critical—is the ideal. Judging from our interviews, the student is helped to achieve this integrative approach when the teacher uses an integrated approach, when the teacher treats the student in the way Bertrand Russell suggests the reader should treat the philosophic.

First believe, then doubt. When we asked students to tell us about teachers who had helped them grow, they told stories of teachers who had "believed" them, seen something "right" in their essays, tried to discern the embryonic thought beneath the tangled prose or the beautiful scupture within the contorted lump of clay. These teachers made connections between their own experiences—often, their own failures—and the students' efforts. Once this had occurred, once the teacher had established a context of connection, the student could tolerate—even almost welcome—the teacher's criticism. Criticism, in this context, becomes collaborative rather than condescending.

I am trying to learn to be this kind of teacher; I have not found it easy. It is easier for me to tell a student what is wrong with her paper than what is right. I can write good specific criticism in the margins; my praise tends to be global and bland: "good point." Connected teaching means working hard to discern precisely what is "good"—what my colleague Mary Belenky calls the "growing edge"—in a student's thinking. Connected teaching is pointing that out to the student and considering what might make a small "next step" for her to take from there. This kind of teaching is anything but "blind"; it does not separate the knower from the known. The point is not to judge the product—the paper—but to use the paper to help you understand the knower: where she is and what she needs.

When we asked women to describe classes that had helped them grow, they described classes that took the form not of debates but of what we called "connected conversations" and the women called "real talk." In these classes, each person serves as midwife to each other's thoughts, drawing out others' ideas, entering into them, elaborating upon them, even arguing passionately, and building together a truth none could have constructed alone.

Current research involving interviews with men may show that learning is different for many of them. We are interviewing men and women about their attitudes toward separate and connected knowing. Although we have only begun to analyze the data, it looks as if men, on the whole, are more comfortable than women with the adversarial style. Some men's responses to our questions about connected knowing reflect an ambivalence similar to the women's attitudes toward argument. They say they know they ought to try harder to enter the other person's perspective, but it is difficult and makes them uncomfortable, so they do not do it much.

It is possible that men like this might feel as constricted in the kind of connected class discussion I envisage as the women seem to feel in the classroom at Smith. In a connected class, these men might grow silent, and the teacher might worry about what in their upbringing had inhibited their intellectual development.

But not all the men would be silent. Although our research suggests that the two modes may be gender related—with more men than women showing a propensity for separate knowing and more women than men showing a propensity for connected knowing—it is clear that these modes are not gender exclusive.

When I first started speaking after the publication of our book, I had a fantasy that a nine-foot male would rise at the end of my talk and launch a devastating attack on our ideas. This has not happened. What has happened is that a normal-sized man rises and says, "Why do you call it 'women's' ways of knowing? I'm a connected knower, too. Why won't you include me?"

A college should be a place where, to paraphrase Sara Ruddick (1984), people are encouraged to think about the things they care about and to care about the things they think about. A college that values connected knowing, as well as critical thinking, is more likely, I believe, to be such a place.

References

Belenky, Mary B., Clinchy, Blythe McV., Goldberger, Nancy R., and Tarule, Jill R. *Women's Ways of Knowing*. New York: Basic Books, 1986.

Buber, Martin. *I and Thou*. New York: Charles Scribner's Sons, 1970.

Clinchy, Blythe and Zimmerman, Claire. Epistemology and agency in the development of undergraduate women. In P. Perun (Ed.), *The Undergraduate Woman: Issues in Educational Equity*. Lexington, Mass.: Lexington Books, 1982.

———. Connected and separate knowing. Paper presented at a symposium on "Gender differences in intellectual development: Women's ways of knowing," at the Eighth Biennial Meeting of the International Society for the Study of Behavioural Development, Tours, France, 1985a.

———. Growing up intellectually: Issues for college women. *Work in Progress*, No. 19. Wellesley, Mass.: Stone Center Working Papers Series, 1985b.

Elbow, Peter. *Writing Without Teachers*. London: Oxford University Press, 1973.

Gilligan, Carol. *In a Different Voice: Psychological Theory and Women's Development*. Cambridge, MA: Harvard University Press, 1982.

Gorra, Michael. Learning to hear the small, soft voices. *The New York Times Sunday Magazine* (1 May 1988): 32, 34.

Perry, William G. *Forms of Intellectual and Ethical Development in the College Years*. New York: Holt, Rinehart and Winston, 1970.

Rich, Adrienne. *On Lies, Secrets, and Silence: Selected Prose—1966-1978*. New York: W.W. Norton, 1979.

Ruddick, Sara. New combinations: Learning from Virginia Woolf. In C. Asher, L. DeSalvo and Sara Ruddick, (Eds.), *Between Women*. Boston: Beacon Press, 1984.

Russell, Bertrand. *History of Western Philosophy*. London: George Allen and Unwin, 1961.

3

Educating for Empathy, Reason, and Imagination

Delores Gallo

In addition to introducing the individual to a rich body of knowledge in literature, history, science, and the arts, education is charged with the development of essential human competencies: a facility for dealing meaningfully with complexity and a capacity for effective personal response. The manifestation of these competencies rests upon possession of a broad knowledge base, clear and resourceful thinking, and the will to act. Thus a major goal of education might be stated as the cultivation of open-minded human understanding and response.

Genuine open-mindedness is multifaceted, at times a seeming paradox, for it is marked by a disposition of distanced engagement and persistence that is free to relinquish. It requires engagement with the issue and investment in achieving a sound understanding that will permit action, while nonetheless demanding distance from any one perspective that might distort perception of the meaning and value of others. It is identified by an ability to probe persistently, yet regularly, to relinquish conceptions in the service of seeing things afresh. It is a posture of chosen commitments held concurrently with a willingness to be proven wrong. It is a capacity to gather information disinterestedly, sensitive to its limits and missing elements; a capacity to revise one's position to accommodate compelling new evidence and questions or new perspectives on extant knowledge. These abilities require a high degree of awareness—awareness of self, of the vantage point from which knowledge is constructed, of the variety of sound assessments available when information is judged against differing criteria and value systems. The exercise of these abilities rests upon personal dispositions and motivations and upon a tolerance for ambiguity, complexity, and deferred judgment, along with a capacity for focused inquiry, sustained investigation, and a drive for problem resolution and task completion. Importantly, these contrasting abilities are predicated on a capacity to function with cognitive and personal flexibility and with an acceptance of the concomitant risks. Thus, fundamentally, the goal of education is the cultivation of the requisite antecedent traits and values: self-esteem and courage, a valuing of the pursuit of truth and the comprehensive, elegant address of complex problems. Therefore, education bears a responsibility for the development of the whole individual—values and voice, disposition and capacity—to imagine and to reason well.

The process by which this development occurs is the maturing process afforded by vicarious experience and the empathic identification with both familiar and remote ideas, events, and persons. To elaborate, what seems essential to the process is not merely intellectual exposure to a variety of culturally identified truths, beliefs, or procedures but empathic engagement with them and with their human sources. This explanation suggests that the long-standing belief that empathy as an emotion can have no positive influence on reason as a distinct mental faculty is mistaken.

The Relations of Thought and Feeling Reconsidered

There is a long tradition in both philosophy and psychology that distinguishes thought from feeling, maintaining that the two are fundamentally different in their capacity to be controlled and in their value to rationality and moral action. There are now reasons to challenge this tradition. Reflection suggests that all feelings are not by nature more weak, transitory, or capricious than rational thought and that the cognitive component in affective response or the intertwining of affect and cognition, in social understanding at the least, is no longer unclear. Further, the specific emotions, often called the altruistic emotions or empathy, may actually have a positive effect on reasoned judgment in a variety of contexts.

It is the purpose of this paper to question the relationship between thought and feeling, specifically the relationship between reason, imagination, and empathy, and to advance the thesis that empathy fosters critical and creative thinking and that its enhancement should be adopted as an important educational goal. Following a clarification of terms, the paper offers a subsidiary thesis that critical and creative thinking are much more integrated processes than is often supposed. Evidence, first theoretical then empirical, to support that empathy, which can have a positive effect on the exercise of both reason and imagination is considered. Although the theoretical evidence draws solely on material from philosophers and psychologists who consider moral reasoning, the empirical evidence establishes that it is not just moral reasoning but reasoning generally that benefits from empathic understanding. Following an overview of reasoning from a psychological perspective, patterns of successful reasoning and impediments to it are identified and related to empathy. Next, the role that empathy plays in successful creative thinking is examined and explained. Finally, role taking strategies are discussed as generative of empathy and remediative of ineffective reasoning and imaginative thinking processes.

Before defining terms, a presupposition relevant to the topic should be identified: it is that thought and action are most meaningfully and comprehensively understood as having both cognitive and affective contributing factors and that these factors are as inseparable as the denotation and connotation of a spoken word. Further, these intellectual and behavioral events occur in a personal and social context and are therefore influenced by factors of disposition and motivation. Given this, it follows that a probing of the contribution of cognitive, affective, and motivational factors and their interaction is necessary to the understanding of effective thinking.

Empathy, Reasoning and Imagination Defined

Since this paper attempts to draw connections across different bodies of literature, the terminological problems faced are enormous; some precision must necessarily be sacrificed for the sake of the attempted synthesis.

As I use the term, an empathic response is one that contains both a cognitive and an affective dimension. In the field of social psychology, one can find the term empathy used in at least two ways: to mean a predominantly cognitive response, understanding how another feels, or to mean an affective communion with the other. In the latter instance, it may refer to putting oneself in the place of another and anticipating his or her behavior. Or it might suggest a still more dramatic transformation, the imaginative transposing of oneself into the thinking, feeling, and actions of another.

Empathy is often equated with role-taking, the capacity to take the role and perspective of the other. (I shall later develop the educational opportunities that this suggests.) Empathy is sometimes used interchangeably with and sometimes distinguished from social sensitivity, intuition, altruism, and projection. Some researchers require that empathy refer to an internal disposition or trait, others that it name a response to external situational circumstance. For this paper, I shall adopt Carl Rogers's definition of empathy: "the state of empathy or being empathic, is to perceive the internal frame of reference of another with accuracy and with the emotional components and meanings which pertain thereto as if one were the person, but without ever losing the 'as if' condition" (1975). Thus it is a condition with both a cognitive and an affective dimension; it includes the ability accurately to perceive and comprehend the thoughts, feelings, and motives of the other to the degree that one can make inferences and predictions consonant with those of the other, while remaining oneself.

One last point requires clarification: often when emotion or its influence is studied, it is the attribute of intensity on which researchers focus. They frequently point out that intense emotion narrows the perceptual field and clouds the judgment. Empathy expands the breadth of perception or range of emotional experience. Empathy does not intensify emotional response; it broadens it.

The terms "reasoning," "logical thinking," "logical problem-solving" and "critical thinking" will be used interchangeably. The salient characterizing feature of the set is the underlying convergent processing that predominates when any of these functions is operating. (To say that convergent processing predominates is not to say that it is used exclusively). From a psychological perspective, the cited operations are identified by the selection and concentrated processing of a few highly related, task-relevant pieces of data or experience, by an ease of coding, and by the infrequent modifying of codes. The process is marked by a focusing or converging on factors that have been determined relevant to the given situation; it moves toward a single, uniquely determined response, highly dependent upon the reproduction of the previously learned and upon the categorization of new experiences as examples of familiar ones. It requires a context of low error-tolerance for optimal performance and is the criterion evaluated by traditional tests of intelligence.

Philosophers often describe critical thinking as the ability to analyze, criticize, advocate ideas, reason inductively and deductively, reach judgments and conclusions based upon sound inferences from statements of tested truth, or the ability to identify the failure of any of the foregoing processes. Thus they also emphasize the convergent process of inference and evaluation against articulated standards.

I shall use interchangeably the terms "imaginative thinking," "imagination," "creative thinking," and "creative problem solving." The salient characterizing feature of this set is the underlying divergent processing that is required and predominates when any of these processes is operating. Divergent processes emphasize highly flexible intellectual functioning, capable of rapid, often drastic changes in problem representation. Less direct than convergent thinking, divergent thinking describes a process of ranging flexibly in the search of relevant factors in connection with a specific task. It is marked by the generation of question, alternatives, hypotheses, and problem statements; it leads to the production of large numbers of varied responses and to the construction of original ideas and logical possibilities. It requires a context of high error-tolerance for optimal functioning. It is the criterion elicited by the popular Torrance Tests of Creative Thinking. Philosophers often prefer to describe critical thinking as imagination and frequently attend to the contribution of intuition to its occurrence.

The Relationship Between Reasoning and Imagination

The common polarizing differentiation made between critical thinking and creative thinking is deceptive, since it often leads one to see creative thinking as the discrete opposite of rational thought. It minimizes the contribution of necessary evaluative, convergent, critical processes to effective creative production and similarly obscures the import of the speculative, divergent, imaginative processes to effective critical thought. While reasoning and imagination do differ, the difference appears not to be accounted for by the operation of discrete functions, but rather by the contribution of the same operations, both divergent and convergent, in differing proportions and in different positions in the sequence of intellective events that constitute addressing the task. Highly well-defined tasks may be approached convergently and may require the minimal or delayed contribution of divergent operations. Highly ill-defined tasks will demand the immediate operation of divergent processing for the construction of possible problem representations prior to the enactment of the selective mode and the establishment of a problem definition. These tasks will likely require the repeated intermittent use of both the generative and evaluative modes to identify possible appropriate rules and operations, then rules to be enacted, possible problem goals, then selected outcomes sought. Allow two brief concrete examples to clarify the description. Asked the mode required for an effective critique of a news article, most persons would cite the evaluative mode, critical thinking, and indeed this does operate in the expected ways to assess the givens and the logical relationships presented. However, a thorough critique requires the operation of divergent processes as well, to generate new and appropriate tests or plausible explanations of the given elements, to raise questions about absent elements appropriate to the issue, and to identify hidden assumptions and presuppositions that demand scrutiny. Similarly, a task such as the development of a product advertisement, which most would describe as a creative thinking activity, also depends on the operation of evaluative processes intermittently with speculative ones to define audience, goal, appropriate materials, and themes and to assess the most elegant or fit response to the task.

The philosopher John Passmore, addressing the issue from another perspective, concurs with this conception of the dual nature of effective thought. In "On Teaching to be Critical," he introduces the term "critico-creative" thinking as a learner's goal, "because critical thinking may suggest nothing more than the capacity to think up objections. Critical thinking as it is used in the great traditions conjoins imagination and criticism in a single form of thinking" (Passmore, 1980).

Reasoning: Theoretical Perspectives

There are several perspectives from which to argue that empathy can have a positive effect on reasoning. To do so, however, requires that one reexamine and depart from longstanding traditions in philosophy and psychology. Several notable scholars in both fields have begun such a reexamination: two among them are Larry Blum and Carol Gilligan, who have focused their attention on moral reasoning. I propose to offer evidence from their work and arguments from others who have studied critical thinking on a range of issues to support my hypothesis that empathy can have a positive effect on reasoning.

In the *Crito*, Socrates advises that to make a sound decision, in this instance a moral decision, one must use reason and avoid the influence of the emotions. This view may be understood as the legacy of the shift from matrilineal to patrilineal socio-political structures and religious beliefs, and of the consequent devaluation of attributes connected to female entities. Whatever its origin, Socrates' advice produced a significant and enduring impact on perceptions of the relationship between the emotions and sound reasoning. It implied that, uniformly, the emotions will have a negative effect on reasoned judgment. It is time to question this advice.

In *Friendship, Altruism and Morality*, Larry Blum argues that contemporary moral philosophy in the Anglo-American tradition has paid little attention to what he terms the altruistic emotions of compassion, sympathy, and human concern (1980). Since compassion is defined as fellow-feeling, or the suffering together with another, and empathy is defined as the entering into the experience of or understanding the emotions of those outside the self, I shall consider Blum's statements about compassion as relevant to empathy as studied here. In assessing the powerful traditions of thought and philosophic orientation that have militated against giving the altruistic emotions a substantial role in the moral life, Blum focuses on the Kantian view. According to this view, "Feelings and emotions are entirely distinct from reason and rationality. They do not yield knowledge, and can in fact divert us from morally-directed thinking and judgment....In order to obtain a clear view of the rights and wrongs in a situation, we must abstract and distance ourselves from our feelings and emotions, [since these] are transitory, changeable, capricious [and] weak" (Blum, 1980). According to the Kantian view, if an action is based purely on a *feeling* of altruism, then it has no moral value: for that, the agent must act from a reason-based *duty* to act altruistically. Actions based on altruistic feelings lack the defining features of universality, impartiality, and obligation that characterize morality which is "first and foremost an enterprise of reason and rationality" (Blum, 1980). Blum continues:

> Taken together, the Kantian view of feelings and emotions and its view of morality constitute a powerful and influential tradition of thought, which would deny a substantial role to sympathy, compassion, and concern in morality and moral motivation. It is important to see that these lines of thought do not spring solely from explicit philosophical thought. Rather, they have roots in our own moral culture. The Kantian view has affinities with a definite protestant tradition of morality—the emphasis on subjection to duty, on control of feelings and inclinations from one's selfish lower nature, on conscientious action on principle, rather than on emotional spontaneity. That tradition has deeply affected the moral thinking and experience of Anglo-Americans.

Offering an argument strongly refuting the Kantian and Protestant view and asserting the moral significance of the altruistic emotions, Blum states, "The emotion itself is often part of what makes the act the morally right or appropriate one in the situation". He continues, "Good judgment is in no way guaranteed by sympathy, compassion, or concern. But neither is it in any way antagonistic to them". Agreeing that empathy in no way guarantees effective functioning, I would suggest that it can predispose the individual to more effective reasoning by increasing one's engagement with the issue and one's motivation for producing a fair judgment.

A second call for the reconsideration of the value of emotion and caring in arriving at sound judgments, again in this instance moral judgments, comes from Carol Gilligan. She asserts that psychological developmental theory has not given adequate expression to the concerns and experiences of women, that the contractual conception of justice is seriously limited, and that a model of an ethical adulthood that encourages becoming principled at the expense of being caring is to be rejected (1982). In so doing, she argues indirectly for the recognition of the value of caring, an altruistic emotion, in arriving at sound ethical judgments.

Having reviewed these theoretical perspectives from which empathy, as an altruistic emotion, can be newly appreciated in its relationship to sound judgment, I will turn to the evidence for this view found in the empirical literature.

Reasoning: Empirical Perspectives

In looking empirically at the process of reasoning, it is necessary to distinguish among the individual's information and theories, the processes used to generate these (where available), and the individual's inferential and predictive performance. Cognitive psychologists frequently identify beliefs and theories as knowledge structures, defining them specifically as "pre-existing systems of schematized, abstracted knowledge" (Ross, 1982). They distinguish these knowledge structures from the methods used to process information often called judgmental heuristics; these general cognitive strategies are the processes used in ordinary perception and problem solving; they allow us to make sense of the flux of experience with speed and little effort.

Two strategies that seem especially important in this endeavor are the "representative heuristic," by which we sort new experience into preexisting categories by matching salient features of the two, and the "availability heuristic...through whose applications objects or events are judged probable or causally efficacious to the extent that they are cognitively and/or perceptually 'available'" (Ross, 1982). How and why a sound of a particular frequency may be categorized, for example, as an infant's cry, a cat's wail, or an oboe's lament is not well understood, but the categorization occurs through the interaction of schema recruitment, representativeness, and availability heuristics.

Adopting a model of the adult lay person as "intuitive social scientist," Lee Ross, in reviewing selected relevant research on reasoning, offers several interesting observations about its effective and ineffective operation. He notes that when persons reason to sound and unsound conclusions, the methods that they employ are not significantly different. Among the factors that appear to differentiate successful from less successful critical thinkers are the initial codings of data, sensitivity to sample size and possible bias in assessing the generalizability of data, and factors affecting belief perseverance; these factors are covariation assessment, causal assessment and prediction, and the testing and revising of theories. Less effective critical thinkers have difficulty detecting and assessing empirical covariations. Ross, summarizing his own studies and those of Amabile, Jennings, and others, notes "Even relatively powerful empirical relationships are apt to go undetected, or to be assessed as trivial in their magnitude, if they could not be predicted from the intuitive scientist's prior theories and preconceptions" (Ross, 1982). With respect to causal judgments, one important source of error has to do with "notions of parsimony"; once an individual has discerned one satisfactory explanation or cause of a phenomenon, he essentially stops looking and/or may fail to recognize other equally sufficient causes. Factors of disposition and motivation clearly enter in here.

Studies of belief perseverance are particularly important to an understanding of open-mindedness and critical thinking. Reviewing work on belief perserverance, Ross notes that theories and beliefs are tenacious; assimilation of new data to preexisting beliefs endures even when the accommodation of those theories is more appropriate. Less effective reasoners exhibit greater rigidity than their more successful counterparts. When subjects were exposed to information that was ambiguous with respect to their current values, they tended to accept the information at face value and to shift their attitudes in the direction of strengthening their existing beliefs. "When the information ostensibly opposes their beliefs, they evaluate it more critically. They seek to formulate alternative, less damaging interpretations and tend to shift their beliefs only slightly" (Ross, 1982). Such belief perseverance occurs not only in response to new evidence but also in response to the discrediting of old evidence. Many studies reveal that "theories about functional relationships in the world can survive even the most logically compelling of challenges to the evidence that initially gave rise to such beliefs" (Ross, 1982).

Perkins in "Difficulties in Everyday Reasoning," a study of broad scope whose subjects ranged from ninth graders to fourth-year doctoral students to older adults with and without college degrees, found that the vast majority of difficulties in reasoning demonstrated across this diverse population were not logical fallacies or other problems of a formal nature but rather what might be called problems resulting from the subjects' underutilization of available information. Assessing subject performance in situations in which subjects were required to generate and judge their own arguments rather than assess given information, he summarizes:

> As to the difficulties subjects encountered in making sound arguments, the analysis of the objections disclosed that only about a quarter concerned problems of a formal character. The rest reflected what might be called inadequate model-building— various failures to use available knowledge in constructing a more elaborate and realistic analysis of the situation under consid- eration. For instance, overlooking a counterexample, one of the most common lapses, is not an error of deductive or probabilistic inference from givens, but one of failing to retrieve relevant information. (Perkins, 1982)

Perkins suggests that the naive reasoner has a "make-sense epi- stemology," while the sophisticated reasoner has "a critical epistem- ology," which includes skills for challenging and elaborating models of a situation. He provides evidence that these skills can be taught.

Several pattens emerge from these studies of reasoning. Successful reasoning requires an alternation between probing persistence and open-minded flexibility. Various impediments to successful reasoning may be identified and affect different stages of the reasoning process: perception and belief construction, maintenance, and the continuance of motivational attitudes and dispositions. Poor reasoners exhibit a pattern of superficial, narrow, undifferentiated, or unelaborated perception of the problem and its elements (e.g., specific datum, quality of sample, or structure of the problem). Often this cannot be attributed to the unavail- ability of data or knowledge of sound empirical procedures. In these instances, the lack of probing persistence appears to be the source of the difficulty and to be rooted in dispositional factors: an unwillingness to invest in the enterprise, a desire for immediate and simple solutions, a contentment with easily available if flawed outcomes. I believe that these attitudes, which impede sustained inquiry, are rooted in a low tolerance for ambiguity and complexity.

The second impediment to effective reasoning is inappropriate belief perseverance. This factor is complex, for some pattern of belief maintenance is necessary not only to learning but also to the individual's mental health. To see all as ineluctable flux is immobilizing, if not maddening. In addition, for all, theory change comes slowly; Thomas Kuhn in tracing the history of scientific revolutions documents the fact that significant, cultural theory change often requires evidence accumulated over centuries, evidence that is often "not seen" by those well-schooled in the scientific method (Kuhn, 1970). Given this, one nonetheless recognizes that what separates the less successful reasoner from the more successful one is the rigidity with which beliefs are held and maintained. I believe that the cognitive flexibility needed to modify beliefs and theories will not be available unless supported by a tolerance for deferred judgment and ambiguity.

The third impediment to effective reasoning is the absence of the necessary underpinnings, the appropriate dispositions and motivation. Some of these factors have already been introduced in relation to belief construction and maintenance. While a valuing of the enterprise of reasoning well and tolerances for deferred judgment, ambiguity, and complexity are especially important to successful reasoning, several other attributes and their relationships deserve mention.

Curiosity, wonder and a desire to understand deeply are also fundamental dispositions for successful thinking. Highly important, too, is the capacity for a modestly skeptical and independent approach to judgment—a capacity whose roots lie in self-esteem and courage, since its exercise requires a self-trusting standing-apart, in which one risks the consequences of self-initiated questioning and challenging.

It is clear that these attitudes would be especially difficult to exhibit genuinely during adolescence, when peer approval is a prime goal and motivator. But the doubting, the taking of initiative and risk remain difficult for the adult as well, since genuine skepticism and probing inquiry uproots the individual from the comfort of an accepted world view. As it often produces temporary confusion, independent reasoning is unsettling and disorienting not only in relation to others (e.g., society and authority), but in relation to *oneself*. Some discomfort and stress and the courage and will to endure them, must be recognized as part of the successful critical process. Programs for developing sound reasoning must attend to the cultivation of the attitudes and dispositions necessary for the manifestation of the target cognitive performances. To neglect this is to fling potent, costly seeds into desiccated, unplowed soil.

Creative Thinking: A Network of Perspectives

There are many perspectives from which to see a relationship between empathy and imaginative production. Traditional biographical sources and recent empirical studies all suggest that the creative individual possesses unusual perceptual and personal openness, and a marked capacity for empathic identification with the other. In the extreme, this produces a condition in which the individual's self-perception is that of egoless vehicle, the instrument of the creative product. Flexible ego-control and low defensiveness indicate a desire and a capacity in the creative person to react beyond the boundaries of self, traits identical to those characteristic of the empathic disposition. Reported research indicates that, although there are some differences in the observable behavior of highly imaginative persons in diverse fields, creative members of the studied professions are more alike than dissimilar. Prominent researchers concur, as Barron states, that the dominant "cross disciplinary correspondences allow one to comment validly on the nature of the creative person across fields" (Gallo, 1973).

Openness is a salient trait of the creative individual. Grounded in self-trust, personally determined values, and independence, the original person's perceptual style is characterized by childlike receptivity, a sense of wonder, and a capacity for nonjudgmental spontaneous response. Providing a succinct account of the traditional view in "Tables Turned," Wordsworth characterizes the creative perceptual style as a condition of attunement, as "a heart that watches and receives." In "Expostulation and Reply," he summarizes the condition when stating,

> The eye—it cannot choose but see;
> We cannot bid the ear be still;
> Our bodies feel, where'er they be,
> Against or with our will.
>
> Nor less I deem that there are Powers
> Which of themselves our minds impress;
> That we can feed this mind of ours
> In a wise passiveness.

Empirical research confirms that a Wordsworthian "wise passiveness" is a prominent characteristic of creative individuals, although the terms denoting the quality vary. Crutchfield calls the attitude an "openness to full contact with reality," while Bruner and Wallach associate the quality with an open cognitive style. Rogers labels it "permeable boundaries" and Maslow "a bold and free perspicuity." Guilford and Torrance refer to the trait as "sensitivity," while Abelson and Brown incline to descriptions like "proceeding with curiosity and an inquiring mind." Mednick and Maltzman identify a pattern of "freedom from pre-existing sets." MacKinnon states succinctly, "The creative person approaches life with perceptual openness" (Gallo, 1973). Thus, the consensus may be captured by Henry James's observation that the creative person is "one on whom nothing is lost" (Gallo, 1983).

Along with perceptual openness and a concomitant tolerance for ambiguity and penchant for complexity, the creative person exhibits flexible ego-control, which in the extreme may be described as possession by the task or object. MacKinnon asserts that, confident of his ability to manage his ego, the creative person can relax his control and release himself from his role without fear of being unable to return to it (Gallo, 1973). In "Ego Diffusion and Creative Perception," Barron reports that in an atmosphere of psychological safety, the creative person can forego "the project of the ego," and can experience no distinctions between self and not-self; instead he can relinquish himself to a fusion with all things that nurture a productive harmony (Gallo, 1973).

Further, the imaginative individual is spontaneous and eschews impulse control through the defense mechanisms of repression. Barron has reported "that creative males score higher on impulsivity scales and score in the direction of undercontrol on an Ego Control scale" (Gallo, 1973). These and other measures suggest low levels of repression of defensiveness. Low defensiveness is related to the creative individual's receptivity to the nonrational in himself and in the world. Assessed by the Myer-Briggs Type Indicator, which classifies a subject's perceptual-cognitive style (using the categories of Intuitive vs. Sensory, Perceiving vs. Judging, Feeling vs. Thinking, Introversion vs. Extroversion), the creative person is found to perceive rather than judge, to respond with feelings as well as thinking. Most striking is the datum that while only 25 percent of the general population rate as intuitive, Barron and MacKinnon found 100 percent of their creative architects and 92 percent of the studied creative writers preferred an intuitive mode (Gallo, 1973).

Paralleling the ability to be possessed by the nonrational within is the creative individual's ability to be possessed by task or product. Bruner calls the condition "an ability to be dominated by the object." Keats terms it "negative capability." The poet describes it as a state of "being in uncertainties, mysteries, doubts without any irritable reaching after fact or reason," for he maintains, the creative character "has no self— it is everything and nothing." This view of the "ego-less" involvement of the artist coincides with the traditional view derived from journals and personal reports; these documents portray the artist as the instrument of the work, the vehicle of its production through insight. In his preface to *The Ambassadors*, Henry James describes his domination of his "fable" and the automatic, involuntary service he rendered it. He records:

The steps, for my fable, placed themselves with a prompt and as it were, functional assurance—an air quite of readiness to have dispensed with logic had I been in fact too stupid for my clue....These things continued to fall together, *as by the neat action of their own weight and form*, even while their commentator scratched his head about them; he easily sees that they were always well in advance of him. As the case completed itself he...[was] breathless and a little fluried. (Emphasis mine)

This is just one of many such accounts of the creative artist's possession by his task. (The reader is referred to Ghiselin's *The Creative Process* for others.)

Thus, the perceptual openness and flexible ego-control characteristic of empathy clearly correlate with the attributes of highly creative individuals. A capacity for spontaneous response is also important. Several relevant attitudinal factors can be identified. Important among them are high self-esteem and task motivation; a great tolerance for disorder, ambiguity, and complexity; the courage to deal with the cognitive and personal disorientations and risks created by the process; and an enormous valuing of the creative enterprise. In comparing these traits to those of successful reasoners, one finds significant similarity. If one accepts the asserted conception of the dual nature of both critical thinking and imagination, this finding is not surprising.

Roletaking: A Strategy for Developing Reasoning, Imagination, and Empathy

The practice of empathic roletaking from multiple perspectives followed by evaluative reflection on the experience can facilitate the development of an individual's reason and imagination.

As I conceive it, a roletaking experience has the following features. It begins with a presented or learner-generated issue or problem, each participant adopts a role, which, when enacted, produces a definition, a detailing, and a resolution of the problem or issue. Roles are rotated among participants, or new roles are generated and enacted. Each participant works through the issue from at least three contrasting perspectives. The practice of having several concurrent groups, working without audience, is recommended in order to provide maximum student involvement, to use instructional time efficiently, and to decrease the psychological threat of the activity. Topics and problems evolve from the more immediate and familiar to the more abstract and remote; the issues of any subject area can be used. Following the series of roletakings, participants engage in a reflective, evaluative discussion in which the issue is defined and detailed from several viewpoints; then these perspectives are incorporated into an elaborated model of the problem. Resolutions and their multiple consequences are evaluated against articulated criteria. Many expository and imaginative writing tasks flow naturally from such experiences and are encouraged, because they provide for the further persistent probing of details, comparisons, conclusions, and consequences, as well as the participants' engagement with them.

It has already been shown that successful and poor reasoners differ from each other in three aspects of their performance: in belief construction, belief maintenance, and the dispositions and attitudes that influence these events. I shall argue that practice with empathic role taking fosters behaviors and attitudes like those exhibited by successful reasoners.

Firstly, roletaking, as described, will facilitate the development of elaborated models of problems and issues. At least temporarily, it will modify the individual's original perception of the issue and its components because the sustained examination of the issue from contrasting perspectives will yield more relevant data, will be likely to produce counterexamples to items generated from different vantage points, and will eventuate in several problem definitions and their subsequent incorporation into one or more elaborated problem models. The activity will raise questions about the meaning of specific data and about the quality of evidence and samples. The activity invites and practices the concurrent consideration of an increasing number of factors and thus facilitates what Piaget calls development from centration to decentration. Regular practice will foster increased participant tolerance for complexity, ambiguity, and deferred judgment.

Something deeply important in human understanding occurs here. I propose that when successful empathic roletaking occurs, it produces from each perspective not only additional and new knowledge, as well as the discrediting of some earlier knowledge, but a new organization of information, a new or variant knowledge structure, with both intellective and feeling-state components. It is the creation of this new or variant structure and the *self-generated* nature of the new and discredited information that account for the impact of the process, an increase in human understanding.

Secondly, there are two ways in which empathic roletaking will tend to increase the flexibility with which beliefs are held. First, the process requires that the participant not only hear but generate views different from his own; as one's on construction, these views will typically be attended to with openness and 'taken seriously," if only temporarily. Also, the regular shifting of perspective will produce some consequent distancing from any one view and provide some greater engagement with perspectives that were originally remote. Thus it will tend to reduce the salience of the original perspective of the self, while increasing the viability of other views. In this way, it will promote development from egocentrism to nonegocentrism, a movement which correlates with more effective formal operational thought (Higgins, 1980).

Lastly, roletaking nurtures the attitudes and dispositions supportive of effective reasoning. It fosters interest in the activity of reasoning, a positive attitude toward the enterprise; it supports the development of initiative, risk-taking, and courage and a tolerance for complexity, ambiguity, and independent judgment. From the evidence of my own teaching experience, I find that roletaking has significant influence on motivation and attitude toward critical inquiry. Roletaking tends to be intrinsically motivating because it involves the whole person, requires initiative, and accords the participant both responsibility and power, or fate control in the learning situation. It is an established principle of learning that active involvement and fate control are motivating factors to child and adult learners and that behavior needs an opportunity to manifest itself.

Beyond the investment of time and effort that genuine critical thinking requires, it is a costly and dangerous activity in that it requires one to separate oneself from comfortable and familiar beliefs held to be right and deliberately and systematically attempt to prove oneself in error in the service of making oneself correct according to a more rigorous and valuable set of standards. The threats are clear. Roletaking fosters a positive attitude toward critical inquiry and nurtures courage because it allows one earnestly to take the risks but in a condition of personal distance and reasonable psychological safety. The naturalistic setting of the roletaking situation may add some of the comfort of the familiar to the complex, ambiguous task.

Thus, having argued that, as an altruistic emotion, empathy is not to be avoided by those who would reason well but more likely should be cultivated through roletaking as a facilitator of sound critical judgment, I shall identify some ways in which empathic roletaking relates to effective creative thinking. (This discussion will be briefer, since the relationship between these is widely recognized in the fields of psychology and education.)

Creative thinking as here discussed is supported by perceptual openness, flexible ego-control, and a capacity for immersion in the task, for spontaneous response, and for seeing connections between apparently unrelated elements. Role shifting both practices and nurtures flexible ego-control and a capacity to see the same event afresh and with openness from different vantage points. It invites immersion in the task by requiring absorption in each role, so that one can effectively analyze, infer, predict, and act in ways consonant with it. In so doing, it fosters spontaneous and original response. Importantly, the procedure of developing what I have called variant knowledge structures, with both affective and cognitive dimensions, and then evaluating them reflectively produces an optimal situation for the finding or constructing of remote associations or novel connections between formerly unrelated elements. Thus, empathic roletaking fosters imagination by providing opportunities for immersive, holistic, spontaneous, and novel responses to problems that are engaging and complex. In so doing, it exercises and nurtures intrinsic motivation for tasks requiring imagination, a tolerance for complexity and ambiguity, as well as self-esteem and courage.

Conclusion

In this paper, I have argued that the attributes that characterize empathy correlate with those of effective critical thinking and imagination. Of course, this correlation makes no causal claim: to suggest that the attributes of the empathic, the creative, and the rational individual overlap is to suggest that these qualities appear to be significant among a set of conditions necessary for the demonstration of empathy, rationality, or creativity. It in no way suggests that they form a set that is both necessary and sufficient.

Nonetheless, the correlation yields significant insights and holds important educational implications. First, it reveals that an affective component can have a positive effect on both rational and imaginative thought. Second, it suggests that empathy is the emotion or affective disposition to cultivate, since it develops emotional range, which is essential to multiple perspective-taking and genuine open-mindedness. Third, in educating for these goals, roletaking is a strategy of promise, since it has a positive influence on problem perception, on belief maintenance, and on relevant attitudes and dispositions. Roletaking discourages hasty and superficial problem examination and facilitates the construction of more fully elaborated, possibly novel, problem models. It discourages belief rigidity and the salience of the perspective of the self and encourages cognitive and personal flexibility. It practices persistent, probing, engaged examination of an issue in alternation with flexible relinquishment and reflective distance. Thus, the strategy has potential for addressing all three of the documented impediments to sound reasoning while practicing the perceptual openness, flexible ego-control, and spontaneity so important to originality. By conjoining and practicing both openness and commitment, flexibility and persistence, empathic roletaking can foster the cognitive and affective patterns that characterize effective reasoning and imagination and can promote open-mindedness and the humanistic response.

References

Blum, L. *Friendship, Altruism and Morality.* Boston: Routledge & Paul, 1980.

Gallo, D. The traits and techniques of creative production. Unpublished doctoral dissertation. Harvard University, 1973.

Gilligan, C. *In a Different Voice: Psychological Theory and Women's Development.* Cambridge, Mass.: Harvard University Press, 1982.

Higgins, E. Role taking and social judgment: Alternative developmental perspectives and processes. In Flavell, J. H. and Ross, L. (eds.) *Social Cognitive Development: Frontiers and Possible Futures.* Cambridge: Cambridge University Press, 1980

Kuhn, T. *The Structure of Scientific Revolutions.* Chicago: University of Chicago Press, 1970.

Passmore, J. On teaching to be critical. In Passmore, J. *The Philosophy of Teaching.* Cambridge, Mass.: Harvard University Press, 1980.

Perkins, D. Difficulties in everyday reasoning and their change with education. Cambridge, Mass.: Harvard Project Zero, Final Report to the Spencer Foundation, November 1982.

Rogers, C. Empathic: An unappreciated way of being. *Counseling Psychologist,* 1975, 5: 2–10.

Ross, L. The 'intuitive scientist' formulation and its developmental implications. In Flavell, J. H. and Ross, L. (eds.) *Social Cognitive Development: Frontiers and Possible Futures.* Cambridge: Cambridge University Press, 1982.

4

Critical Thinking, Rationality, and the Vulcanization of Students

Kerry S. Walters

A Spockean Prologue

Any fan of the old "Star Trek" television series knows there is something remarkably gripping about the character Spock. When he elevates an eyebrow on an otherwise expressionless face and matter of factly declares an argument "logical, flawlessly logical," we can't help but tingle with awe at his analytical expertise. We even exult (albeit somewhat uneasily) when Spock uses his laser-sharp logical skills in the dispassionate and indisputable demolition of his human companions' crude attempts at reasoning. Spock's cold-bloodedness may exasperate us at times, but we generally admire and envy his ability to get to the heart of an argument by stripping through rhetorical gloss, emotional ephemera, and cognitive confusion. We might be amused and perhaps even occasionally sympathetic with McCoy's sputtering accusations that Spock is nothing more than an organic calculating machine, but we do not take them too seriously. More often than not, it is the ultralogical Spock we admire, not the likeable but rather excitable Bones.

Spock, as everyone knows, is a Vulcan (actually a half-Vulcan, but never mind), a member of a species characterized by its innate and total fidelity to logic. Vulcans are constitutionally incapable of thinking or behaving nonlogically. They never jump to conclusions, never act rashly, never let emotional smokescreens get in the way of sound inferential reasoning. They draw conclusions only when there is enough evidence to warrant them and refuse to go beyond the limits of logical probability. When Captain Kirk occasionally asks Spock to speculate in the absence of compelling evidence, for example, the usual response is something like, "Speculate, Captain? Speculation is not logical." Spock is contemptuous (insofar as a Vulcan is capable of contempt) of what he sees as the unfortunate human propensity to bypass logical procedures by playing hunches and going with intuition. Such flagrant disregard of the established rules of inference comes as close as anything does to unsettling otherwise unflappable Vulcans.

Because they are so good at sticking to the evidence and drawing properly logical conclusions from it, Vulcans shine when it comes to problem solving and critical analysis. Ask a Vulcan for help in cracking a logical chestnut, and chances are he or she will have the answer for you before you have finished the request. This is because Vulcans possess a computer-swift alacrity in reducing an argument or problem to its simplest constituents, eliminating irrelevances, checking for informal fallacies, and examining inferential connections between premises and conclusions. A Vulcan never resorts to sophistries in the defense of an argument or the analysis of a problem. Instead, he or she follows the dictates of logic regardless of where they lead.

Perhaps this is one of the reasons we admire Vulcans. They are scrupulously honest in their thought processes and evaluations, never succumbing to prejudices, hidden agenda, or emotional obfuscations. They represent the epitome of the objectivity that traditionally has been one of Western epistemology's sacred cows. They are symbols of what we suspect we ought to be but unhappily realize we are not: impeccably logical thinkers.

But every specialization has its price, and the Vulcan's hyper-trophic logical acuity is no exception. Spock, like all his fellow Vulcans, may be a master at logical justification, but he is astoundingly devoid of imagination, intuition, insight, or appreciation for metaphorical thinking. One suspects he doesn't have a creative bone in his body and hasn't had an original idea in his life. He is, as Bones never tires of pointing out, a marvellous computing device and can see through the weakness in any line of reasoning in a flash. But he is innately incapable of moving beyond a mechanical search for justification of ready-to-hand arguments. There is a disarming literalness to his thinking that retards imaginative speculation and practical adaptability to novel situations. His reasoning is always reactive, never innovative. It follows with maximum fidelity the rules of logical analysis but is incapable of sus-pending those rules if a predicament calls for it. He is genetically incapable of nonanalytic "what-if" reflections or intuitive shots in the dark. His immaculately logical orientation, in short, is his greatest strength but also his greatest weakness.

Spock's problem (or more correctly, every Vulcan's problem) is that he identifies good thinking, or what may be called rationality, with logical thinking. So far as he is concerned, the rational person is one whose thought processes unequivocally conform to the formalistic rules of problem solving and logical analysis. But, as I shall argue here, rationality involves much more than merely logical processes, or what I call the "calculus of justification." It also includes nonlogical but quite legitimate cognitive acts such as imagination, conceptual creativity, intuition, and insight. These are functions of what I generically call the "pattern of discovery." Unlike the analytical functions characteristic of the calculus of justification, pattern of discovery processes are not formalistically rule-oriented or inferentially transparent. Nor are they purely reactive. They go beyond analyses of ready-to-hand problems and enable the reasoner to formulate new, alternative paradigms and problems. They are often tacit in nature and arrive at conclusions in a nonsequential fashion. As such, they complement the analytic functions definitive of the calculus of justification and serve as essential, albeit nonlogical, conditions for the possibility of rationality.

Unfortunately, however, the dual nature of rationality is a point that most proponents of critical thinking in the college and university curriculum have missed. As any educator knows, the training of students in critical thinking, analytic skills, and problem solving has become a top educational priority in recent years. Courses in critical thinking are now standard in institutions of higher learning. At least one state university system—California—requires its students to take nine hours of critical thinking or its equivalent (Moore, 1983). In addition to courses in critical thinking proper, usually taught by philosophy faculty, academic departments from anthropology to zoology are increasingly mainstreaming the technique in their specific offerings. This in turn has created a booming industry in the publication of critical thinking texts and manuals. Moreover, it has sparked a dramatic upswing in the number of regional and national faculty workshops that train teachers how to incorporate the critical thinking technique in their classes. Finally, the professional literature reflects the pedagogical emphasis upon critical thinking. Paul (1985) calculates that 1,894 discussions of the method made it into print between 1977 and 1984 alone. Although statistics are unavailable, there is no reason to suppose this swell has abated in the last five years. If anything, it probably has increased.

The disturbing thing about this educational championing of critical thinking is that it assumes the same model of rationality accepted by Spock and his fellow Vulcans. From an epistemological perspective, it argues that thinking is legitimate—that is, rational—if and only if it is logical. From a pedagogical one, it focuses almost exclusively upon drilling students in the rather mechanical rules of the calculus of justification and ignores (as well as devalues by omission) training in the cognitive functions of the pattern of discovery. In a word, conventional instruction in critical thinking technique leans toward the vulcanization of students. Advocates of the critical thinking model usually are horrified by this sort of accusation. They counter that it is a fallacious stereotype of critical thinking as uncreative fault-finding and insist that their goal in fact is to train students in responsible, free, and flexible thinking. But the epistemological assumptions and pedagogical techniques they espouse belie such an ideal. Regardless of what their intentions are, the practical consequence of their model of rationality is student vulcanization. This is disconcerting. Pedagogical emphasis upon critical thinking's calculus of justification may enable students to analyze texts with some degree of Spock's logical brilliance, but it will not make them, in the broadest sense of the word, rational.

In what follows, I defend this claim by doing two things. First, I examine the conventional model of critical thinking and show that its epistemology and pedagogy focus exclusively upon the calculus of justification, thereby supporting my contention that it identifies rational thinking with logical thinking. Then I show how this model of rationality needs to be complemented, both epistemologically and pedagogically, with attention to and training in the cognitive functions characteristic of the pattern of discovery. Students *can* be educated in responsible, free, and flexible thinking, but only when the model of critical thinking currently pushed across the curriculum drops its exclusive allegiance to the vulcanizing calculus of justification and recognizes that the Spock ideal is disingenuous as well as dangerous.

Critical Thinking and the Calculus of Justification

Conventional critical thinking mainstreamed in college and university curricula claims to be a technique that schools students in the rational justification of beliefs by providing a set of rules with which to analyze propositional arguments. The method it defends, as I have argued elsewhere (Walters, 1986) is best described as "analytic reductionism." This method teaches how to break arguments down into their simplest constituents—premises and conclusions—and then investigate whether or not the latter are logical inferences, either deductive or inductive, from the former. As a means of testing the presence or absence of logical soundness, critical thinking drills students in the evaluation of evidence, provides them with tips for distinguishing between relevant and irrelevant propositions, teaches them to be on the watch for hidden premises and conclusions, and warns them against an array of informal fallacies that may camouflage noncogent but good-sounding arguments. Moreover, standard critical thinking texts typically include overviews of certain semantic points: the criteria for adequate definitions, denotative and connotative meanings of words, and the various functions of language. Finally, standard presentations of the technique stress its universality, claiming that its analytical tools are applicable for the evaluation of any propositional knowledge claim. Some textbooks (Beardsley, 1975; Copi, 1986; Kelly, 1988; Ruggierio, 1984; Scriven, 1976) supplement their primary focus upon critical thinking's technique of reductionistic analysis with brief theoretical discussions of its epistemological foundations and assumptions, but most do not. Usually the standard text either completely ignores or only cursorily mentions conceptual issues (Walters, 1989) and concentrates instead upon providing rules for the analysis of arguments and exercises by which to train students in their concrete application. Logic, not epistemology, is the central theme. As Kurfiss (1988, p. 14) correctly points out, "Teaching 'critical thinking,' at least at the introductory level, has become synonymous with the methods of applied informal logic."

In order to explore the epistemological assumptions behind the critical thinking technique, then, one must turn from textbooks to the professional literature. Although there are a few dissenting opinions (De Bono, 1977, 1984; McPeck, 1981, 1985; Walters, 1986, 1987, 1988, 1989, 1990a, 1990b, 1992), most educators, psychologists, and philosophers who champion the critical thinking method as a top educational priority do so because they identify it, either implicitly or explicitly, with rational thinking. Glaser (1941, p. 5), for example, argues that the technique's formalistic rules of "logical inquiry and reasoning" enable its practitioners "to consider in a thoughtful way the problems and subjects that come within the range of one's experiences." The comprehensive applicability of critical thinking to all human experience suggested by Glaser is echoed in Ennis (1985, p. 45), who defines critical thinking as "reflective and reasonable thinking that is focused on deciding what to believe or do," in addition to the "disposition" to behave and think rationally. Consequently, critical thinking is a sufficient condition for "the correct assessment of statements" in any discipline or subject matter (Ennis, 1962).

The most explicit postulation of an identity between critical think - ing and rationality is the "reasons conception" defended by Scheffler (Scheffler, 1965, 1973, 1980) and Siegel (Siegel, 1988). This model argues that the educator "ought to keep uppermost the ideal of rationality and its emphasis on the critical, questioning, responsible free mind" (Scheffler, 1973, p. 64). Rationality, in turn, is best understood as being "co-extensive with the relevance of reasons" (Scheffler, 1965, p. 107). That is, an individual is rational if and only if he or she is capable of defending his or her arguments and opinions with sound justifications (reasons) and evaluating the justifications (reasons) of others' arguments and opinions. One determines whether a given justification is sound or not by affirming or denying its logical relevance to the conclusion it claims to defend, and the best way to do that is through an application of critical thinking's principles and rules of inference. Consequently, critical thinking is "the educational cognate of rationality" (Siegel, 1988, p. 32). In order to teach persons to be rational, therefore, one must school them in the logical skills of critical analysis, problem solving, and textual criticism. As Siegel (1988, p. 32) says, "critical thinking involves bringing to bear all matters relevant to the rationality of belief and action; and education aimed at the promulgation of critical thinking is nothing less than education aimed at the fostering of rationality and the development of rational persons."

These and other (Binkley, 1980; Johnson & Blair, 1980; Passmore, 1967; Scriven, 1980; Woods, 1980) proponents of the conventional critical thinking model, then, tend to identify rationality or good thinking with the rule-oriented inferential procedures of critical thinking. This, of course, reduces rationality to the canons of informal and formal logic. The clear implications of such a reduction are (a) good (or rational) thinking is defined in terms of cognitive processes that are exclusively logical, analytic, and conducive to problem solving, and (b) cognitive processes that are nonlogical, nonanalytic, and not directly conducive to problem solving are immediately suspect. A good (or rational) thinker cultivates the processes characteristic of (a) and avoids those which fall into (b). Moreover, the good (or rational) educator likewise focuses upon instruction in (a) and tries to wean his or her students away from (b).

This model of rationality represents what I call the "calculus of justification." It identifies good thinking with cognitive processes exclusively oriented by the logical principles of analytical computation and reduces rationality to little more than the critical scrutiny of ready-to-hand arguments. From this perspective, rationality's only proper function is to examine justifications that claim to support arguments or solve problems. More specifically, the calculus of justification model of rationality suggests that thinking is legitimate if and only if (a) It is *formalistic* in operation, exhibiting unswerving fidelity to logical rules of inference that define correct procedures for the justification and evaluation of arguments.   These inferential rules correspond to the methodological steps characteristic of conventional critical thinking's analytic reductionism discussed at the beginning of this section; (b) The process of inference defined by the principles of analytic reductionism is *transparent*. There must be no ambiguity or tacit assumptions embedded within the set of justificatory premises that lead up to a conclusion. Moreover, all premises must be supported by clearly established or at least highly probable evidence.   Otherwise, they are speculative and hence nonjustifiable; (c)   The process of inference defined by the principles of analytic reductionism must be *sequential*.   Premise A must lead immediately to premise B, premise B to premise C, and so on until the entire set of premises inevitably points to the conclusion. Any gaps in the inferential continuity of a line of reasoning indicate either that hidden premises have not been properly ferreted out or that the line of reasoning in fact is rationally indefensible; (d) The process of inference defined by the principles of analytic reductionism must be *predictable*. This characteristic follows from the previous three.   Because rational thinking conforms to logical rules of inference that mandate transparency and sequentiality, the steps in constructing and evaluating arguments are procedurally determinate.   A good thinker routinely identifies premises, checks for evidence to support them, eliminates irrelevancies, searches for fallacies, analyzes the flow of logical continuity from one premise to another, and concludes by ascertaining whether or not the set of premises justifies the conclusion.

Two general features of the calculus of justification's model of rationality follow from its four specific characteristics. First, it is what I call "evidentialistic"—that is, it insists that any legitimate premise, in addition to being logically consistent with its fellow premises, must conform to rigidly strict standards of evidential propriety. Barry (1984) speaks for most critical thinking proponents when he argues that empirical premises in inductive arguments are properly analyzed in terms of a consideration of the physical conditions under which the observation is made, the sensory acuity of the observer, the reliability of background knowledge the observer brings to his or her observation, the "objectivity" of the observer, and the presence or absence of corroborating testimony from other "objective" observers.   These five conditions are jointly necessary for determining the truth or probability of a given premise. Consequently, a premise that fails to conform to each of them is prima facie suspect. This rigorously evidentialistic imperative immediately disenfranchises intuitive and imaginative assumptions not solidly founded on empirical bases that might otherwise serve as working premises in a creatively exploratory context. They are dismissed by the calculus of justification as vague, speculative stabs that not only transgress the limits of acceptable evidence but also violate the standards of formalistic rule-adherence, logical transparency, inferential sequentiality, and methodological predictability.

Moreover, the calculus of justification model of rationality is reactive. Because it identifies good thinking with logical analysis, it concentrates upon the critical examination of already existing arguments and problems. The rational thinker, therefore, is one who responsibly searches for logical justifications through the formalistic application of computational analysis and avoids creative "what-if" shots in the dark that violate reductionistic canonicity. This evaluation epistemologically ignores the cognitive acts of intellectual or aesthetic discovery and invention and pedagogically minimalizes training in thought processes that, although perhaps not immediately logically justifiable, are necessary conditions for the envisioning of alternative paradigms and problem construction (as opposed to conventional problem solving).

The upshot of conventional critical thinking's tendency to identify logical thinking with rational thinking and its concomitant pedagogical emphasis upon training in the calculus of justification is that it undercuts the very goals its proponents espouse. Critical thinking advocates usually defend their method by appealing to any or all of three justifications. One (Barry, 1984; Johnson, 1980; Nosich, 1982; Scriven, 1976) is that the ability to analyze arguments critically is a pragmatic necessity in today's world because it prepares students to withstand the onslaughts of deceptive advertisers or unscrupulous ideologues. Another (McPeck, 1981) is that critical thinking is pedagogically necessary because the very possibility of education rests upon the ability of students to analyze arguments correctly. A third (Siegel, 1988) is that training in critical thinking is a necessary condition for fostering self-sufficiency in students, preparing them for responsible adulthood and initiating them into the "rational traditions" of science, mathematics, history, and so on. But none of these clearly admirable ideals are well served by an exclusive drilling in the calculus of justification. As I have argued in detail elsewhere (Walters, 1986, 1987, 1989), mere facility in the logical deconstruction and criticisms of propositional arguments, although possessing some pragmatic value in the 'real world,' is in itself insufficient to prepare students for careers as responsible adults and citizens. Its essentially reactive nature fails to provide training in the creative adaptability, cognitive daring, and tolerance of dissenting perspectives fundamental to survival as well as self-sufficiency. Moreover, the assumption that skill in critical analysis is a necessary condition for effective education is correct but incomplete. The ability to think logically is certainly essential for the comprehension of academic texts as well as initiation into the "rational traditions," but it is not sufficient. The successful student, in the richest sense of the term, is not one who merely learns how to analyze the ideas of others. He or she also begins to manipulate those ideas creatively, using them as springboards for imaginative leaps from the conventional to the unconventional, the known to the unknown, the orthodox to the heterodox. Anyone who teaches is sadly familiar with straight A students who follow all the rules and study all the texts but are absolutely incapable of thinking for themselves. Such students are virtuosos in the mechanical manipulation called for by the calculus of justification. They are scrupulously logical; but for all their logical acuity, they are well on the way to becoming hopelessly uninspired pedants. This is because they have been vulcanized. However, as I pointed out at the beginning of this discussion, vulcanized thinking is not rational thinking. Spock is a curious figure whose impeccable logical acuity intrigues us, but he is not a representative of good thinking. And neither are students who have been vulcanized by the calculus of justification's narrow model of rationality. Yet it is precisely this model that is canonized by curricular training in conventional critical thinking.

Creative Thinking and the Pattern of Discovery

Just as the calculus of justification is not identical to rational thought, neither is it the only cognitive game in town. Logical inference, critical analysis, and problem solving are fundamental qualities of good thinking, but only if they are complemented by the cognitive functions of imagination, insight and intuition—essential components of the pattern of discovery. The last two serve as necessary conditions for innovative speculations, intellectual and artistic creativity, and the discovery of alternative conceptual paradigms and problems. They facilitate flexibility and adaptability of new ideas, as well as novel situations and are thereby essential to the nurturing of responsible, free, and reflective adults and citizens. Along with the analytic functions characteristic of the calculus of justification, the creative functions of the pattern of discovery provide those skills, abilities, talents, and capacities that properly can be characterized as rationality or good thinking. Critical thinking and creative thinking, then, are not incompatible with one another nor are they mutually exclusive. Indeed, genuine success in one entails facility in the other. It follows that the education of good thinkers requires training in both. Effective teaching of thinking slides neither into a lopsided Spockean emphasis upon the calculus of justification (as critical thinking technique currently does) nor an equally skewed concentration upon the creative functions of the pattern of discovery. Instead, it focuses upon both, examining their complementary but irreducible natures and providing students with pedagogical opportunities for enhancement in imagination as well as analysis, creativity alongside justification, problem construction in addition to problem solving. Contrary to the claims of critical thinking's proponents, critical thinking is not the sole educational cognate of rationality.

Perhaps the central cognitive function of the pattern of discovery is imagination. Etymologically, the word is derived from the Latin imago, which means "image" or "representation." But clearly this sparse etymological definition is insufficient for our purpose inasmuch as it incorporates simple empirical images produced by visual perception, in addition to what we associate with imaginative flights of fancy, under the same rubric. Still, the Latin derivation provides us with an essential starting point: imaginative processes are characterized by nonanalytical imagings. Imaginative constructs are not reductionistic. They are attempts at capturing whole representations rather than analyzing their components. They strive for comprehensiveness and frequently sacrifice details for the sake of the broader pattern. Consequently, imaginative paradigms are often more vague than analytical deconstructions of ready-to-hand conceptual models.

What is the nature of these nonanalytical writings? Wittgenstein provides a clue in his *Philosophical Investigations* (1963, p. 213) when he says, "Doesn't it take imagination to hear [or see] something as a variation on a particular theme?" For Wittgenstein, the imaginative function typically goes beyond a merely passive perceptual absorption of a particular object of experience by examining it from a new perspective, focusing upon aspects of the image that are usually so taken for granted that they bypass our scrutiny, and "seeing" them in new, fresh ways. The process of taking this uncommon view he calls "seeing-as" (1963, p. 197). Imagination does not merely "see-that" this square, dense, reddish object is conventionally called a "brick" and possesses a conventional pragmatic use. Instead, it envisions new possibilities by "*seeing* the brick as," for instance, a wall hanging or a bookend, or as a source, when pulverized, or red pigment. This imaginative reconstruction of a conventional object with a conventional utility presupposes the ability on the part of the perceiver to go "beyond the actualities in which [he or she is] immersed," to "know that something other than this immediate temporary reality is possible" (Hanson, 1988, p. 138). It requires that he or she temporarily suspend fidelity to a literalistic "seeing-that" mode of representation and move beyond the obvious and conventional to a "seeing-as" imaging. It involves, as Arnheim (1974, p. 142) says, the invention of a strikingly alternative pattern that constitutes "the finding of new form for old content or...a fresh conception of an old subject."

Wittgenstein's distinction between seeing-that and seeing-as points to a characteristic of imagination that is often missed. Imaginative constructs are never created in a vacuum. They always arise within a discrete context and on the basis of a background of established knowledge and conventional perceptions (what Wittgenstein calls "language games"). They envision new possibilities by taking uncommon views of given aspects, not by shutting out reality and creating *ex nihilo*. This suggests three qualitatively necessary features of imaginative envisionings. First, they are unusual, insofar as they go beyond common modes of seeing-that, but their unconventionality is always rooted in and emerges from a given evidential base. As Barrow (1988) correctly argues, the mere generation of unusual ideas may not constitute imagination. Odd or unorthodox ideas can be nonconventional without necessarily being imaginative, particularly when they are absurd, incoherent, whimsical, or delusional. This points to the second feature of imaginative construction: it must be effective, genuinely capable of extending cognitive comprehension and enriching practical utility. It also underscores the earlier point that imaginative constructs are formulated in a given context and on an evidential basis. But mere effectiveness by itself is not, of course, a sufficient condition for designating an idea as imaginative. Effective or pragmatic ideas that lack the quality of unusualness or novelty are properly described as competent or sound, not imaginative. Finally, imaginative constructions are not merely disguised inductive inferences. They do not arise from a sequential and logical consideration of data that point to a probabilistic conclusion. This is because seeing-as is nonreductionistic, as well as nonanalytic. The imaginative function generates whole imagical patterns on the basis of a given set of assumptions or perceptions, but it does not do so in a step-by-step, rule-oriented way. It is, if you will, a process of refocusing upon hitherto ignored or overlooked aspects, not a transparently logical inference from A to B. This is not to suggest that imaginative paradigms subsequently may not be analyzed according to the logical rules of the calculus of justification and accordingly strengthened, modified, or rejected, but only that their initial discovery is based upon a wholistic imaging rather than a reductionistic computation.

Closely related to the pattern of discovery's imaginative function is intuition. Intuition may be described as a perception that occurs spontaneously in the absence of conscious deliberation or logical calculation (Stewart, 1988; Westcott, 1968). Intuitive insights often follow intensive reflection upon a particular problem within a specific context, but, when and if they arise, they are unexpected and not consciously premeditated. Characteristically they hit the subject with a sudden and comprehensive "Aha!" impact. Their realization is often visual rather than propositional and frequently entails an initial nonverbalizability (Bruner & Clinchy, 1966). They are immediate representations that bestow comprehensive "meaning" (Noddings & Shore, 1984) or an awareness of "verisimilitude" (Bruner, 1986) rather than analytic definition. As Arnheim (1985, p. 94) suggests, "Intuition is privileged to perceive the overall structure of configurations. Intellectual analysis serves to abstract the character of entities and events from individual contexts and defines them 'as such'."

Although the process of intuition clearly is similar in nature to the imaginative mode of seeing-as, there appears to be at least one fundamental distinction that differentiates the two. The imaginative mode is deliberate and conscious. A subject who attempts imaginative construction is aware of what he or she is doing and cognizant of the fact that he or she is engaged in an attempt to capture the uncommon perspective. It is often the case that the product of imaginative speculation is surprising to or unexpected by the subject, but the act of imagination itself is intentional. Intuitive insight on the other hand is not. Consequently, it is always unanticipated. It simply happens, and often when the subject least expects a breakthrough. As with imaginative construction, intuitive insights are capable of being examined and tested according to the standards of the calculus of justification after their emergence. Moreover, they likewise may arise from an evidential base defined by the specific problem with which the subject is wrestling. But they are not the final product of a sequential logical inference, precisely because the subject who experiences an intuition is unable to account for the reasons for its appearance.

On the basis of these descriptions of the two cognitive processes essential to the pattern of discovery's creative mode of thinking, we now see that this function of rationality is characterized by its noninferential and constructive going beyond ready-to-hand arguments and paradigms toward the invention and discovery of new ones. The calculus of justification process analyzes received knowledge claims, while the pattern of discovery adds to and extends them. More specifically, the functional qualities of imagination and intuition suggest the following about the pattern of discovery's creative mode of thinking. (a) Unlike the logical analysis of the calculus of justification, creative thinking is *nonformalistic*. It is constrained in operation by neither deductive nor inductive procedural rules, although it clearly takes as its starting point knowledge claims that have been arrived at through formalistic logical analysis. This is just another way of saying that creative speculation emerges from a context and is not performed *in vacuo*; (b) The process of discovery characteristic of creative thinking is often *opaque* rather than transparent. Imaginative as well as intuitive modes of thinking aim toward the invention or discovery of comprehensive imagings characterized by harmony and verisimilitude. The specific contents of these harmonious forms may not be any more immediately apparent than the process or steps by which they were arrived at. This implies that the justifications of creative imagings are always after and never prior to their actual emergence. They are evaluated in terms of their effectiveness and coherency, not in terms of the process from which they arose; (c) Moreover, the specific processes leading to their emergence are *nonsequential* (or what De Bono [1977, 1984] calls "lateral"). The intuitive thinker does not follow a consistent and premeditated chain of reasoning any more than the imaginative thinker. Instead, the process of discovery is better characterized as a series of leaps from the given to the unknown. These leaps may culminate in dead ends or, conversely, may serve as solid foundations for further explorations, but they are not computationally inferential in the way calculus of justification processes are. Instead, they are often disjointed, spontaneous, and seemingly random, resembling what Polanyi (1964, 1985) designates as "tacit jumps" or Koestler (1964, 1979) calls "infolding" or "holonistic" knowing; (d) Finally, creative thinking is *indeterminate* in regard to both its processes and the specifics of its products. This characteristic follows from the previous three. Unlike the calculus of justification, there is no predictable procedural blueprint that regulates the pattern of discovery. Nor is there an entailment or high degree of inductive-like probability that imaginative constructs or intuitive flashes will in fact prove effective or innovative. This is not to suggest, however, that creative thinking is arbitrary or whimsically fantastical. Again, imaginative speculations and intuitive insights are not *ex nihilo*. Instead, they are constrained and influenced by the context from which they spring.

All of this points to two general features of the pattern of discovery that functionally differentiate it from the calculus of justification. First, it is "evidential" rather than evidentialistic. Creative imagings and intuitive insights are always contextual, emerging from a given base of received knowledge or data. Moreover, they are testable after their discovery according to their degree of coherency, their effectiveness in expanding comprehension and construction of new problems and paradigms, and their consistency to available evidence. But the process by which they are arrived at need not conform to the strict evidentialistic standards insisted upon by the calculus of justification. This is just to underscore the fact that the cognitive acts of discovery and invention are not sequentially inferential and should not be judged in terms of either the standard of logical transparency or an immediate fidelity to the five standards of evidentialistic propriety that Barry (1984) defends. Second, the pattern of discovery is active, not merely reactive. Its imaginative and intuitive functions serve as the necessary conditions for going beyond the straightforward analysis of ready-to-hand arguments toward the construction of new ones. These functions do not aim at the critical reduction of conventional beliefs so much as the synthetic elaboration of comprehensive models and patterns. True, the alternative paradigms provided by imagination and intuition are more susceptible to error than the formalistic analyses characteristic of the calculus of justification, but this is an inevitable as well as acceptable risk of innovative thinking. Moreover, as pointed out earlier, there are ad hoc strategies for testing the credibility of such conceptual inventions.

Scientists and mathematicians have long acknowledged, albeit sometimes reluctantly, the role of pattern of discovery processes in the formulation of new theoretical paradigms and problems. Einstein, James Clerk Maxwell, Michael Faraday, von Helmholtz, Francis Galton, Nikola Tesla, John Herschel, Henri Poincare, James Watson, and others claim to have broken new ground in their respective fields through the use of noninferential imagination and nonverbalizable intuitions (Shepard, 1988). Evidence such as this, as well as an increasing appreciation of the cognitive limitation of analytic reductionism, have prompted an increasing number of educators, psychologists, and philosophers (for example, Adler, 1982; Belenky, Clinchy, Goldberger & Tarule, 1986; Brown, 1967; Bruner, 1962, 1966, 1986; De Bono, 1977, 1984; Freie, 1987; Girle, 1983; Hausman, 1976; Kagan, 1967; Koestler, 1964; Matthews, 1988; McPeck, 1985; Nadaner, 1988; Noddings & Shore, 1984; Polanyi, 1985; Stewart, 1988; Torrance, 1976; Walker, 1988; Weininger, 1988) to argue that exposure to the pattern of discovery is as essential an ingredient in quality education as training in the calculus of justification. None of these individuals argues for the curricular elimination of the conventional model of thinking. Nor do I. Instead, the claim is that rationality involves cognitive functions characteristic of the pattern of discovery, as well as the calculus of justification, and that, consequently, the pedagogical cognate of rationality will emphasize training in both. But the current emphasis upon the calculus of justification, which stems from conventional critical thinking's erroneous identification of logical inference with rationality, by and large ignores classroom strategies that enhance receptivity to imagination and intuition. This is indicated by a recent study (McDonough & McDonough, 1988) that discovered that only 76 out of 1,188 surveyed American colleges and universities offered opportunities for course work in creativity enhancement, even though most of those same institutions required or at least offered training in critical thinking. Curricular instruction in thinking, then, focuses upon a Spockean model of rationality, which results, unfortunately, in the vulcanization of students. Such a model is promotive of neither true rationality nor the formation of responsible and free adults and citizens, which are the stated aims of critical thinking.

A Bonesian Epilogue

I have argued here that rationality or good thinking encompasses both logical (calculus of justification) and nonlogical (pattern of discovery) cognitive functions. Moreover, I have claimed that the two are complementary: good thinking incorporates the ability to analyze critically given arguments and knowledge claims as well as the capacity for envisioning alternative ideas, paradigms, and problems. This comprehensive account of rationality, which focuses upon critical *and* creative thinking, not only better reflects the nature of human thought than a model that emphasizes one at the expense of the other. It also suggests a pedagogical cognate that is broader in scope than the lopsided one currently endorsed by conventional critical thinking. Education in thinking, if it truly aims at the nurturing of responsible adults and citizens, must do more than train students in the formal procedures of analytic reductionism. It must also cultivate in them a receptivity to imaginative and intuitive apprehensions. Good thinkers are not merely mechanical, Vulcan-like computational devices. They are also creative adventurers who are willing and able to at least temporarily suspend their fidelity to rule-oriented inferential analysis in order to venture into unexplored speculative regions. I do not take this to be a terribly original thesis. Nor do I claim to have done any more here than to highlight the broad characteristics of critical and creative thinking; clearly much work remains to be done. But I do insist that the conventional critical thinking model, inasmuch as it tends to identify logical thinking with rationality, has missed the basic point that the goals of training in thinking are ill served by an exclusive concentration upon the canons of formal and informal logic. Such an approach does not school students in rationality. Instead, it vulcanizes them by overplaying the calculus of justification and underemphasizing—if not outright ignoring—the pattern of discovery.

If I am correct, the impeccably logical Spock, intriguing as he may be, is neither a proper representative of good thinking nor an example that we educators should want our students to emulate. Instead, he is an illustration of the disconcerting consequences of hypertrophically cultivating one set of cognitive functions at the expense of the other. A much more fruitful model of rationality, I would suggest, is McCoy, the "Enterprise's" Chief Medical Officer. Bones is constitutionally incapable of Spock's immaculate logical acuity, but this is a strength rather than a weakness. There is no question that he possesses logical aptitude and is able to evaluate arguments on the basis of their inferential soundness and evidentialistic support. He is, after all, a scientist and medical diagnostician and consequently relies upon both inductive and deductive reasoning when confronted with a problem. But Bones, unlike Spock, is also remarkably receptive to the imaginative and intuitive functions characteristic of the pattern of discovery. He is willing to play hunches and explore nonconventional speculations, even if they cannot immediately be justified on strictly logical grounds. This is not to imply that he is illogical, as his Vulcan friend usually concludes, but rather that he appreciates the value of nonlogical cognitive processes as well as the necessity of logical ones. Sometimes Bone's willingness to suspend allegiance to analytic reductionism gets him into trouble, but it just as often enables him to reach a level of effectiveness and comprehension that is quite beyond Spock's purview.

Bones, in short, is a well-rounded thinker who calls upon both critical and creative thought processes. He does not sacrifice creativity for the sake of literalistic security, nor critical analysis for the sake of self-indulgent whimsy. His logic is tempered by his willingness to take imaginative and intuitive risks. His creativity, in turn, is properly mediated by his awareness of the importance of inferential reasoning and evidence. The upshot is that Bones is rational, in the best sense of the word. Spock is not. Curricular education in critical thinking would do well to drop its implicit epistemological and pedagogical allegiance to the latter and adopt the former as its role model. Exclusive concentration upon the calculus of justification may be appropriate for Vulcans because they are genetically incapable of going beyond a lockstep fidelity to logic. But it is inappropriate, as well as dangerous, to attempt to vulcanize humans. We are less, and at the same time much more, than Spock-like thinkers.

References

Adler, M.J. (1982). *The Paideia Proposal: An Educational Manifesto.* New York: Macmillan.

Arnheim, R. (1974). *Art and Visual Perception: A Psychology of the Creative Eye.* 2nd ed. Berkeley: University of California Press.

Arnheim, R. (1985). The double-edged mind: Intuition and the intellect. In E. Eisner (Ed.), *Learning and Teaching the Ways of Knowing*, 84th year-book of the National Society for the Study of Education, part 1, pp. 77–96. Chicago, Ill.: University of Chicago Press.

Barrow, R. (1988). Some observations on the concept of imagination. In K. Egan and D. Nadaner (Eds.), *Imagination and Education*, pp. 79–90. New York: Teachers College Press.

Barry, V.E. (1984). *Invitation to Critical Thinking.* New York: Holt, Rinehart & Winston.

Beardsley, M.C. (1975). *Thinking Straight: Principles of Reasoning for Readers and Writers.* 4th ed. Englewood Cliffs, N.J.: Prentice-Hall.

Belenky, M.F., Clinchy, B.M., Goldberger, N.R., and Tarule, J.M. (1986). *Women's Ways of Knowing: The Development of Self, Voice, and Mind.* New York: Basic Books, Inc.

Binkley, R. (1980). Can the ability to reason well be taught? In J.A. Blair and R. H. Johnson (eds.), *Informal Logic: The First International Symposium*, pp. 79–92. Inverness, CA: Edgepress, 1980.

Brown, J.D. (1967). The development of creative teacher-scholars. In J. Kagan (ed.), *Creativity and Learning*, pp. 164–80. Boston: Beacon Press.

Bruner, J.S. (1986). *Actual Minds, Possible Worlds.* Cambridge, Mass.: Harvard University Press.

——. (1962). *On Knowing: Essays for the Left Hand.* Cambridge, Mass.: Harvard University Press.

Bruner, J.S., & Clinchy, B. (1966). Towards a disciplined intuition. In J.S. Bruner (Ed.), *Learning About Learning*. Washington, D.C.: Bureau of Research, Office of Education, U.S. Department of Health, Education and Welfare.

Copi, I. M. (1986). *Informal Logic*. New York: Macmillan.

De Bono, E. (1984). Critical thinking is not enough. *Educational Leadership* 42, 16–17.

——. (1977). *Lateral Thinking: A Textbook of Creativity*. Harmondsworth, England: Penguin.

Ennis, R. H. (1962). A concept of critical thinking. *Harvard Educational Review* 32, 81–111.

——. (1985). A logical basis for measuring critical thinking skills. *Educational Leadership* 43, 44–48.

Freie, J.F. (1987). Thinking and believing. *College Teaching* 35, 98–101.

Girle, R.A. (1983). A top-down approach to the teaching of reasoning skills. In W. Maxwell (Ed.), *Thinking: The Expanding Frontier*. Philadelphia: Franklin Institute Press.

Glaser, E.M. (1941). *An Experiment in the Development of Critical Thinking*. New York: Teachers College of Columbia University, Bureau of Publications.

Hanson, K. (1988). Prospects for the good life: Education and perceptive imagination. In K. Egan and D. Nadaner (Eds.), *Imagination and Education*, pp. 128–40. New York: Teachers College Press.

Hausman, C.R. (1976). Creativity and rationality. In A. Rothenberg and C.R. Hausman (Eds.), *The Creativity Question*, pp. 343–51. Durham, N.C.: Duke University Press.

Johnson, R.H., & Blair, J.A. (1980). The recent development of informal logic. In J.A. Blair and R.H. Johnson (Eds.), *Informal Logic: The First International Symposium*, pp. 3–30. Inverness, Calif.: Edgepress.

Kagan, J. (1967). Personality and the learning process. In J. Kagan (Ed.), *Creativity and Learning*, pp. 153–63. Boston: Beacon Press.

Kelly, D. (1988). *The Art of Reasoning*. New York: W.W. Norton.

Koestler, A. (1964). *The Act of Creation*. New York: Macmillan.

Koestler, A. (1979). *Janus: A Summing Up*. New York: Vintage.

Kurfiss, J.G. (1988). *Critical Thinking: Theory, Research, Practice, and Possibility*. Washington, D.C.: ASHE-ERIC Higher Education Report No. 2.

Matthews, G. (1988). The philosophical imagination in children's literature. In K. Egan and D. Nadaner (Eds.), *Imagination and Education*, pp. 186–97. New York: Teachers College Press.

McDonough, P., and McDonough, B. (1988). A survey of American colleges and universities on the conducting of formal courses in creativity. *Journal of Creative Behavior* 21, 271–82.

McPeck, J.E. (1981). *Critical Thinking and Education*. New York: St. Martin's Press.

——. (1985). Critical thinking and the 'trivial pursuit' theory of knowledge. *Teaching Philosophy* 8, 295–308.

Moore, B. (1983). Critical thinking in California. *Teaching Philosophy* 6, 321–30.

Nadaner, D. (1988). Visual imagery, imagination and education. In K. Egan and D. Nadaner (Eds.), *Imagination and Education*, pp. 198–207. New York: Teachers College Press.

Noddings, N., and Shore, P.J. (1984). *Awakening the Inner Eye: Intuition in Education*. New York: Teachers College Press.

Nosich, G.M. (1982). *Reasons and Arguments*. Belmont, Calif.: Wadsworth.

Passmore, J. (1967). On teaching to be critical. In R.S. Peters (Ed.), *The Concept of Education*, pp. 192–211. London: Routledge & Kegan Paul.

Paul, R.W. (1985). Critical thinking research: A Response to Stephen Norris. *Educational Leadership* 42, p. 46.

Polanyi, M. (1985). *Personal Knowledge: Towards a Post-Critical Philosophy*. New York: Harper & Row.

——. (1964). *The Tacit Dimension*. New York: Peter Smith.

Ruggierio, V.R. (1984). *The Art of Thinking: A Guide to Critical and Creative Thought*. New York: Harper and Row.

Scheffler, I. (1965). *Conditions of Knowledge*. Springfield, Ill.: Scott Foresman.

——. (1973). Philosophical models of teaching. In I. Scheffler (Ed.), *Reason and Teaching*, pp. 67–81. London: Routledge & Kegan Paul.

——. (1980). Critical thinking as an educational ideal. *Educational Forum* 45, 7–23.

Scriven, M. (1976). *Reasoning*. New York: McGraw-Hill.

——. (1980). The philosophical and pragmatic significance of informal logic. In J.A. Blair and R.H. Johnson (Eds.), *Informal Logic: The first International Symposium*, pp. 147–60. Inverness, Calif.: Edgepress.

Shepard, R. (1988). The imagination of the scientist. In K. Egan and D. Nadaner (Eds.), *Imagination and Education*, pp. 153–85. New York: Teachers College Press.

Siegel, H. (1988). *Educating Reason: Rationality, Critical Thinking and Education.* New York: Routledge.

Stewart, W.J. (1988). Stimulating intuitive thought through problem solving. *The Clearing House for the Contemporary Educator in Middle and Secondary Schools* 62, 175–76.

Torrance, E.P. (1976). Education and creativity. In A. Rothenberg and C.R. Hausman (Eds.), *The Creativity Question*, pp. 217–26. Durham, N.C.: Duke University Press.

Walker, R. (1988). In search of a child's musical imagination. In K. Egan and D. Nadaner (Eds.), *Imagination and Education*, pp. 209–11. New York: Teachers College Press.

Walters, K.S. (1986). Critical thinking in liberal education: A case of overkill? *Liberal Education* 72, 233–44.

———. (1987). Critical thinking and the danger of intellectual conformity. *Innovative Higher Education* 11, 94–102.

———. (1988). On bullshitting and brainstorming. *Teaching Philosophy* 11, 301–13.

———. (1989). Critical thinking in teacher education: Towards a demythologization. *Journal of Teacher Education* 30, 14–19.

———. (1990a). Critical thinking and the Spock fallacy. *Innovative Higher Education* 15, 17–28.

———. (1990b). How critical is critical thinking? *The Clearing House* 64, 57–61.

———. (1992). Critical thinking, logicism, and the eclipse of imagining. *Journal of Creative Behavior* 26, 130–44.

Weininger, O. (1988). 'What if' and 'as if': Imagination and pretend play in early childhood. In K. Egan and D. Nadaner (Eds.), *Imagination and Education*, pp. 141–49. New York: Teachers College Press.

Westcott, M.R. (1968). *Toward a Contemporary Psychology of Intuition.* New York: Holt, Rinehart and Winston.

Wittgenstein, L. (1963). *Philosophical Investigations.* Translated by G.E.M. Anscombe. New York: Macmillan.

Woods, J. (1980). What is informal logic? In J.A. Blair and R.H. Johnson (Eds.), *Informal Logic: The First International Symposium*, pp. 57–68. Inverness, Calif.: Edgepress.

5

Toward a Gender-Sensitive Ideal of Critical Thinking: A Feminist Poetic

Anne M. Phelan and James W. Garrison

The last decade or so has witnessed the appearance of what Jane Roland Martin calls "the new scholarship on woman."[1] A very short list of these scholars would include Mary Belenky[2] and colleagues, Carol Gilligan,[3] Evelyn Fox Keller,[4] Sarah Ruddick[5] and Jane Roland Martin.[6] Reading the writings of these and many other women opens up windows that allow us to look out upon lively new educational landscapes. One such window has been opened with the renewed role that unreconciled paradoxes, contradictions, and contraries are often allowed to take in our images of rational thinking and the rational thinker. We have been repeatedly struck by the way that writers within the new scholarship will explicitly present some of their most important insights and results in the form of permanent paradoxes and irreconcilable but complementary contraries.

Almost as remarkable as the willingness of the new scholarship to embrace contraries is its unwillingness to appeal to dialectical thinking to resolve them. We believe that there are good grounds for the new scholarship's hesitation to embrace dialectical thinking with the same eagerness that it appears willing to embrace contraries. The two dominant forms of dialectical thinking, the classical dialectic of Plato and Aristotle as well as the modern dialectic of Hegel and Marx, both display elements of gender bias. We will try to show why the new scholarship would most likely be better served by the dialectic of the poets rather than the truth-seeking dialectic of the philosophers. The refusal to reconcile some crucial contraries points to the possibility of a radical reconstruction of what it means to be a rational person, one that accords the logical principle of noncontradiction considerably reduced status.

If we are right about the role of irreconcilable paradox, poetic dialectic, and the possibility of a radical reconstruction of what it means to be rational, then one of the things we as educators will want to reconsider is our ideal of critical thinking and the critical thinker. In our conclusion we will want to consider the contribution of Peter Elbow, Jane Roland Martin, and Deanne Bogdan toward the development of the idea of embracing contraries as providing a possible feminist poetic of critical thinking.

Paradoxes* in the Images of Relationships

In her book, *Maternal Thinking*, Sarah Ruddick relates the experience of a mother whose feelings for her newborn child sway from intense love to hate. Ruddick's tale of preservative love is spun on a night when Julie, the mother, along with her baby, slept lightly. As usual, the baby was wailing. Or, rather, the baby was screaming. Ruddick quotes Julie:

> I stumble towards your room and switch on the low lamp so the light will not startle you. You toss your body back and forth, arch your back and wail and call. Trembling, I walk to your bed and check your diaper. I try to speak, to soothe, to give voice to my presence, but my throat constricts in silent screaming and I find I cannot touch your tangled blankets. I force myself to turn and walk away, leaning against the door jam. My knees buckle beneath me and I find myself huddled on the floor. "Please do not cry. Oh child I love, please do not cry. Tonight you can breathe, so let me breath." And I realize my chest is locked and I am gasping for breathe. I picture myself walking towards you, lifting your tininess in both my hands and flinging you at the window. Mixed with my choking I can almost hear the glass as it would smash and I see your body, your perfect body, swirl through the air and land three stories below on the pavement."[7]

We are told that, sickened by her vision, Julie vomited and then felt calmer. Ruddick explains that, "After changing the baby's diaper and propping a warm bottle so that she could drink, Julie shut the door to the baby's room, barricading it against herself with a large armchair...."[8]

"Thought-provoking ambivalence is a hallmark of mothering," Ruddick concludes.[9] The thinking in which Julie engaged is indicative of a mother-love intermixed with hate, sorrow, impatience, resentment, and despair. In Julie's case, thinking was not an affectless activity. Instead, it was the very passionate feelings of love and hate and Julie's attachment to her baby that facilitated her preservative thought and subsequently, her protective action. Ruddick calls this kind of thinking "protective thinking," and she insists that thinkers have feelings about the subjects they think about.

> In maternal thinking, feelings are at best complex but sturdy instruments of work quite unlike the simple and separate hates, fears, and loves that are usually put aside and put down in philosophical analyses....Rather than separating reason from feeling, mothering makes reflective feeling one of the most difficult attainments of reason.[10]

Sarah Ruddick's understanding of protective thinking stands in stark contrast to our inherited Western tradition of reflective, critical thinking. While reflective thinking relies on a division between "inner" self and "outer" world, protective thinking relies on the connection between the self and one's world. Moreover, while "truth" and the logic of noncontradiction are the hallmarks of reflective thinking, ambivalence and contradiction characterize Ruddick's formation. On hearing Julie's narrative, we are left to deal with notions of "passionate thought" and "thoughtful feeling." Ruddick writes that,

> In protective work, feeling, thinking and action are conceptually linked; feelings demand reflection, which is in turn tested by action, which is in turn tested by the feelings it provokes. Thoughtful feeling, passionate thought, and protective acts together test, even as they reveal, the effectiveness of preservative love.[11]

Protective thinking is paradoxical in nature. In being at the same time true and not true, paradox violates the accepted logical categories of sense—in this case, emotion/reason, passion/thought, feeling/reflection—defined and established since the Enlightenment. A colleague of ours, Leigh Garrison, points out that

> the very violation of those logical categories serves at the same time to expose their limitations by revealing dimensions of experience in which they do not apply, but which nonetheless yield meaning on investigation.[12]

Motherhood seems to be one of those dimensions.

Toward the end of the second chapter of her *In a Different Voice,* titled "Images of Relationships," Carol Gilligan considers two images of self and society. She contrasts "the imagery of hierarchy and web, drawn from the texts of men's and women's fantasies and thoughts." The image of hierarchy follows a masculine gender construction that tends to emphasize domination, self-assertion, and moral judgment resting upon arbitrary and abstract rules and principles. The contrary image of the web follows a feminine gender construction and tends to emphasize intimate relationships, caring response, and personal moral responsibility. One of Gilligan's respondents explained:

> There are no moral absolutes. Laws are pragmatic instruments, but they are not absolutes. A viable society can't make exceptions all the time, but I would personally...I feel an obligation...not to hurt....[13]

"But these images," declares Gilligan, "create a problem in understanding because each distorts the other's representation."[14] She then goes on to observe "the power of the images of hierarchy and web, their evocation of feeling and their recurrence in thought, signifies the embeddedness of both these images in the cycle of human life."[15] Gilligan then closes with this antinomy/paradox:

> These disparate visions in their tension reflect the paradoxical truths of human experience—that we know ourselves as separate only insofar as we live in connection with others, and that we experience relationships only insofar as we differentiate other from self.[16]

The two visions are contrary—they can never be fully reconciled, but the relation is a complementary one and their connection is dialectical, although the exact nature of this tense dialectical connection remains unstated.

The paradoxes upon which we want to focus attention are all in one way or another paradoxes in the images of relationship. Some, like the one framed by Ruddick, focus on the complementarity of emotion and reason in the context of the mother-child relationship and maternal thinking. Others, such as that presented by Gilligan, explore the moral and sociopolitical relationships between self and society. Still other paradoxes, like that posed by Evelyn Fox Keller, are concerned with the epistemological relationships between knower and known.

In her biographical work about Barbara McClintock, titled *A Feeling for the Organism*, Keller describes the scientist's wholistic approach to science. Barbara McClintock seeks to honor "the complexity she sees in nature and the individual uniqueness of the organisms she studies."[17] Keller recalls McClintock's words from a conversation:

> ...when I was really working with them I wasn't outside, I was down there. I was part of the system. I was right down there with them, and everything got big. I even was able to see the internal parts of the chromosomes—actually everything was there. It surprised me because I actually felt as if I were right down there and these were my friends.[18]

McClintock speaks about her materials affectionately, referring to her corn plants as unique entities. She continues, "No two plants are exactly alike. They're all different....I know them intimately, and I find it a great pleasure to know them."[19]

McClintock's way of doing research cannot be easily subsumed within dominant metascientific theories. Instead, rejecting the subject-object dualism, the scientist's relationship with the "objects" of her research—corn plants (ears, kernels, and cells)—can be best described as intimate and connected. McClintock's research methodology contrasts sharply with the pervasive scientific approach that reifies "objectivity." Keller uses the term "objectivism" to refer to the currently dominant androcentric ideal of objectivity. Objectivism requires that the subject contribute nothing to the act of coming to know an object. Objectivism is founded upon metaphysical realism, the idea that there is a totally mind-independent reality, and, epistemologically, upon the correspondence theory of truth, i.e., the idea that knowledge arises only when our previously entirely detached minds correspond to external reality. Any contribution of the subject to knowledge acquisition is discredited and reduced to mere subjectivism. This sharp separation between subject and object gives rise to such unfortunate and untenable structuralist dualisms and discontinuities as the subject/object, theory/fact, fact/value, and primary/secondary quality distinctions.

After deconstructing objectivism, Keller attempts to reconstruct objectivity by reconnecting the subject to the object. She calls the result "dynamic objectivity" and says that it is "a pursuit of knowledge that makes use of subjective experience." In what Keller calls "an exquisite balancing act," dynamic objectivity recognizes the role of the self in the act of knowing although it refuses to allow itself to be reduced to the romance of mere subjectivism. In contrary fashion it also recognizes the role of other persons, things, and events in the act of knowing, although, again, it refuses to allow itself to be reduced to the romance of objectivism. The relation is a paradoxical one. As Keller indicates, dynamic objectivity is "premised on continuity, it recognizes difference between self and other as an opportunity for a deeper and more articulated kinship. The struggle to disentangle self from other is itself a source of insight—potentially into the nature of both self and other."[20] Genuine knowledge of others (persons, objects, or events) requires self-knowledge, a state that can only arise as the result of self-reflection.

As writers Ruddick, Gilligan, and Keller have shown, our cultural assumptions about "objectivity" and "detachment" as foundational to knowledge do not apply in the realm of women's experiences. For many women a natural foundation for knowledge is in "closeness, connectedness, and empathy."[21] This insight presents us with a different cultural narrative of the self as thinker.

Similar to these paradoxes in the images of relationships—emotion and reason, web and hierarchy, objective and subjective knowing—we find the paradox of critical thinking in the contrary but complementary relationship of doubting and believing. It is the distinct logic of such paradoxical thinking that we wish to legitimate. The "new" logic is grounded in intersubjectivity—shared conversation and community. It constructs knowledge and meaning by using separate and connected ways of knowing—i.e., from paradoxical circumstances in the context of ordinary everyday living.

Separate and Connected Knowing, Doubting, and Believing

Mary Belenky, Blythe Clinchy, Nancy Goldberger, and Jill Tarule borrow and build on the terms *separate* and *connected* used by Carol Gilligan and Nona Lyons to describe two different senses of self. Belenky et al., borrowing phrases from Lyons, describe the differences this way: "The separate [autonomous] self experiences relationships in terms of 'reciprocity,' considering others as it wishes to be considered. The connected self experiences relationships as 'response to others in their terms'"[22]—claim that, if correct, contains tremendous consequences for our understanding of the golden rule. Belenky and her colleagues build this idea into a distinction between two modes of *knowing*, separate and connected, adding that when they "speak of separate and connected knowing we refer not to any sort of relationships between the self and another person but with relationship between knowers and the objects (or subjects) of knowing (which may or may not be persons)."[23] They then conjecture that "the two modes may be gender related."[24] They are careful to note that these modes are not gender specific and that they are somewhat mixed in most people.

Separate knowers rely on argumentative reasoning and objective facts. "At the heart of separate knowing," declare Belenky et al., "is critical thinking [as we know it], or, as Peter Elbow puts it, 'the doubting game.'"[25] The game is played by the laws of discursive logic following the belief that "Laws, not men, govern the world."[26] It is, they say, an "essentially adversarial form."[27]

Separate knowing is characteristic of Elbow's rationalist model of education. Teaching and learning become matters of abstract, dispassionate, and detached rationality. For Elbow there is a distinct connection between teaching and the giving of reasons on the part of the teacher. He cites Scheffler to make his point: "To teach, in the standard sense, is at some points at least to submit oneself to the understanding and independent judgment of the pupil, to his demand for reasons, to his sense of what constitutes an adequate explanation."[28] Teacher and students are participants in some ritualized cognitive combat to which there is always a resolution—a rational, logical, knowing victor.

"Connected knowing," write Belenky et al., "builds on the subjectivists' conviction that the most trustworthy knowledge comes from personal experience,"[29] especially personal experience of others (which may or may not be persons) that emphasizes empathetic modes of knowing. In so far as possible, connected knowers are prone to seeing the other not in their own terms but in the other's terms. Elbow calls this procedure the believing game.[30] Where the doubting game suspends belief, the believing game suspends doubt. Connected knowers suspend judgment in order to understand and arrive at meaning rather than invoke (predicative) judgment in order to explain and arrive at truth. Elbow's doubting and believing games are dialectically contrary but complementary; eventually they will help us move closer to a feminist poetic of critical thinking.

Connected knowing is reminiscent of Martha Nussbaum's "love's knowledge." Nussbaum is concerned with how one comes to know "the condition of one's heart where love is concerned"[31]—whether one loves someone or not. One view, she explains, is that love's knowledge

> can best be attained by a detached, unemotional exact intellectual scrutiny of one's condition, conducted in the way a scientist would conduct a piece of research. We attend carefully, with subtle

intellectual passion, to the vicissitudes of our passion, sorting, analyzing, classifying.[32]

The writer-philosopher rejects this sort of "objective," disconnected, scientific scrutiny as both unnecessary and insufficient for the requisite self-knowledge. Nussbaum argues that knowing love is "knowing how to go beyond…skepticism and solitude."[33] She explains that

> …this view does not simply substitute for the activity of the knowing intellect some other single and simple inner attitude or state of the person, holding that knowledge consists in this. It insists that knowledge of love is not a state or function of the solitary person at all, but a complex way of being, feeling, and interacting with another person. To know one's own love is to trust it, to allow oneself to be exposed. It is, above all, to trust the other person, suspending…doubts.34

To know our own love we must sometimes suspend all doubts and simply believe or trust in ourselves in intimate connection to others. Recall Gilligan's paradoxical conclusion cited earlier.

The Position of Constructed Knowledge

Belenky and her colleagues propose "The Position of Constructed Knowledge"[35] as a way of relating and integrating, without necessarily reconciling, separate versus connected knowing. They seem to see the two modes of knowing as contrary but complementary (as in doubting and believing).

At the core of the constructivist position is the claim that "All knowledge is constructed and the knower is an intimate part of the known."[36] Such a view insists that since knowledge is constructed it is open to the permanent possibility of reconstruction. Belenky et al. write:

> Women constructivists show a high tolerance for internal contradiction and ambiguity. They abandon completely the either/or thinking so common to the previous positions described. They recognize the inevitability of conflict and stress and, although they may hope to achieve some respite, they also, as one woman explained, 'learn to live with conflict rather than talking or acting it away.' They no longer want to suppress or deny aspects of the self in order to avoid conflict or simplify their lives.[37]

This leads many back toward trust and intimacy, a respect for individual uniqueness in the context of a deep and articulated kinship. Through shared conversations meaning is made with many others, moment to moment, here and now, in the context of ordinary concrete everyday living in all its wonderful complexity.

Embracing Contraries: A Poetic Dialectic

As we have seen, at the center of connected knowing is the "believing game," whereas at the center of separate knowing is the "doubting game" and, we assume, at the core of constructivist knowing lie both games. Believing and doubting are contraries; they cannot be engaged in simultaneously. They are, however, complementary. By alternating between belief and doubt, it is possible to enhance our understanding. The relationship is dialectical. The dialectic, though, is poetic rather than philosophical; it is directed toward disclosing meaning and enhancing understanding rather than determining the truth and arriving at discursive explanation. Our examination of the philosophical dialectic reveals its shortcomings.

The locus classicus of traditional dialectic is Plato's *Republic*.[38] As described by Aristotle in the *Topics*, dialectic "reasons from opinions that are generally accepted," and "the prius of everything else."[39] Traditional dialectic is an a priori means of resolving conceptual puzzles and paradoxes by unifying them under a higher, universal, true principle that is the prius of everything else. In classical dialectic the ultimate a prior principles sought are, ideally, static, hierarchical, timeless truths.

Modern or Hegelian dialectic presents paradoxes that show the impossibility of unconditional knowledge. Hegel emphasized the role of temporality in the process of reconciling paradoxes and contraries. Contraries and contradictory things can be true—at different times. Being and 'nonbeing, for instance, can be reconciled in the process of becoming. Hegel's dialectic is binary, it blends thesis and antithesis together into a single unified synthesis. The ultimate unifying principle is The Absolute, the one and final transcendent telos. For philosophers, then, in either dialectic, the goal is to ascend the hierarchy of truths.

By contrast, poets are, in their dialectic, concerned with meaning, interpretation, and semantic insight. Rather than a flaw to always and immediately be eliminated, poets find in paradox an opportunity to forge new connections. At first finding and describing a poetic dialectic of critical thinking and drawing the alternate games of doubting and believing into it might appear a Herculean task; fortunately most of the hard work has been done for us by Peter Elbow in his excellent *Embracing Contraries: Explorations in Learning and Teaching.*[40]   As Elbow observes: "A person who can live with contradiction and exploit it—who can use conflicting models—can simply see and think more."[41] This is the epistemological cash value of Emerson's affirmation that "A foolish consistency is the hobgoblin of little minds, adored by little statesmen and philosophers and divines. With consistency a great soul has simply nothing to do."[42]

Contraries in Critical Thinking

In attempting to establish new connections in critical thinking, Elbow posits a series of oppositions between doubting and believing that help restore their intimate dialectical relation as "contraries in inquiry." The first opposition declares, "Doubting is the act of separating or differentiating and thus correlates with individualism: it permits the loner to hold out against the crowd or even—with logic—to conquer. Belief involves merging and participating in a community; indeed a community is created by—and creates—shared beliefs."[43]

The second opposition, closely associated with the first, asserts, "Methodological doubt is the rhetoric of propositions; methodological belief is the rhetoric of experience. Putting our understanding into propositional form helps us extricate ourselves and see contradictions better; trying to *experience* our understandings helps us see as someone else sees. Thus believing invites images, models, metaphors, and even narratives."[44]   Such "oppositions" and "the rhetoric of "experience" characterizes the constructivist way of knowing.

The third opposition is that doubt "implies disengagement from action or holding back while belief implies action."[45] If we agree with the pragmatic philosophers' theory of meaning, a belief is a disposition to act; suppression of this disposition by doubting demands a suspension of the act it directs.

Elbow's ultimate opposition brings us full circle. He writes, "with respect to gender, doubting invites behaviors which our culture associates with masculinity: refusing, saying No, pushing away, competing, being aggressive. Believing invites behaviors associated with feminity: accepting, saying Yes, being compliant, absorbing, and swallowing."[46] Elbow concludes, "If I am not mistaken, much feminist theory and criticism points to the cognitive and methodological processes I am exploring here—processes that have been undervalued in a culture deriving its tradition from methodological doubt and male dominance."[47]   If Elbow is correct, then we must identify and address the androcentric assumptions that, in the context of critical thinking, systematically distorts what Michael Oakshott has called the continuing conversation of humankind.[48]   Given such distortion, then we must, borrowing twice from Jane Roland Martin, reclaim the conversation of critical thinking and develop a gender sensitive ideal for teaching critical thinking.

A Gender Sensitive Ideal of Critical Thinking

"It is time for the voice of the mother to be heard in education."

—Ned Noddings

In her groundbreaking work, "Excluding Women from the Educational Realm," Jane Roland Martin has clearly articulated how the educational realm is defined in terms of productive processes of society, not the reproductive processes.[49]   In academic debates and curriculum inquiry, attention has been given to certain kinds of educational problems, definitions, approaches, and solutions. Predominantly, there is an emphasis on a certain kind of reflective thinking, one that reinforces the traditional dualisms of reason/emotion and doubt/belief. The idea of the individual as a community member is disregarded. Instead, the ideal of the educated person is the old Cartesian rational self, devoid of connection and community. This masculine-bias is evident in the popularly acclaimed work of analytic philosopher of education, R. S. Peters. He describes the educated person in the following terms:

> We would not call a man who was merely well informed an educated man. He must also have some understanding of the "reason why" of things.[50]

Martin suggests that at the center of Peters's description of a liberal education and the educated person is the importance of initiating the student into worthwhile activities, "the impersonal cognitive content and procedures"[51] of which are publicly sanctioned. In one way or another, she maintains, the disciplines reflect Peters's curriculum for the educated person.[52] There is no recognition of the importance of the reproductive processes—keeping house, raising children, handcrafts—because they are "not enshrined in public traditions," and hence, are not included in the curriculum. According to Martin, this lack of acknowledgement of the reproductive processes of society accounts for the exclusion of maternal thinking with which it is associated.[53] Along with Ruddick, Martin insists that "'maternal' is a social not a biological category: although maternal thought arises out of childrearing practices, men as well as women express it in various ways of working and caring for others."[54] Martin concludes that children have to learn this kind of thinking process because they are not born with it. With Nel Noddings and others, she challenges us to return the mother to the field of education. In this way, we can revive the reproductive processes, introduce maternal thinking, and help restore balance to our curriculum.

The need to reconsider our ideal of critical thinking and the critical thinker is further underscored by the literary theorist, Deanne Bogdan. In "Censorship, Identification, and the Poetics of Need," she recounts her first experience of teaching a graduate course titled "Women, Literature, and Education."[55] It was that semester that Bogdan realized the rationalist, masculinist bias of the thinking she required of her students.

In the course, Bogdan asked her students to explore "how the aesthetic mechanism intersects with female stereotyping in John Updike's short story "A&P".[56] The writer quotes from Updike's book to illustrate its content.

> In walks three girls in nothing but bathing suits. I'm in the third checkout slot, with my back to the door, so I don't see them until they're over by the bread. The one that caught my eye was the one in the plaid green two-piece. She was a chunky kid, with a good tan and a sweet broad soft-looking can with those two crescents of white under it, where the sun never seemed to hit, at the top of the back of the legs. I stood there with my hand on a box of HiHo crackers trying to remember if I rang it up or not. I rang it up again and the customer starts to give me hell. She's one of those cash-register watchers, a witch about fifty with rouge on her cheekbones and no eyebrows, and I know it made her day to trip me up. She's been watching cash registers for fifty years and probably never seen a mistake before.[57]

Bogdan, expecting her students to engage in a literary critique of the story, is shocked by her students' reaction, which she describes below:

> Instead of dispasionately considering nuances of tone, mood, irony, ambiguity, verismilitude, and the like—all elements of what I had come to regard as a fully literary response—they committed

what I thought was critical heresy by ignoring the distinction between author and narrator, foreshortening aesthetic distance, and appearing arbitrarily to dismiss the work in a stock response to its sexist overtones. Stock response it apt to hanker after some form of censorship....[58]

Implicity, Bogdan had expected her students to disregard their instinctive reactions to the sexist images presented by Updike and to theorize the work. Instead, the students refused. One class participant named Judy challenged the existence of the book in the course, asserting that she did not need "to learn how yet again sexism gets rationalized within a masculine poetics."[59] When asked what should be done with the short story, Judy replied—and was supported by her fellow students—"I am not a censor, but burn the damned thing!"[60]

Through this particular classroom incident Bogdan began to realize how "powerfully experiential the confrontation of the personal and the ideological in reader response" can be.[61] She saw identification elevated over reason.[62] She has expected the students to academise the material. She learned that many women cannot deal "objectively" with such writing because it touches "too raw a nerve."[63] Indeed, if Judy and her colleagues had agreed to theorize Updike's story they would, in effect, have had to undergo a "double immasculination."[64] Bogdan draws from Jane Roland Martin's work to explain,

> For both Martin's educated woman and Judy and her sisters, 'To be unalienated they must remain uneducated'(104)....to engage the logical structure of her oppression, [they] must submit to the androcentric order of symbolic thought and language itself.[65]

As women in patriarchy, Bogdan's students have already experienced themselves as "other" to the male subject. To engage in a critique of Updike's story would entail the objectification of themselves as "other," yet again. Hence, the "double immasculination."

To transform the experience of alienation in education we must first reclaim and then revise our current notion of critical thinking. The reclamation requires that we restore the missing dialectical contrary, i.e., belief, in order to overcome the masculine gender biased dogma that currently defeats the dialectic of critical thinking. The process of reclamation will involve a valuing of irreconcilable paradoxes and, hence, a radical reconstruction of what it means to be rational. The result will resemble a poetic of critical thinking.

Notes

We would like to thank the reviewers of an earlier version of this manuscript for many helpful comments. We would also like to thank Leigh C. Garrison for sharing with us her highly insightful unpublished essay. Needless to say, we are responsible for any dogmas of the dialectic that remain.

Paradox: "'Paradox' is defined by The Oxford English Dictionary as 'a statement or tenet contrary to received opinion or belief,' and secondly, as a statement that appears on the face of it absurd or self-contradictory but proves on investigation to be well-founded. These two definitions converge in an interesting way when related to modern Western thought in that they tend to explain or account for each other. In being at the same time true and not true, paradox necessarily and blatantly denies the law of noncontradiction, which has been since Aristitle the foundation of logic and rational thought and the very touchstone of 'truth.' Paradox appears especially absurd to the modern mind of rational Enlightenment since Bacon because it violates accepted categories of 'sense' that have been defined and established according to that tradition.

What paradox does, in effect, is force the 'rational' mind into a confrontation with what it cannot immediately or completely encompass. Now we can begin to see why, and how, paradox is dangerous and how many of our cultural assumptions it is dangerous to." Cited from an Unpublished Manuscript by Leight Garrison.

1. Jane Roland Martin, "Science in a Different Style," *American Philosophical Quarterly* 25 (1988): 129–40.

2. Mary Field Belenky, Blythe McVicker Clinchy, Nancy Rule Goldberger, and Jill Mattuck Tarule, *Women's Ways of Knowing* (New York: Basic Books, 1986).

3. Carol Gilligan, *In a Different Voice* (Cambridge, Mass.: Harvard University Press, 1982).

4. Evelyn Fox Keller, *Reflections on Gender and Science* (New Haven, Conn.: Yale University Press, 1985).

5. Sarah Ruddick, *Maternal Thinking: Towards a Politics of Peace* (Boston: Beacon Press, 1989).

6. Jane Roland Martin, "Redefining the Educated Person: Rethinking the Significance of Gender," *Educational Researcher* 15 (1986): 6–10.

7. Ruddick, p. 67.

8. Ibid.

9. Ruddick, p. 69.

10. Ibid.

11. Ruddick, p. 70.

12. Leigh Garrison, Unpublished manuscript. (Blacksburg: Virginia Polytechnic and State University.)

13. Gilligan, p. 65.

14. Gilligan, p. 62.

15. Ibid.

16. Ibid.

17. Martin, "Science," p. 129.

18. Evelyn Fox Keller, *A Feeling for the Organism* (San Francisco: W.H. Freeman & Co., 1983).

19. Ibid., p. 198.

20. Ibid., p. 117.

21. Susan Bardo, "The Cartesian Masculination of Thought," *Signs* 11 (1986).

22. Belenky et al., p. 102.

23. Ibid.

24. Ibid.

25. Ibid., p. 104.

26. Ibid., p. 107.

27. Ibid., p. 106

28. I. Scheffler, *The Language of Education* (Springfield, Ill.: Thomas, 1960), pp. 57–58.

29. Belenky et al., p. 112.

30. Ibid., p. 113.

31. Martha Nussbaum, *Love's Knowledge: Essays on Philosophy and Literature* (New York: Oxford University Press, 1990).

32. Ibid.

33. Ibid.

34. Ibid.

35. Belenky et. al., p. 137.

36. Ibid.

37. Ibid.

38. Plato, *Republic*, see especially 510 c-e.

39. Aristotle, *Topics*, 110a, 40–101b1.

40. Peter Elbow, *Embracing Contraries: Explorations in Learning and Teaching* (New York: Oxford Unversity Press, 1986).

41. Ibid., p. 241.

42. Ralph Waldo Emerson, "Self-Reliance," in *Essays by Ralph Waldo Emerson* (New York: Thomas Y. Crowell, 1926), p. 41.

43. Elbow, p. 264.

44. Ibid.

45. Ibid., p. 265.

46. Ibid., p. 266.

47. Ibid.

48. Michael Oakeshott, *Rationalism in Politics and Other Essays* (New York: Basic Books, 1962).

49. Jane Roland Martin, "Excluding Women from the Educational Realm," *Harvard Educational Review* 52 (1982).

50. R.S. Peters, *Ethics and Education* (Atlanta: Scott, Foresman, 1967), p. 8.

51. Roland Martin, "Excluding Women," p. 141.

52. Ibid.

53. Ibid., p. 142.

54. Ibid.

55. Deanne Bogdan, "Censorship, Identification and the Poetics of Need," in *The Right to Literacy*, ed. Andrea A. Lunsford, Helen Moglen, James Steven. (New York: The Modern Language Association of America, 1990).

56. Ibid., p. 131.

57. John Updike, "A&P", in *Pigeon Feathers and Other Stories* (New York: Knopf, 1962), pp. 187–92.

58. Bogdan, "Censorship," p. 132.

59. Ibid., p. 132.

60. Ibid.

61. Ibid.

62. Ibid., p. 141.

63. Ibid., p. 136.

64. Ibid.

65. Ibid., p. 136.

II.

Critical Thinking in Context

The mainstream identification of critical thinking with logical thinking usually leads to two obvious pedagogical consequences: students are encouraged to examine claims, arguments, and beliefs in isolation from their broader contexts, and they are likewise encouraged to assume that an individual's thinking is "good" only if it is "objective"—i.e., neutral. But both assumptions are unacceptable reifications. Arguments and claims do not exist in vacuo. They arise from concrete forms of life, from specific historical contexts that give rise to the very conceptual frameworks within which discourse itself emerges. Moreover, given the contextual nature of arguments and beliefs, the individual thinker cannot neutrally separate herself from her analysis of them, particularly if she is personally invested in them. This does not mean that objectivity is impossible, but only that its meaning must be rethought in order to accommodate the contextual nature of thinking.

In this section's first essay, John McPeck disagrees with the mainstream model's abstractionist assumption that critical thinking is either a set of specific skills with across-the-board applicability or a content-free general ability. Instead, he argues, critical thinking is better understood in a more concrete way as knowledge-based skills: one learns to think critically within the context of particular disciplines. To assume otherwise is to implicitly accept a theory of knowledge that McPeck calls the "Trivial Pursuit" model, and which he claims pervades critical thinking textbooks and classroom strategies. The Trivial Pursuit theory of knowledge has it that knowledge is unambiguous, conceptually simple, and noncontroversial, such that it can be analyzed and evaluated by a single, abstract set of logical rules and standards. But, McPeck concludes, such a model is simplistic from an epistemic perspective and dangerous from a pedagogical one.

Although Connie Missimer disagrees with McPeck's insistence that critical thinking is subject-specific, she concurs that it must be understood contextually. In her essay, she distinguishes between the received model—what she calls the "Individual View"—and her alternative—the "Social View." The Individual View of critical thinking, she argues, is atemporal. It focuses on isolated arguments, ignores their historical background, and evaluates the quality of the arguer (how successfully has he manipulated logical rules?) rather than the argument. In place of this reified model, Missimer advocates an approach that is frankly historicist in nature. The Social View of critical thinking accepts that arguments are historical artifacts (as, indeed, are styles of arguing), and that the good thinker must therefore compare and evaluate competing arguments before she can determine which ones are sound. Such a model of critical thinking is historical, evolutionary, and focuses on the merits of the argument rather than the arguer (how well does this argument stack up against its competitors?).

Karl Hostetler's essay likewise takes on the traditional critical thinking assumption that neutrality is a necessary condition for examining arguments and beliefs. In opposition to this "neutral high ground," he argues that critical thinking is necessarily a communal inquiry carried out within and between particular forms of life. But this acknowledgment of the contextual nature of thinking does not inevitably reduce to a vapid relativism. Objectivity and neutrality are not necessarily conjoined. Hostetler concludes with a brief discussion of strategies for encouraging "nonobjectivist" critical thinking in the classroom.

Finally, Karen Warren concludes the discussion by reminding us that styles of thinking as well as particular beliefs emerge from specific contexts, or "conceptual frameworks," and that the good thinker consequently needs to analyze received models of critical thinking in order to check for context-specific biases. Warren argues that in fact mainstream critical thinking's exclusivistic insistence on traditional logical standards does reflect a bias: a patriarchally based one. She explores the dimensions of this bias by comparing patriarchal and feminist ways of doing science and ethics and concludes that a feminist deconstruction of the received model of critical thinking is necessary.

6

Critical Thinking and the "Trivial Pursuit" Theory of Knowledge

John E. McPeck

A cousin of mine, who is a businessman, recently asked me what my book on critical thinking has to say about that subject. After giving him a brief summary of the major thesis of the book, he responded by saying: "You mean to say that you had to write a book to say that? Boy, you academics have a way of making the obvious sound complicated!" Needless to say, I had several qualms about this response. But despite these, I confess to sharing a certain sympathy with it. Because, at times, my general view about the nature of critical thinking seems so obvious and commonsensical to me that it is almost embarrassing that it need be said at all, particularly to the learned audience for whom it was originally intended. That audience, incidentially, is what has been called the "Informal Logic Movement," and now has an official executive body, a journal, several annual conferences in the United States including such familiar textbook authors as Michael Scriven, Robert Ennis, Howard Kahane, Perry Weddle, Walton and Woods, and a growing cadre of informal logic teachers. However, given the discussion (not to mention criticism) that my view has generated within this movement, I am beginning to feel vindicated insofar as what I took to be common sense turns out *not* to be so common at all. There remain some very real differences over what the ingredients of critical thinking are and how best to teach it.

The view of critical thinking that I have been defending simply tries to account for certain common, and what I think are obvious, facts about human reasoning. At no place does my description of critical thinking appeal to, nor attempt to explain, any mysterious or complex cognitive processes. I would, as it were, be content with a garden variety account of critical thinking that at least covered the obvious properties of it. I'll leave its more esoteric dimensions for some rainy day.

Here are some of the more obvious points that I attempt to account for. I thought it important to point out that *thinking*, let alone critical thinking, is always about some particular thing or subject (let us call this thing X), and that it therefore makes little or no sense to say "I teach thinking *simpliciter*," or "I teach thinking in general but not about anything in particular." All such talk is literal nonsense. (Parenthetically, similar arguments apply to such notions as "creativity" and "problem solving" as well.) No matter how general or abstract the subject matter, if the thinking involved is not about *some* kind of X, then it is not describable as thinking at all. This consideration, then, *binds* thinking, and thus critical thinking, to particular subjects or activities. This conclusion represents the first point of departure between my view of critical thinking and what has come to be the standard approach to this subject. Those committed to the standard approach purport to teach courses in critical thinking, *simpliciter*, and it doesn't matter what the subject may be about. In my view, this borders on being an absurdity, because there are almost as many ways of thinking as there are things to think about. To claim to teach critical thinking *in general*, even about mundane "everyday problems," is to make promises that cannot be kept. What is worse, it simply confuses conscientious teachers who are trying to improve the various thinking capacities of students.

A second corollary that my analysis of critical thinking tried to take into account was the fact that an effective thinker in one area is not necessarily an effective thinker in all other areas. For example, while Einstein could communicate remarkably in physics he was rather inept at poetry. I have suggested that this is because the knowledge and skills required for the one activity are quite different from the knowledge and skills required for the other. And while it is possible that one person can be quite accomplished at many different activities, common sense suggests such a person possesses several *different kinds* of knowledge and understanding: it is *not* one skill, generically referred to as "reasoning" that one then uniformly applies to all these tasks. It is possible that there may be some common elements in the various tasks requiring reasoning, but a little reflection suggests that the *differences* among the kinds of reasoning are far greater, and more obvious, than whatever they may have in common. After the fact, a logician might want to describe some inference by an historian as "inductive," as he might also describe some mathematician's or astronomer's inference as "inductive," but this logical nomenclature is merely a handy *theoretical* (or formal) *description* of the two inferences. It is not meant to suggest that the knowledge and skills required for making these inferences are in any way identical.

Moreover, almost all of the empirical studies that have searched for transfer-of-training effects, particularly in the cognitive domain, have been notoriously unpromising to say the least. This result, I suggest, is what common sense would predict. My analysis of critical thinking tries to take these considerations into account. But the Informal Logic Movement, by contrast, continues to press for its small bag of tricks (e.g., the fallacies) to make one a critical thinker in any area no matter what the subject matter.

The final commonsense property of critical thinking that I tried to account for was that what we typically *mean* when we say that someone is a critical thinker is that they somehow think for themselves; they do not simply believe everything that they may hear or read. I have argued that such people have *both* the disposition (or propensity) *and* the relevant knowledge and skills to engage in an activity with reflective scepticism. That is, not only are they *prone* to question things, but they have the relevant knowledge and understanding to help them do so productively. And if one thinks long enough about what this might entail, particularly from a curriculum point of view, I suggest you will find that its major ingredients are close to what we have always thought of as a good liberal education. There are ways of improving this kind of education, and hence, critical thinkers, but there are no shortcuts to it. This is because the various "forms of thought" (to use Paul Hirst's phrase) have a logic, texture, and relevant background knowledge that are peculiar to themselves. And a course, or two, called "critical thinking" cannot begin to capture these relevant peculiarities.

In sum, I take these points to be a matter of common sense to any who take the time to think about it. As promised, they contain nothing mysterious nor esoteric. Yet each of them is incompatible with, and flies in the face of, the standard or most common approaches to critical thinking to be found in the literature (particularly the Informal Logic Movement). Each of these commonsense points is either denied, or somehow swept under the rug, by the Informal Logic approach to critical thinking. If I were to put my basic disagreement with the Informal Logic Movement into one bold-relief sentence, it is this. In their attempt to develop critical thinking, they have the order of cause and effect *reversed*. They believe that if you train students in certain logical skills (e.g., the fallacies) the result will be a general improvement in each of the other disciplines or qualities of mind. Whereas I contend that if we improve the quality of understanding through the disciplines (which may have little to do with "logic" directly) you will then get a concomitant improvement in critical thinking capacity. When the difference between us is put this way, one might be tempted to ask: "Are these two approaches really all that incompatible?" Well, put this way, no, they are not *logically* incompatible. But from a pedagogic and practical point of view they are clearly at odds, because to me, they have the tail wagging the dog. They make much the same error as teaching someone how to use a computer by teaching them only what all computer languages may have in common, and then leaving the rest to chance or personal interest. Whereas I would suggest teaching people how to program in the various computer languages and leave whatever these languages may have in common to chance or personal interest. From an instructional point of view such a difference makes all the difference.

Critical Thinking: "General Ability" or "Specific Skills"?

I would now like to look at critical thinking from a slightly different perspective, a more psychological perspective. I want to consider the question of just what kind of thing it is that one has when they can think critically. Specifically, is it some kind of *general ability*, like, say, verbal ability, or perhaps intelligence? Or is it rather more like a *specific skill* that can be directly taught, and the person can then either do it or not do it depending on whether they have been taught that skill? This difference is sometimes described by psychologists as the difference between a "general aptitude" versus a "specific skill."

It is important to raise this kind of question for two reasons. First, if we have a fairly clear idea of what kind of competence it is, then we should have some better ideas of how to teach and test for it, and we should have more realistic expectations of what courses designed to promote critical thinking might hope to accomplish. The second reason this kind of question is important is that several government reports and prestigious commissions have strongly recommended that schools start teaching people to be critical thinkers, yet neither they nor the programs that they have spawned are at all clear about what kind of thing critical thinking *is*, nor what these initiatives are supposed to accomplish. There is, therefore, no clear acid test for the success or failure of these expensive programs (cf. California's Executive Order #338).

A review of the literature on critical thinking tests reveals a fairly clear body of opinion that treats critical thinking as a "general ability" that can be measured independently of context and subject matter. The "Watson-Glaser Critical Thinking Appraisal" is perhaps the best known, but I know of at least twenty-six other tests designed to measure critical thinking ability that also treat critical thinking as a general ability. My purpose here is not so much to criticize these tests per se but to draw out some of the implications of conceptualizing critical thinking as a generalized ability, as these tests seem to do.

If we take the Watson-Glaser test as a typical example, a perusal of the accompanying test manual clearly reveals that critical thinking is to be thought of as a "general ability" and not as a specific skill.   The discussion in the manual makes plain that the test is committed to three propositions:

1.   that the ability to perform on the test items is content and context free; that is, no specific knowledge or information is required. The test items themselves provide all the required information.
2.   the manual explicitly states that *critical thinking ability* is a composite of five subabilities:
    i.   the ability to define a problem
    ii.   the ability to select pertinent information for the solution of a problem
    iii. the ability to recognize stated and unstated assumptions
    iv. the ability to formulate and select relevant and promising hypotheses
    v.   the ability to draw valid conclusions and judge the validity of inferences.
3.   that the test is measuring a unique or *sui generis* human ability (albeit a composite one).

These propositions almost define what is usually meant by a general ability.

Now, if we consider critical thinking to be the kind of general ability that Watson and Glaser's test purports to measure, then we can begin to notice several things about it.   First, we might notice that given the description of the abilities involved and their context-free measurement, *critical thinking* turns out to be very similar to what we normally mean by general scholastic ability, or *intelligence*.   That is, not only are critical thinking and intelligence both supposed to be general abilities, but in this case they look very much like *the same* general ability.   From a conceptual point of view, it is difficult even to imagine a person being able to score well on one of these tests without also being able to score well on the other—particularly when one remembers that the items on both tests are designed to be relatively content and context-free.   And if critical thinking is the kind of content-free general ability that Watson and Glaser appear to think it is, at least two things follow: (1) it is not at all clear what the test is measuring apart from intelligence, and (2) we should be leery of programs purporting to teach it directly given the recalcitrance of IQ to improvement by direct teaching. The variance on IQ seems to remain substantial despite massive compensatory education programs. This is not to suggest that bona fide critical thinking can never be improved, but it is to suggest that there may be something *conceptually* limiting in considering it to be a "content-free general ability."

On the *empirical* side, things are even worse for Watson and Glaser's conception of critical thinking. They cite the high correlation coefficients with various intelligence tests as an index of the Critical Thinking tests' validity. In effect, they are saying: Bright people tend to score well in the critical thinking appraisal. (Draw your own inference if you do poorly!) But Watson and Glaser are trying to have it both ways, it seems to me. They want to cite the tests' high correlations with general intelligence as a psychometric virtue, yet they want to claim that they are measuring something else (i.e., some *other* general ability). However, if they are measuring something quite distinct from intelligence then we should be able to find cases of people with low IQ yet high critical thinking ability, and conversely we should find people with high IQ and low critical thinking ability. As I have pointed out elsewhere, however, even according to Watson and Glaser's own norming data, this doesn't happen. The situation with critical thinking tests and IQ is analogous to the situation between "creativity" and IQ, viz., they correlate so highly with one another that they appear to be measuring one thing and *not* two distinct things. Watson and Glaser's conception of "critical thinking," like "creativity," would appear to have little discriminant validity. For these reasons, then, I suggest that critical thinking is *not* a content-free general ability, and, furthermore, we should be sceptical about educational programs and initiatives that assume that it is.

There is, however, a competing conception of critical thinking in the literature that conceives of it as a small set of specific skills that once learned can then be applied in any area requiring critical thought. This view of critical thinking is predominant among those advocating Informal Logic programs for critical thinking. In fact, some of these programs use the phrases "informal logic" and "critical thinking" more or less interchangeably, as though this is what "critical thinking" obviously *means*. Perhaps I should reiterate that none of the views discussed here are particularly clear about precisely what kind of an ability critical thinking is. There is a considerable amount of slipping and sliding over this question. So one has to dig beneath the surface, as it were, in order to unearth what is meant by critical thinking ability.

In the case of the Informal Logic Approach, one can see certain similarities to *and* certain differences from the "general ability" approach. (Perhaps this is what renders the slipping and sliding so tempting at times.) The major *difference* embedded in the "specific skills" view (e.g., the informal logic approach) is that critical thinking consists in a relatively small number of specific teachable skills, which, once mastered, enable one to deploy these skills across any problems, arguments, or questions where critical thinking might be called for. On this view, those who have had the advantage of the specific training will be much more capable of critical thought than those who have not. The major *similarity* of this view with the "general ability" view, is that these specific skills are likewise content and context-free and can therefore be deployed *generally* across different subjects and tasks.

Incidentally, Informal Logic teachers frequently report large gains on the Watson-Glaser test following courses in Informal Logic. (I confess to similar findings myself in years past.) And this finding tends to reinforce the belief that critical thinking is developed by mastering their specific skills. They take such results as clear evidence for the necessity of their specific skills for critical thinking. However, there are at least two reasons why such results should not be taken too seriously. The first is that there is so much overlap between the Watson-Glaser test items and what is taught in these Informal Logic courses that it amounts to direct training or "coaching." Thus, improved results are hardly surprising. Second, there is no evidence that I know of which comes near to establishing that such direct skill-training can be transferred to examples or situations unlike those on the test. Thus, there is a curious kind of mutual propping-up exercise going on between the Watson-Glaser test and the specific skills that are allegedly required for critical thinking.

The difficulty that I have with the "specific skills" view of critical thinking is that these putative skills appear to be neither *necessary* nor *sufficient* for true critical thinking, and that there is a much more plausible view that is congruent with our commonsense intuitions about critical thinking. That certain specific skills are *not necessary* for critical thinking is evidenced by the fact that many people can and do display critical thinking who have never been directly taught, and perhaps never heard of, the specific skills supposedly required of critical thinkers. As the Watson-Glaser norm data shows, people with conventional liberal arts educations tend to score highest on their test; and there is little reason to believe that these people have been directly trained in any of these specific skills (e.g., the informal fallacies). Secondly, if certain specific skills were necessary for critical thinking, then you would expect to find that only those people with the requisite training able to do it. What we find, however, is that it appears to be normally distributed just as IQ is.

To *show* that certain specific skills are also *not sufficient* for critical thinking would require an analysis of the specific skills alleged to compose it. Unfortunately, the list of specific skills is subject to change from program to program. However, all the specific skills that I have seen, and those mentioned on the Watson-Glaser test are typical, turn out not to be skills at all. For example, consider two of the putative "skills" included by Watson and Glaser in their definition of "critical thinking":

1. the ability to select pertinent information for the solution of a problem
2. the ability to formulate and select relevant and promising hypotheses.

I submit that while the grammar of these phrases might suggest that bona fide abilities are being described, upon analysis, they *do not describe* any singular or specific abilities at all, but rather they describe large collections of different kinds of skills and abilities. They are somewhat like "the ability to win at games"; it doesn't matter what kind of game, any game from tiddlywinks to chess and football to cricket: "the ability to win at games" means just what it says. But there is not specific *ability* or *skill* to win all kinds of games. Instead there are literally hundreds of skills, and kinds of skills, involved. And so it is with Watson and Glaser's "ability to select pertinent information for the solution of a problem." Does this mean any and all problems? And aren't "problems" and their solutions at least as diverse as games? The moral to be drawn from this is that these phrases do not really denote true abilities at all, let alone specific ones. If they were describing specific abilities, then you should be able to train a person in that specific skill and it could then be deployed on all other problems (or games). Thus, such phrases as these often masquerade as describing specific abilities, but we should not be seduced by the grammar of such talk, because further analysis usually reveals that they are not *one* but *many* abilities or skills.

However, setting aside these conceptual difficulties for a moment, let us suppose that there are certain directly trainable skills that we believe to be important to critical thinking somehow (say, for example, the informal fallacies). There remains two important questions that we would have to answer about these skills. The first is, are they really as broadly deployable across all or most questions requiring critical thought as we might initially think? We should be aware that this question is not merely an empirical question about the transfer-of-training across multiple domains and contexts, but more importantly it is a question about the different kinds of reasoning which are ingredient in, and characterize, the different domains of knowledge. That is, scientific thinking or mathematical thinking would appear to be substantially different from moral thinking or literary thinking. Not only are the cannons of validity different, but what might be fallacious reasoning in one context or domain, might be perfectly correct in another. This fact about the different forms of thought casts serious doubt upon the inter-field validity of any small set of specific trainable skills. However, even if we could find some common elements of reasoning that equally apply across fields or domains, we should have to ask whether these common elements are *sufficient* to enable one to make the required critical judgments that various problems require.

My own view is that these common or specific skills account for such a small portion of the total reasoning required vis-à-vis the complex of cognitive demands posed by different problems, that they are far from *sufficient* for regarding a person as a critical thinker in all (or even most) domains. Just as knowing how to spell and to type would be nowhere near *sufficient* for writing philosophy essays or literary criticism, so these specific skills would be nowhere near sufficient for bona fide critical thinking across multiple domains. The vast array of problems, and types of understanding required, are simply too diverse to regard any set of specific skills *sufficient* for critical thinking in all or even most of them. And when one stops to consider that most problems or questions that require critical thought (e.g., public issues) are complexes, or combinations, of different *types* of knowledge and understanding, then the sufficiency of any set of specific skills appears even more remote and unlikely.

The second question that must be faced by any claim that certain specific skills are *sufficient* for critical thinking is this: What is the major ingredient of critical thinking? Is it having knowledge and understanding or is it having certain specific skills? Here again, I am afraid, I must appeal to your common everyday experience. But when there is a discussion or argument about some public issue, be it the war in El Salvador, disarmament, Reaganomics, or what have you, who is usually able to make the more useful contribution to such a dispute? Is it the person who possesses the relevant knowledge and information or is it the person who has been trained in certain specific skills? If your experience has been anything like mine, it is the person who has the relevant knowledge.

Incidentally, for those of you familiar with Michael Scriven's treatment of *extended arguments* (in his book *Reasoning*), where he is trying to teach the skills of "argument analysis," you might notice that these arguments are usually resolved by bringing into the argument some additional relevant information or knowledge not given in the original argument. We should notice this is not a matter of skill, but again, a matter of knowledge.

For these reasons, then, I submit that possessing certain specific skills is neither *necessary* nor *sufficient* for true critical thinking and that it is unproductive to conceive of it this way.[1]

The "Trivial Pursuit" Theory of Knowlege

Since I have argued that critical thinking is not a content-free "general ability," nor is it a set of "specific skills," I suppose you think it time that I come out of the closet and declare what kind of cognitive entity I think critical thinking *is*. After all, if I'm opposed to monogamy and polygamy, I must be in favor of something. So what is it? I shall try to oblige this question in a moment. But my answer will be more clearly understood if I contrast it with an assumption that I think underlies both of the views discussed above. This assumption consists of a certain view about *knowledge* and facts, which I shall call the "Trivial Pursuit" theory of knowledge. I call it this because both views tend to treat the substantive knowlege and information for critical thinking as though they typically consist of facts that are relatively simple and discrete. Like "Trivial Pursuit," knowledge is assumed to be the kind of thing that can be fitted into one-sentence questions, with one-sentence answers. Moreover, such knowledge is more or less unambiguous, noncontroversial, and conceptually simple. Television quiz shows exploit this same type of knowledge. The reason that the standard views of critical thinking unwittingly treat knowledge in this same way is that it is only by holding substantive knowledge constant, and unproblematic, that direct training in their skills or abilities takes on any plausibility. The operative strategy seems to be: first, you get the relevant facts, and, as in quiz shows, this step is assumed to be relatively straightforward, *then* you use these various skills to derive clever solutions or arguments. Since knowledge is usually assumed to be common knowledge (e.g., "every-day knowledge"), as in quiz shows, all that one needs to be a critical thinker is to have facility with certain skills and abilities. This assumption about knowledge pervades the simplistic textbook examples designed to teach reasoning skills. All the relevant knowledge is given in the premises, and one is taught how to draw appropriate conclusions from it. The knowledge itself is always assumed to be complete and nonproblematic. In real life, however, this assumption about knowledge cannot be maintained. For actual problems, the required knowledge is seldom complete, almost always problematic, and susceptible to several interpretations.

Moreover, the criteria for what should count as relevant knowledge are themselves problematic. The relevant knowledge cannot be assumed to be complete nor obvious. And a person's critical assessment of things, such as knowledge claims and so on, will necessarily be influenced by their experience, understanding, cognitive perspective, and values. The knowledge component of critical thinking will not stand still, as it were, but is constantly being added to, reinterpreted, and assessed from different perspectives. This complex processing of knowledge is always involved in real-life problems that require critical thought, and it is the *norm* not the *exception*. The only instances where this complex processing of knowledge is not required is when the knowledge is assumed to be complete and unproblematic, as in the simple textbook examples, or in Trivial Pursuit. But such problems are themselves trivial and hardly require critical thought. It is only by denigrating or ignoring the complexities of substantive knowledge and information that the specific skills approach can be made to even sound initially plausible. They treat "knowing" as a kind of "recall," or simply something essentially mindless.

The intimate connection between the *kinds of knowledge* and their corresponding *kinds of skills* helps to clarify my view of critical thinking. I would now like to state my view as succinctly as I can. First it includes a *knowledge component*, that is, knowledge-based skills whose general range of applicability is limited by the form of thought or kind of knowledge being called upon. The second component, which we might regard as the specifically *critical component*, consists of the ability to reflect upon, to question effectively, and to suspend judgment or belief about the required knowledge composing the problem at hand. This *critical* component, it should be noted, is parasitic upon the *knowledge* component since the epistemic status (i.e., its certainty *and* its vulnerability) of the different kinds of knowledge varies considerably. That is, there are some data, say, that enjoy a much higher degree of certainty and reliability than others. All so-called "data" is *not* on an equal footing. The critical thinker, therefore, knows what and when it might be reasonable to question something. But this requires comprehensive understanding of the kind of information that it is and perhaps how it is gathered or generated. Critical thinking ability, therefore, varies directly with the amount of the knowledge required by the problem. Enough, then, about the cognitive ingredients of critical thinking.

The Purpose of Critical Thinking

Since it is theoretically possible to train people for critical thinking in very narrow domains and practical tasks, just as it is for very broad domains and theoretical tasks, we therefore have to ask ourselves *what kind* of critical thinking we are interested in developing? For *whom* and for *what*? Certain kinds of knowledge and information will lay the groundwork for critical thinking about some kinds of problems but not others. And since school time and human capacities are limited, choices have to be made. Such choices will reflect society's values and the very purpose of public schooling. Here enters the normative side of education, it is not a value-neutral enterprise.

In our society, at least since the time of Thomas Jefferson, the chief purpose of schools has been to produce an informed citizenry, capable of making intelligent decisions about the problems that might face it. Ostensibly, we would like students to become critical thinkers for every such problem and perhaps more personal ones as well. But when one reflects upon both the diversity and complexity of such problems, in the present as well as the future, the goal is nothing short of staggering. The briefest list would include such diverse problems as the morality of abortion, pornography, and minority rights, the multidimensions of pollution, nuclear disarmament, the feasability and equality of various taxation schemes, television hype and propaganda, etc., etc., etc. When one considers how complex and knowledge-dependent rational solutions really are for any one of these problems, the odds against a sufficiently informed citizenry are almost demoralizing. Indeed, the odds finally led Walter Lippmann to conclude (in his book *Public Opinion*), after forty-five years of covering public issues from Washington, that the democratic citizenry is no longer up to the task of adequately responding to the increased complexity of the problems that face it. Gone are the days of "the town meeting," he argued. Increasing complexity of contemporary problems makes appeal to "the experts" and their technocracy inevitable. Similar observations led Carl L. Becker to say: "Round every next corner democracy works less well than it did." This circumstance might also explain why modern mass communication largely consists of *image-making* and *slogans* rather than clear explanations of the issues: the real issues, and real explanations, are too complex for mass consumption. So, as in advertising, the catchy phrase, or image, increasingly forms our views on reality.

All of this, believe it or not, is not intended as a "doom and gloom" prophecy for democracy. The practical alternatives to an informed citizenry remain as abhorrent to us now as they did to Thomas Jefferson. The point is simply to dramatize the enormity of the task that one sets for oneself when one says "Let's make critical thinkers out of our students." To perceive the task from this perspective helps to explain why quick-fix solutions for the critical thinking problem are so tempting to some people: one or two courses in the right critical thinking skills, and most of these problems can be handled—or at least so the rhetoric goes. However, the main point of looking at critical thinking from this broader perspective is that it underscores the real limitations that any critical thinking program is bound to have. Since we could not possibly provide the requisite knowledge for every kind of problem, we are forced to ask the most fundamental of all curriculum questions: What kind of knowledge is most worthwhile for our students? Given the kinds of problems that are imbedded in the Jeffersonian ideal of an informed citizenry, we can see that any answer to this question must involve some very broad domains of understanding.

Another way of putting this basic question is "what kinds of knowledge and understanding are likely to have the most universal value?" When the question is put this way, notice, it is not a question about transfer-of-training effects, which is a psychological question, but it is a question about what kinds of knowledge we consider to possess the most value. Will it be, for example, how to repair one's automobile or the study of history? Will it be public speaking or literature? These are the sorts of questions that must be faced for education in general and *a fortiori* for critical thinking in particular.

It seems to me, therefore, that when all of these points are taken into consideration, there is no other plausible candidate for our curriculum besides a broad liberal education. No other curriculum can provide quite the same breadth of understanding into the human condition and the problems that perennially face it. The disciplines that make up a liberal education (e.g., those in the arts, the sciences, and humanities) are not separate from, nor alien to, the everyday problems requiring critical thought, but rather they are the fundamental constituents of such problems. To attempt to think rationally at all is to employ the various forms of rational discourse that are the disciplines. This, indeed, is the core of Paul Hirst's defense of a liberal education. However, there has come to be a strong and widely held belief that standard disciplinary knowledge is somehow technical, esoteric, abstract, or primarily of academic interest. This view fails to recognize that the disciplines had their *origins* in the human condition and are substantively *about* the human condition. Their *raison d'être* is to provide insight and understanding to the problems faced by humanity. If the disciplines are believed to consist in merely esoteric or academic knowledge, then this says more about the poor way this knowledge is perhaps often taught, but this should not confuse us about the basic purpose and power of the disciplines. Despite rhetoric to the contrary, the disciplines do not exist for *their own sake*. Rather they enable rational discourse about the problems that confront us. It is the job of educators to convey this power and purpose of the disciplines because they are the basic ingredients of rationality itself.

Having reasserted the case for the liberal arts as the most efficacious vehicle for critical thinking, two further clarifications must be emphatically stressed. First, I am not claiming that typical, everyday problems of the sort we are interested in will always, or indeed *ever*, fall neatly into one domain or the other. The typical problem is many-faceted and multidimensional, therefore several types of knowledge and understanding will be needed for most problems. I am simply claiming that because the disciplines provide knowledge and understanding that go "beyond the present and the particular," (to use Charles Bailey's felicitous phrase) they provide the *best set* of knowledge and skills for coping with problems affecting society.

The second point that must be stressed about liberal education is that it does not consist in merely taking in or absorbing a lot of different types of information, but its major characteristic is that it enables one to understand and appreciate both the strengths and weaknesses, and the power and limitations, of the various forms of thought that make up our thinking. That is, the liberally educated student should understand the epistemic status of different types of knowledge claims within the different forms of knowledge. Liberal education is not, of course, the passive acquisition of different types of information, as it is being able to enter the various forms of rational discourse as an autonomous thinker. The liberally educated person must understand the different *processes* of reasoning every bit as much as the *products* of that reasoning. Moreover, such a person is not someone who merely possesses arcane knowledge in a half dozen specialty areas, but rather possess a broad cognitive perspective (to borrow a phrase from R. S. Peters) that enables him or her to see significance in the most mundane events.

The proponents of various courses in critical thinking will often say, at this point, that they have never denied the value of liberal education and that they have no desire to displace it. Rather, they typically make either one or both of the following claims to justify their courses. One claim is that liberal arts courses seldom if ever contain so-called "everyday problems" and "everyday reasoning" within their syllabi, thus critical thinking courses are designed to compensate this deficiency. The other claim often made is that these courses are intended to specifically teach people how to think critically, as such, *within* and *about* the disciplines. Both of these claims for critical thinking courses justify their purpose as a kind of topping-up exercise designed to offset or rectify the perceived deficiencies of the liberal arts curriculum.

If we disregard those deficiencies that are due to poor or inadequate teaching, since these are present in any kind of program, it seems to me that both these claims for critical thinking courses misrepresent or misunderstand the nature of liberal education and what it is intended to do. The first claim that liberal education fails to teach reasoning about "everyday problems" simply fails to appreciate that this is precisely what the disciplines are about—the disciplines simply study these problems one dimension at a time. And the second claim for critical thinking courses, viz., that it teaches how to be critical within the disciplines themselves, fails to recognize that the standards and criteria for rational thinking are uniquely determined by the disciplines themselves, and not by some external criterion separate from them.

The strongest cast that I have heard made for critical thinking courses is that they *can* serve a kind of *remedial* role for those whose education has been otherwise so inadequate that they are seriously deficient in any kind of autonomous thinking. To give credit where it is due, perhaps such courses can help to remedy this. But we should recognize that this is a rear-guard action and not the vanguard of a new and promising curriculum for all. The glitter of such programs is for those with little light to begin with. Even in these cases I would suggest the more direct remedy of improving the quality of the normal curriculum, where teachers feel more at home, rather than laying on yet another specific course in an already crowded curriculum.

How to Improve Critical Thinking

It may not be obvious, I'm afraid, but there is a point to my leading you through these disagreements about the nature of critical thinking. The point is a very practical one, namely, we should now have a better idea of what is involved in teaching for critical thinking. If there is any truth to my view that critical thinking skills are primarily dependent upon, even peculiar to, the various forms of rational discourse (e.g., morality, art, science, history) then at least two conclusions follow from this: (1) that general courses in critical thinking are either over-zealous or simpleminded since, unlike "Trivial Pursuit," the relevant knowledge is not all cut from the same conceptual cloth, and (2) that the so-called "thinking skills" are an inherent part of the warp and woof of the various disciplines, and must, therefore, be taught as part of them.

Happily, most teachers are already fairly knowledgeable in their parent disciplines, at least in secondary schools and beyond, so there really is no need for an entirely new specialty, or alien expertise, in order to improve critical thinking skills in their classes. It requires more of a shift in emphasis or redesigning their material and tests to reflect this emphasis on independent thinking. I am not claiming that teachers are now capable of doing this effectively on their own, but it is to suggest that with a little guidance and a few suggestions, teachers are already more than halfway there by virtue of their understanding of their discipline.

The really useful and concrete suggestions for teachers would, of course, have to be discipline-specific (e.g., how to improve historical thinking skills). Here, you will appreciate, I have neither the space nor the competence to provide suggestions for each of the disciplines. But I can at least indicate two potentially rich sources of suggestions for each of the disciplines. Both of these sources might provide the necessary skills and understanding required for critical thinking. The University of Chicago's Joseph Schwab once described this understanding as follows:

> Let [a body of knowledge] be taught in such a way that the student learns what substantive structures gave rise to the chosen body of knowledge, what the strengths and limitations of these structures are, and what some of the alternatives are which give rise to alternative bodies of knowledge.[2]

One source that could help a teacher provide this kind of understanding to students can be found in the "philosophy of" their specific discipline.

Many teachers are not even aware that such a philosophical literature exists for their own discipline. But much of this literature consists in explaining and laying bare, as it were, the epistemic foundations and logical peculiarities of the various disciplines. If teachers possessed this fresh and somewhat different perspective on their discipline, they could better see what kinds of questions and material would give rise to this kind of understanding. As a starting place and general guide to this literature, I would first recommend reading a very clear and important paper by Israel Scheffler titled "Philosophies-of and the curriculum" (in *Educational Judgments*, ed. James F. Doyle [RKP, London, 1973]). This paper provides an exceptionally clear rationale for using this literature and what teachers can hope to get from it for teaching the structure and logic of their discipline.

In addition to the "philosophy-of" literature, there are many discipline-specific monographs by educators in these fields that are extremely perceptive about the logical and conceptual peculiarities of their field. And many of these monographs contain useful pedagogic strategies for making these peculiarities manifest to students. The names, indeed disciplines, are too numerous to list here, but I have in mind the kind of work that, say, Gerald Holton has done in physics education, and Schwab in biology, Northrop Frye in literature, and Elliot Eisner in art education. Much of this kind of literature can take teachers a long way toward teaching critical thinking in their respective fields.

The Medievals used to say that there is nothing really new under the sun. And I realize that I have said nothing that is really new. But sometimes old ideas remain good ideas and need another day on top— particularly when there are so many bad ideas seeking to displace them.[3]

Notes

1. I use the phrase "true critical thinking" here, not to beg the question, but to rule out those few authors who almost *define* "critical thinking" in terms of possessing certain preferred skills (e.g., those who use "informal logic skills" as synonymous with "critical thinking")—this move *does* beg the question.

2. J. J. Schwab, "Structures of the Disciplines: Meanings and Slogans." Quoted from I. A. Snook, "The Concept of Indoctrination," *Studies in Philosophy of Education* 7:2, Fall, 1970.

3. I would like to thank my colleague, James T. Sanders, for his copious editorial suggestions on an earlier draft of this paper.

7

Why Two Heads Are Better Than One: Philosophical and Pedagogical Implications of a Social View of Critical Thinking

Connie Missimer

Consider, if you will, the following two conceptions of critical thinking (CT). I will call one the Individual View, the other the Social View. Central to both Individual and Social views is the belief that reasoned judgment is a necessary condition for critical thinking. A "reasoned judgment" means proposing a conclusion (i.e., argument, hypothesis, solution) and supporting it by means of noncontradictory reason(s). And both views accept two basic rules about reasoned judgment: the judgment must be relevant to the evidence upon which it was made and the judgment must not contradict the evidence upon which it was made. Finally, both individual and social views assume the existence of objective knowledge.[1] Along with these significant commonalities, however, lie important differences.

The Individual View conceives of critical thinking as a reasoned judgment by an individual at any given moment. The Individual View is concerned that each act of critical thinking be not only sound by logical principles but free of bias and prejudice, reflecting an impartial mind. The assumption is that if each act of critical thinking is as error-free as possible, knowledge ensues. Therefore, the Individual View is concerned about the character of the critical thinker, because only an impartial, fair-minded person will be able to consistently produce good critical thinking. At its essence, then, the Individual View concerns itself with the *discrete act* of critical thinking, judging it by *atemporal* criteria, e.g., whether it is free of fallacies and reflects a fair-minded *individual*. The Individual View is the dominant view of critical thinking.[2]

The second view is of critical thinking as *social*. A person makes a reasoned judgment, *which must take account of other reasoned judgment(s),* on an issue. Within the Individual View a well-wrought and accurate argument is sufficient to count as critical thinking. Within the Social View, however, one argument, no matter how well-wrought, cannot count as critical thinking unless it takes account of one or more alternatives and compares their evidence. Of course, one can do critical thinking upon encountering a single-minded argument, but to do so one must call up the alternative(s) for oneself.

Within this Social framework, the person doing critical thinking does not see out of the eye of one argument alone (monoscopic vision), but must see a hypothesis from the point of view of two or more arguments or lenses (stereoscopic, even multiscopic, vision). Why does the Social View add this stereoscopic requirement? Within the Social View, critical thinking in its totality is conceived as the accretion of reasoned judgments on a myriad of issues by many people over time. The Social View is by definition a *historical* view. It assumes that there has been progress in critical thinking over time, and that such progress is directly predicated upon the building of hypotheses in relation to what has gone before. Thus, as in vision, one can achieve "depth perception" only by seeing an issue through the lenses of two or more theories. The Social View requires consideration of some (not all) extant alternative theorizing on an issue. Finally, the Social View is an *evolutionary* view in which terms like good and bad, appropriate or reasonable, and critical thinking are meaningless without historical and social reference points. A piece of CT is good for a particular historical time to the extent that it links itself to a socially wrought fabric of pre-existing argument; the piece of critical thinking is even better if it provides a new theoretical thread that others add to until in time it becomes a contrasting fabric within the larger weave of critical thought. The Social View assumes that the more thoroughly alternative arguments are taken into account, the more knowledge ensues.

In sum, the Social View concerns itself that a piece of critical thinking reflects an awareness of at least some of the existing theoretical fabric, thereby attaching itself to that fabric. The Social View is a *longitudinal* view, the view of critical thinking as a historico-evolutionary process—in its largest conception, one that has gone on for millenia and is responsible for the moral and material progress we see. (Conversely, moral and material progress are halted whenever this stereoscopic consideration of hypotheses is forbidden.)

One might say that the stipulative definition or operating principle of the Social View is to take account of alternative argument, by dialogical reasoning[3] or other means. In contrast, the Individual View has as its main principle to be "appropriately moved by reasons" or to engage in "reasonable reflective thinking concerning what to believe or do."[4] Such words as "appropriate" and "reasonable" are fundamental to the Individual View, which holds that the onus of rightness or justification falls on each act of critical thinking and on the individual doing the critical thinking. Let us consider these individual principles in more detail.

How does one decide that a reasoned judgment is reasonable or appropriate? It must be free of bias and reflect an impartial mind.[5] But how does one know if one is free of bias and is reflecting an impartial mind? The answer cannot be that one's judgment is reasonable because one makes reasoned or appropriate judgments, for that argument is circular. Perhaps it is that the critical thinker has the disposition and skill to ask whether a piece of evidence actually provides compelling reasons for a proposition, or justifies that proposition.[6] But surely this does not mean that merely to *ask* "In this case does the evidence warrant the conclusion?" is sufficient for critical thinking, although everyone would agree that it is necessary. Critical thinking, of course, demands that one go on to answer yes or no to that question of justification and to support the answer with reasons. But it is precisely here that one cannot proceed without information outside the argument in question. Any argument will look reasonable or seem the appropriate view if it is the only argument that one is aware of.[7]

The power that most reasons have is therefore a power that must be assessed in relationship to alternative reasons. The most impartial and able critical thinker could not assess the force of reasons of an argument torn from its social fabric. The Individual View is therefore an artifact, born of close scrutiny of the relation of logic to critical thinking. While basic logical operations are important and necessary for good critical thinking, they are far from sufficient. Logic alone will not produce the impartiality and lack of bias that the Individual View seeks.

Unlike the Individual View, the Social View avoids the terms *reasonable* or *appropriate*. One must have reasons for one's judgment, such reasons argued to be better than those in contrasting theories, but the onus of being right or correct does not fall on the individual. As history has shown, that is too large a burden; most critical thinking would be poor. This is a crucial point. The Social View invites new threads of argumentation, many of which at first blush may seem—indeed, have seemed—far from reasonable or appropriate. Consider quantum mechanics, Darwin's Theory, or Trembley's claim that small animals reproduce asexually—all flew against what seemed reasonable at the time.

Oddly, the individual within the Social View has a much more important role than she does within the Individual View. In the latter the expectation seems to be that the impartial individual will determine by and for herself the most reasonable, appropriate view. The individual's principal job is to be right, or justified, for the right reasons. Within the Social View the individual, whose individuality is achieved thanks to social influences, is expected to make a contribution to the socially wrought conceptual fabric of theories that have helped to make her the individual who she is.

In both Individual and Social views, a critical thinker might, upon examining an issue, change things in three ways: (1) add, (2) subtract, and/or (3) innovate. She might add to an existing theory; she might suggest reasons why a theory be modified or scrapped; or she might create a new theory.

Since the Social View as historical invites change, it takes the innovative critical thinking that starts a new intellectual trend as the superior of the three. The Individual View cannot explain why intellectual innovators who produce more powerful theories with better evidence are given greater recognition than someone who is merely seen as justified in coming to the conclusion that an extant theory is warranted. The Individual View does not permit as close a connection between critical thinking and creativity.

As was noted, alternative-argument requirements are absent from the definitions offered by the Individual View; the appropriateness or reasonableness requirements are absent from the Social View. One might attempt to meld principles from the two views into one principle, for instance, "appropriately moved by alternative arguments." The problem with this, however, is that the phrase would hold an entirely different meaning, depending upon the framework from which one viewed it. Within the Individual View, "appropriate" is intimately connected with the most proper, impartial decision. Within the Social View the prescription to be "appropriately moved by reasons" is either redundant or *inappropriate*. It is redundant in that every reasoned judgment that takes account of alternative argument is appropriate, in the sense of "suitable," for further elaboration and improvement, either by its author or by someone else. But if one takes appropriate to mean "in accordance with established ideas or customs" it is misplaced because maintenance of the view that is perceived, even by those with the most intimate knowledge of available evidence, to be the most appropriate at the moment is *not* a requirement of the social theory, which views the adequacy of arguments as a long-range judgment rather than a short-range one, and it is a judgment that requires the presence of alternative hypotheses to the piece of critical thought in question. The Social View, therefore, deliberately eschews the requirement of reasonableness or appropriateness at each step of the way. Maverick ideas count as good critical thinking, so long as they are supported by reasons and placed in association with related arguments so we can judge the adequacy of their evidence.

From the framework of the Individual View, alternative argument could of course be included in a piece of critical thinking, but it is hard to see how alternative argument would constitute a *requirement*. If one is fair-minded and impartial at the moment about an issue, one might well construct an appropriate, reasonable argument without need to take account of an alternative argument. To impose an alternative argument is therefore unnecessary within this framework, and, in fact, might simply encumber the most appropriate argument.

From the perspective of the Social View, the demand to "properly assess reasons" and to be appropriately moved by them or by the most impartial view is chimeric. What is the "impartial view" in question? That view that an impartial person decides is impartial? But that possibility begs the question. That view that agrees most closely with the views of the person to whom it is addressed? Surely not. That view that agrees most closely with the views of (most) experts in the field? But we can point to numerous historical examples in which that view that appeared partial, prejudiced, wrong, even crazy was seen in later light to be a more appropriate view than the dominant one. Cases such as Einstein, Galileo, and Socrates spring to mind. If we immediately pass judgment on the partiality of another position, who is to say that we are not more akin to the spirit of the Inquisition than to Galileo? How much evil might have been avoided by taking a "wait and see" attitude to new ideas, to shifting their evidence?

It is precisely because the Individual View takes a "freeze-frame" snapshot of an act of critical thinking and evaluates it on the spot as "partial or not," "reasonable or not," that the Individual View becomes mired in these difficulties. The Individual View does not make sense unless one borrows elements from the Social View, for example, that alternative theories play the dominant role in theory-assessment, or that a piece of critical thinking that was excellent in the eighteenth century could now be poor because the network of alternative theories is at present much richer. The Individual View that one person should perfectly assess an argument is a false ideal. No man is an impartial island. No argument is an intellectual island.

For these reasons I would conclude that the Social and Individual views are incompatible. We can see critical thinking out of the lens of the Individual View, then switch lenses and view it from the perspective of the Social View, but like the Gestalt theorists' famous "duck-rabbit," one cannot point to crucial features and get them to mean the same thing under both views.

But what of the difficulties engendered by the Social View? Are we not awash in a sea of relativism regarding the immediate judgment of a piece of critical thinking? After all, the Social View eschews the requirement of reasonableness or appropriateness of arguments. Isn't argument assessment then dead? I believe not.

The Social View encourages the judgment of *adequacy in light of alternative arguments*. The relevant question here is "Does the argument evaluate its evidence in light of alternative arguments? If so, how well?" To say that an argument is inadequate is not to say that its author was inappropriately moved by reasons—it's just to say that we're requesting the author to go back to the drawing board and give an explanation how the evidence in a well-known alternative argument fits (or doesn't fit) with the author's claims. As we well know, there can be arguments about the adequacy of arguments, and again these can only progress if each side considers others' judgment in constructing future arguments on the subject. Let me note in passing that although the Social View does not make it a *requirement* that a theory be reasonable or appropriate, its originator can offer reasonableness or appropriateness in light of alternatives as warrants to (partially) justify her theory.

The Individual View has far less latitude in giving high marks for critical thinking than does the Social View, whose adherents can declare a piece of critical thinking good even though they do not consider the judgment to be correct or justified (except in the sense of noncontradictory). We might, for example, find a piece of critical thinking excellent while thinking its assumptions incorrect, and its reasons not nearly as compelling as those in a competing theory discussed in that piece of critical thinking. The author (let's say) clearly understood the competing theory and explained why he believed his reasons to be superior. The same is true for an argument whose conclusion we might think quite prejudiced or biased. Again, the question is not whether the conclusion is biased *in our eyes*, but whether and how thoroughly the argument has dealt with alternatives and their evidence that should be the deciding factor in its counting as (good) critical thinking. This is far more important, because the best way that we can remain open to change is to welcome the notion that perhaps we are the biased ones, after all. Like the financial markets, the stock of arguments may be up at some times, down at others (although the stock of arguments that stay in business climbs over the long haul). Neither the arguments nor their assessment need be perfect; all is provisional, subject to an improved perspective with the influx of new theories and better evidence. Like the stock market, the Social View is a form of long-range gambling: the gamble is that over time with enough people producing alternative arguments in a field, the truth will out—we just can never be sure when. This is Popper's notion of approximationist verisimilitude, that by reason we can get to the truth. I appeal to your reason and experience whether this is more the way that critical thinking works. In any event, within the Social View, what any individual believes about a given argument at any moment—for instance, whether it is reasonable, appropriate, biased—is not very important—except, of course, to that individual. It is widespread use of critical thinking by many people over the long haul that produces greater reasonableness.

As noted, in the Social View one judges *new* critical thinking in light of how well it takes into account extant theorizing on the issue, as well as how innovative it is. One takes *past works* of critical thinking in their historical context, for instance making a judgment like "a great piece of thought for the 17th century, but incomplete because people had not yet thought of X."

Interestingly, the Individual View is inextricably bound up with concerns about character formation,[8] while the Social View holds that the habit of "stereoscopic" critical thinking will produce character, not vice versa. The outcomes differ vastly when a piece of critical thinking is thought to be lacking. The Individual View will have it that a *critical thinker* is inappropriately moved by reasons or has not engaged in reasonable reflective thinking; the Social View would hold that *an argument* is inadequate, i.e., *not yet adequate* if it has not taken account of the foremost extant alternatives. The Social View entails no judgment about the individual doing the thinking in question.

That which might further point up this difference concerns the recent discovery of high-temperature superconducting materials. Two years ago the reasonable or appropriate view was that such materials did not exist. It required courage to pursue the course deemed unreasonable under the Individual View. According to the Social View, as long as an upstart scientist understood the theory(ies) that he was contesting and knew the kind of evidence needed to challenge extant theories, his critical thinking would be good before evidence was found for superconducting materials—his critical thinking would be good for its time even if such superconducting materials were not found.[9] Again it can be seen that a piece of critical thinking that would be considered excellent by the Social View could be considered poor in the Individual View.

To sum up: in the Social View, it is not so much that one should be appropriately moved by reasons as that one continually takes account of others' ideas. The Social View assumes that the more people take account of alternative theories about an issue, the better everyone's chances are of getting closer to the truth. The Individual View, however, assumes that the more impartial the character, the more appropriate (correct) the judgment.

What are the pedagogical implications of the Social and Individual views of critical thinking? There are many, but I wish to concentrate on three: (1) critical thinking and theoretical innovation, (2) critical thinking as transdisciplinary, and (3) critical thinking as bound up with *theoretical* content.

The tension between critical thinking and mental creativity or imagination is well known. It is not hard to see how this tension exists if one accepts the strictures of reasonableness and appropriateness placed by the Individual View. The Individual View works against theoretical innovation, since what is new is often thought odd or unreasonable. As the late Peter Medawar put it, "The mind takes to a new idea the way the body takes to a microbe: it rejects it." In its quest for the impartial, the Individual View fixes the "reasonable" view as against new candidates. (If the Individual View permits a multiplicity of equally impartial views, I have never seen that position stated. In any event, it is not clear what this would mean.)

As just noted in the case of superconducting metals, the Social View permits the weird, the outre, as good critical thinking. It lets imagination run wild, so long as the imagination comes up with relevant supporting reasons and takes account of alternatives. The Social View is biased toward the new, in the sense that the very idea of history requires change. Within the Social View, critical thinkers come up with new ideas and superior evidence, thereby creating intellectual history as they build upon one another's ideas over time.

What might this mean for us and our students? In the Social View, students are potential creators of intellectual history as much as we. If they come to us with ideas that we think are wrong, biased, hackneyed, inappropriate, we are careful not to teach them that they are wrong. Rather, within the social perspective we would encourage students to pursue their arguments in *light of alternatives*. Thus, the student may end by altering his or our opinions, or neither might happen. A student may maintain her original conclusion or not.   The relevant question is whether the new argument that she makes adequately takes account of alternative arguments, not whether it is reasonable or impartial in our eyes. And as I have tried to show, these are two very different things.

I recently ran across a marvelous sentence in a P. D. James mystery, *The Black Tower*, which neatly illustrates this point.   "He reminded [Inspector] Dalgliesh of a school master he had much disliked who was given to initiating frank discussion as a matter of duty but always with the patronizing air of permitting a limited expression of unorthodox opinion provided the class came back within the allotted time to a proper conviction of the rightness of his own views." I would not argue that this classroom atmosphere is an inevitable outcome of the Individual View; I do worry that it is a possible outcome.

What does it mean for students to *"take adequate account* of alternative arguments"?   Answering this question requires brief inspection of a second issue, whether critical thinking is discipline-specific. McPeck has criticized theories of the Individual View as oddly divorced from content.   He points out that it requires a sophisticated knowledge of the particular subject matter to do critical thinking in, say, biophysics or sociology.[10]   McPeck concludes that critical thinking is discipline-specific. The Social View would be in agreement that it is virtually impossible for someone unaware of the rich, intricate accretion of theories in a subject to estimate whether a given argument *"adequately* takes account of alternative arguments," much less to construct such an argument. But the Social View does not entail McPeck's conclusion that critical thinking is discipline-specific, as I will explain in a moment.

But regarding student work, it is crucial to distinguish between "state of the art" critical thinking in a subject and what might be called "state of *student* art" in critical thinking. Of course all instructors make use of this distinction.   It is possible for a student to do a quite respectable job as a beginner in a field, marshalling some alternative argument(s) that she has read concerning an issue and coming to a reasoned judgment about them in light of her opinion. Partially our judgment about the quality of her critical thinking has to do with her academic level—Is she a graduate student or a freshman? Along with the student's academic level, the judgment about her critical thinking also has to do with whether she has barely mentioned alternative theories (poor critical thinking, but critical thinking nonetheless in the Social View) or she has raised sustained consideration of alternative theories (good critical thinking).   In either case, for purposes of the Social

View she has done critical thinking, that is, taken account of alternative arguments. One might think of the classroom as a micro-social environment in which a student's work is judged "in light of the level of alternative arguments made by her peers." But judgments about her critical thinking should not entail that the student's assessment of "the force of reasons" be the same as that of her professor. In fact, emphasizing how well a student gauges the force of reasons could be dangerous, in that our opinions, which always seem to us to carry greater "force of reason," could easily become synonymous with "good critical thinking" in our classrooms. This would create an ideological atmosphere antithetical to critical thinking. In the Social View, students should always be entitled, even encouraged, to see a reason or piece of evidence as having more or less force than we.

In the sense of "state of the art critical thinking," then, all student critical thinking is poor just as all science in 200 B.C. is poor in retrospect. But that does not take away from the achievement either of students or of ancient scientists. If students can grasp how to critically think, appreciating that this process of evolving alternative theories within each field forms the heart and guts of the intellectual life, then students are becoming educated.

Let us further pursue McPeck's charge that critical thinking is discipline-specific. In his view, the idea of a general critical thinking course is an oxymoron, since each subject has its own epistemology. This claim would seem to confuse the structure of theorizing, which is transdisciplinary, with the type of evidence alleged in various disciplines. For instance, Siegel makes the argument that "skills such as identifying assumptions, tracing relationships between premises and conclusions...do not require the identification of specific subject matters."[11] In support of Siegel's claim that critical thinking is transdisciplinary, consider the following abstract from a scientific journal. It ought to be incomprehensible content-wise to most. Yet the theoretical structure is apparent to critical thinkers, thanks to the uniformity of our language in indicating critical thinking moves. Its title is "Enstopped Neurons in the Visual Cortex as a Substrate for Calculating Curvature." A critical thinker can calculate that, true to contemporary writing conventions, this title is the authors' conclusion or hypothesis. Now here is the abstract:

Neurons in the visual cortex typically respond selectively to the orientation, and velocity and direction of movement, of moving-bar stimuli. These responses are *generally thought to provide information about* the orientation and position of lines and edges in the visual field. Some cells are also endstopped, that is selective for bars of specific lengths. Hubel and Wiesel *first* observed that endstopped hypercomplex cells could respond to curved stimuli and *suggested* they might be involved in detection of curvature, but the *exact relationship* between endstopping and curvature *has never been determined. We present here a mathematical model relating* endstopping to curvature in which the difference in response of two simple cells *gives rise to* endstopping and varies in proportion to curvature. *We also provide physiological evidence that* endstopped cells in area 17 of the cat visual cortex are selective for curvature, whereas non-endstopped cells are not, and that some are selective for the sign of curvature. *The prevailing view* of edge and curve determination *is that* orientations are selected locally by the class of simple cortical cells and then integrated to form global curves. *We have developed a* computational *theory* of orientation selection *which shows that* measurements of orientation obtained by simple cells are *not sufficient because* there will be strong, incorrect responses from cells whose receptive fields span distinct curves. If estimates of curvature are available, however, these inappropriate responses can be eliminated. Curvature *provides the key to* structuring the network *that underlies our theory and distinguishes it from previous* lateral inhibition schemes.[12]

This abstract from the science journal *Nature* certainly requires a sophisticated grasp of the subject to know whether the authors' theory has adequately taken account of the previous schemes they discuss. Although we (presumably) know absolutely nothing about this subject we can, however, still tell that the authors have (1) offered a new hypothesis, (2) set it in relation to previous theorizing, (3) offered physiological evidence for it, and (4) argued that a competing hypothesis was not as strong. Thus, contra McPeck, critical thinking *is* transdisciplinary: we can "know how to reason within an area without knowing the area."[13] We can always see *whether* critical thinking has been done and trace the reasoning, although we cannot estimate whether it is adequate unless we are steeped in the subject.

What is the advantage of being able to see whether critical thinking has been done in areas one knows little or nothing about? I would argue that the advantage is enormous. First, it greatly helps in learning new subjects to know to look for their predominant theories. Otherwise one is swept away in a sea of data. Second, a course in critical thinking is of retroactive help as well. It helps to understand the significance of past learning or to ponder how one might have missed out if theoretical constructs don't spring to mind. Finally, a course in critical thinking is needed to show students what theorizing is, how it is the same in all disciplines, yet how supporting *evidence* for theories must be different for science (experiment/control), social science (often correlation), and humanities (often a principle supported by appeal to reason and experience). McPeck's claim about discipline-specific evidence conceals commonalities, the awareness of which would be of great benefit to students.

It requires the time and coordination of a separate course to explain theoretical structure and show its occurrence across disciplines. McPeck was critical of de Bono for failing to appreciate that "a 'mere' fact or piece of information such as 'The minister resigned because of political pressure from his constituency'...may take a competent teacher weeks to convey."[14] How much longer it should take to teach McPeck's definition of critical thinking:

> The process of justifying one's beliefs, however, has two distinguishable dimensions. One is to assess the veracity and internal validity of the evidence as presented, and the other is to judge whether the belief, together with its supporting evidence, is compatible with an existing belief system. If it is not compatible, then an adjustment somewhere in the system will be required: there is something amiss either with the new evidence or with the system of beliefs. The importance of this process of assessing, fitting and adjusting beliefs cannot be overemphasized.[15]

Leaving aside disagreements over this prescription, any instructor who has students for whom the understanding and application of this information would be trivial has far more advanced students than most.

Finally, the question of critical thinking versus content. One could imagine that we are caught between the Scylla of syllogisms, skills and/or attitudes and the Charybdis of endless information. But the Social View charts a middle course, insisting upon teaching *information that forms part of* the major theories of a subject.[16] That is a lot of information. To teach information as part of alternative theoretical structures is the essence of education, in my opinion. Information qua information is an absurdity, but so is it absurd to pillory information. It would be wonderful to know enough about the visual system to enjoy the abstract just quoted.

A part of most writing about critical thinking contains a disturbing distrust of information. McPeck notes that "informal logic books discuss 'the fallacies' with a touch of paranoia, as though mistakes in reasoning were always perpetrated by unscrupulous souls."[17]   But for all his insistence on subject-specific information, McPeck himself creates a wary tone.   Any new idea requires "reflective skepticism"; an idea already held requires "suspend[ing] a given belief long enough to assess the internal coherence of the evidence for it and to integrate the belief within [an] existing belief system."[18] These prescriptions work to undermine acquiring the very knowledge that McPeck believes is necessary for critical thinking.   Rather than advocating reflective skepticism (believe less), why shouldn't we work hard to *believe more*, read more, absorb more theories? This does not mean to believe everything with equal fervor but to establish a sliding scale of *provisional* belief, for instance to say "This seems very likely, that somewhat likely, and such and such quite unlikely," but fundamentally going in search of *as many new things to believe* as possible (this might be termed "learning"). Furthermore, why should anyone be required to suspend their beliefs? The stereoscopic act of considering one or more alternatives could, and most times does, entail that one keep one's belief while inspecting others. I don't see how suspending belief is psychologically possible, in any event. We want (for ourselves and our students) to be able to *shift or expand* belief, but I would argue that this ability is the result of careful stereoscopy; it does not come from suspension of one's belief. Again, critical thinking practice will provide the character that the Individual View seeks, not vice versa. Further, one often comes across an insistence that all of one's beliefs or theories must be consistent. This too seems odd; people often adopt new viewpoints that they only gradually come to see are at loggerheads with other theories that they accept. To exhort this kind of consistency only gets in the way of learning.

The educated person is like Hydra, many-headed.   The best theories of many other heads, perhaps long dead, live, grow, and change inside an educated person's head. This metaphor may be ghoulish. Hydra, you may recall, is the many-headed monster whom Hercules slew.   Two heads are better than one, and, by Herculean efforts, cultivation of a thousand heads in each brain is best.

Notes

1. Karl Popper, *Objective Knowledge* (London: Oxford University Press, 1972), p. 59.

2. Robert Ennis, "A Concept of Critical Thinking," *Harvard Educational Review* 32 (Winter 1962): 83–111; Edward D'Angelo, *The Teaching of Critical Thinking* (Amsterdam: B. R. Gruner, 1971); Harvey Siegel, "Educating Reason: Critical Thinking, Informal Logic, and the Philosophy of Education," *American Philosophical Association Newsletter* (1985): 10–13; see also John McPeck, "The Prevailing View of the Concept of Critical Thinking," *Critical Thinking and Education* (Oxford, England: Martin Robertson, 1981), pp. 39–65.

3. Richard Paul's work has elements of the Social View: "[Critical thinking] questions, structuring the very warp and woof of everyday life, are typically dialectical, settled, that is, by general canons of argument, by objection (from one point of view) and reply (from another), by case and counter-case." "McPeck's Mistakes," *Informal Logic* 7 (1985): 37. Since John McPeck stresses knowledge in a field as a necessary condition for critical thinking in that field, he also qualifies as a participant in the Social View; but to the degree that he sees this knowledge as discrete bits of "information" rather than as the major contending *hypotheses* in a field, he is not in accord with the Social View. McPeck, Ibid., p. 64 and passim. Information is only important to the degree that it is (can be) incorporated into theories. Edward De Bono touts generations of alternatives but not of *full alternative arguments in the context of historically derived theories.* His view is not "social" in the sense discussed here. Cf. *Teaching Thinking* (London: Maurice Temple Smith, 1976).

4. Ennis; Siegel.

5. Harvey Siegel, "The Critical Spirit," adapted from *Educating Reason: Rationality, Critical Thinking, and Education* (London: Routledge and Kegan Paul, 1987).

6. Siegel, "Educating Reason," p. 11.

7. Siegel offers the counter-example that he can foil Jehovah Witnesses' arguments without the need to appeal to "subject-specific information." He need only show that their argument that the Bible is divinely inspired because the Bible says it is divinely inspired is circular. Ibid., p. 12. It is much likelier that he and anyone else hearing the Jehovah Witnesses thinks first of alternative religious (or agnostic) arguments. We live in such an argument-rich society that we forget its importance to our thinking. If someone were raised having learned only one religion, I would predict that the person would more readily appreciate the problematic elements of their creed after a course in comparative religions, rather than in a class that taught fallacies, although having benefit of both would be ideal.

8. Passmore: "'being critical' is more like the sort of thing we would call a 'character trait' than it is like being skilled in a performance." John Passmore, *The Philosophy of Teaching* (Cambridge, Mass.: Harvard University Press, 1980), p. 168; cf. R. F. Dearden, *Theory and Practice in Education* (London: Routledge and

Kegan Paul, 1984), p. 119. McPeck is also in agreement: "training in particular critical thinking skills is not sufficient to produce a critical thinker. One must also develop the disposition to use those skills." Ibid., p. 19.

9. The scientist is C. W. Chu, The *New York Times,* March 10, 1987.

10. McPeck, p. 64.

11. Siegel, "Educating Reason," p. 11.

12. Allan Dobbins, Steven Zucker, and Max Cynader, *Nature* 229 (1987): 438.

13. McPeck, p. 81.

14. Ibid., p. 112.

15. Ibid., p. 35.

16. McPeck insists upon "basic knowledge of the field in question" and "norms and standards of [a] field" as necessary conditions for critical thinking. Ibid., p. 7. He does not mention that competing theories are important. Yet it is theories that determine what the basic knowledge is; it is theories which, by dint of working well in a subject, *set* that subject's norms and standards.

17. Ibid., p. 93.

18. Ibid., pp. 7, 37, and passim.

8

Community and Neutrality in Critical Thought: A Nonobjectivist View on the Conduct and Teaching of Critical Thinking

Karl Hostetler

Critical thinking is an important educational ideal, one line of reasoning for this being that critical thought is essential if people are to achieve autonomy and self-fulfillment in their intellectual, professional, and ethical lives. Such autonomy requires the ability to question rationally the social norms that are professed to govern those aspects of human lives. Without such a critical ability, people are susceptible to domination by authority and mere convention.

In this article, I assume the value of critical thinking, although there is certainly a need to be critical about that as well. I do not wish to imply that critical thinking is central or appropriate in every situation. Still, the question I wish to consider is how we are to understand the nature of critical thinking. Focusing on the examples of scientific and ethical inquiry, I contend that there are two fundamentally different ways that the nature of critical thinking has been understood. At stake in the debate is not only our understanding of critical thinking but our understanding of ourselves as moral beings.

A strong tradition in philosophy holds that a critical perspective on social norms requires a point of view neutral to particular social situations. Without such a neutral high ground, thought cannot hope to escape from the mire of community biases and relativistic argument. However, recent work in philosophy challenges this objectivist view.[1] While holding that objectivity is important for a critical perspective, it denies the *objectivist* claim that critical thought requires a neutral vantage point. It suggests that critical thought is and must be carried out in communal inquiry within and among particular forms of human life, not divorced from them. Objectivity is possible within such inquiry, but it is not achieved by reference to some perspective that is neutral to all views. Indeed, it is suggested that community "prejudices" are a necessary basis for critical inquiry. A critical perspective is not pursued by attempting to abandon these prejudices for a neutral view. Rather, it is achieved in the clash of divergent views that are always views from somewhere and so are not neutral.

Far from being something to be overcome, community plays an essential role in critical thought, according to this nonobjectivist view. This article aims to indicate the plausibility and importance of a non-objectivist orientation to critical thought. First, I attempt to characterize the objectivist view, which is the target of our objections. I then try to develop a nonobjectivist alternative, considering how this alternative responds to the charge of relativism and how community plays a central role in this conception of critical thought. I close by offering some brief reflections on what our discussion suggests for teaching critical thinking.

In the space we have here it is not possible to consider all aspects of critical thinking, for certainly a number of significantly different processes and contexts are subsumed under that broad heading. The discussion here focuses on the sort of critical thinking that has as its object the question of what social norms, values, and purposes ought to guide human thought and action. This is a critical activity in that it aims to investigate the real value of these norms, values, and purposes and their proper place in human affairs. Their value and place are not to be taken for granted. This sort of critical activity spans a wide range of human endeavors. For example, it has its place in academic disciplines such as literature, where norms that govern the composition and criticism of literary works (for example, norms having to do with characterization, creativity, and subtlety of plot) may be in need of critical examination. This sort of critical reflection has its place in the nonacademic workplace as well. For example, an architect planning a building has a repertoire of standards and principles to guide her work, but she still faces the problem of what standards ought to guide her work in particular situations and how these should be applied, for the particular physical and political environment in which the building is to be erected precludes straightforward or automatic application of archi-tectural standards.[2]

So, my ultimate goal is to suggest how community is essential for this sort of critical thinking in these diverse realms of human activity. However, in attempting to make that point, I will be focusing on two specific domains, science and ethics, which are useful for bringing out relevant issues. The example of science is used primarily because much of the inspiration for the nonobjectivist view I advocate comes out of the philosophy and history of science, particularly the work of Thomas Kuhn. The focus on ethics is significant because it is a domain different from science but where critical thinking is strikingly similar to critical thinking in science. Of course, there are also significant ethical reasons for attempting to understand the nature of critical thought in ethics.

The Objectivist View

As an example of an objectivist view in ethics, I will utilize Immanuel Kant. Kant provides a worthwhile example, not only because his work has been exceedingly influential in moral philosophy but because with his notion of moral autonomy he provides a vital issue with which we should deal.

A central aspect of Kant's moral philosophy is the Categorical Imperative. For Kant, this principle provided the ground for critical reflection on the fundamental maxims by which moral agents proposed to guide their lives. To consider critically whether one's maxims were ethically right or not, one had to pass these through the test of the Categorical Imperative: Could these maxims be willed to be universal laws of nature?[3]

Kant's belief that critical ethical thought required a neutral test via the Categorical Imperative reflects an objectivist orientation with associated views on the restricted role of community in critical thought. Certainly, this did not imply disregard for community. Kant was deeply concerned with the human community in the sense that he saw ethics as being essential to improving the personal and social lives of people. Furthermore, it was not Kant's contention that the Categorical Imperative alone was sufficient for ethical judgment. For Kant, one's specific social context provided the content of one's particular ethical beliefs and served to suggest concrete forms in which broad ethical virtues were to be enacted.[4]

So Kant's objectivist ethic was not asocial or antisocial. Nevertheless, a critical ethical perspective required examining one's socially developed notions about ethically proper conduct from a perspective that in some sense enabled one to rise above one's particular social context, in Kant's case through a principle that was taken to be a standard for a rational being as such, and so a standard that was neutral to any particular human community. This requirement of neutrality is the focus of our objection.

To be clear, while the objection here is focused on Kant's objectivist views specifically, it is aimed ultimately at the broad assumption Kant shares with others, namely, that a critical ethical perspective requires recourse to some standard or set of standards that in some way offers access to a point of view unaffected by particular personal or social beliefs. Kant manifests this idea with his Categorical Imperative, but so does John Rawls with his neo-Kantian notion of the Original Position.[5] It is also manifested by non-Kantians such as utilitarians with their notion that the principle of utility provides a neutral ground for examining proposed standards or actions. Hare's requirement of universalizability in ethical judgments is another example. This requires that "the universalizing reasoner must somehow compile the views of all standpoints in reaching her normative conclusions."[6] While such a reasoner need not deny the presence and legitimacy of her own particular viewpoint, a critical ethical judgment requires that she move beyond that to the stance of a neutral spectator.

A Nonobjectivist View

Having spent some time considering the target of our criticisms, I turn now to the positive task of constructing an alternative nonobjectivist conception of critical thought. A basic premise of the proposed conception is that critical thinkers are autonomous beings. While rejecting the objectivist aspects of Kant's philosophy, the nonobjectivist view advocated here seeks to preserve the Kantian notion of moral autonomy.[7] This idea captures an essential element of critical thinking in ethics and, as I suggest below, raises a vital issue for a nonobjectivist view. Kant argued that moral agents are autonomous beings in that they are legislators of ethical standards who give themselves these standards rather than have them determined by the mere fact that these same standards are accepted by other people. Moral agency requires, among other things, that the agent be able to judge socially accepted norms critically.

This requirement of autonomy raises the vital issue of objectivity. To be autonomous in the sense of giving oneself the standards that guide one's activities implies an ability to recognize possible alternative standards and objectively judge their relative worth. Thus our nonobjectivist view, with its claims for the nonneutrality of critical thought, is opposed to ethical subjectivism, ethical relativism, or ethical egoism that would have ethical agents inescapably confined to the realm of their own subjective or community beliefs or of their self-interested desires.

However, if the notion of autonomy, and related notions of objectivity and impartiality, is to be preserved in critical thought in ethics (and other areas of inquiry), as our nonobjectivist perspective says it must, there must be some significant sense in which people can question their society's ethical norms.

In the eyes of objectivist critics, however, it is just such a possibility for which a nonobjectivist view cannot provide. For such critics, a nonobjectivist view can only be relativistic.[8] The argument is that only neutral standards or procedures can permit inquirers to gain a critical perspective upon the particular beliefs held by themselves and their society.

We must deal with this challenge. The crucial question to be addressed by the nonobjectivist is how a person can critically question the norms of a society in a nonneutral way, that is, from within that social framework.

Objectivity and Relativism

In this section, I try to develop further our alternative to the objectivist view of critical thought. The issue of relativism serves as a focus. The principle concern is to show how a nonobjectivist view is not relativistic, how it can preserve significant notions of autonomy, objectivity, and impartiality. This nonobjectivist alternative holds that inquiry can be objective, and so go beyond relativism, while at the same time going beyond objectivism.[9]

First, the nonobjectivist position I propose should not be equated with contextualism, although it is a sort of contextualist view. A contextualist view of knowledge has largely supplanted foundationalism. Foundationalism is a species of objectivism that holds that claims to knowledge can only be justified on the basis of rationally indisputable standards of procedures. Thus the Categorical Imperative was taken to be the solid standard against which claims to ethical knowledge could be evaluated. Contextualism rejects the foundationalist assumption, suggesting that knowledge claims can be rationally justified on the basis of standards that may be disputable but that are not disputed in the case at hand. Recent philosophy of science has done much to prompt this shift to contextualism. For example, in his notion of scientific research programs Imre Lakatos acknowledges that scientific theories are conventions and so cannot be considered unshakable, yet these provide rational guidance to scientific research and serve to justify claims to scientific knowledge.[10]

The shift to contextualism is significant for the issue of relativism. The contextualist holds that knowledge is a human construction and that knowledge can be gained without requiring a foundation in rational certainty. Thus one may legitimately claim to be critical and objective in one's judgments without claiming that these judgments are based on some neutral, immutable standards or procedures. This represents an important challenge to objectivism, but it does not go far enough in itself. Objectivism is consistent with contextualism in that one could agree that the ethical norms one might appeal to in cases of ethical disputes are not timeless and infallible, yet argue that these are neutral to any particular point of view in the particular dispute at hand. For example, Harvey Siegel argues for a fallibilist absolutism that holds that "claims to knowledge can be *neutrally and objectively* evaluated and assessed."[11] Or again, while Rawls's recent position indicates a move toward the sort of communitarian position advocated here, it still "seeks its ground upon shared uncontroversial ideals such as the Kantian ideal of normative self-determination in the private and public spheres of modern society."[12]

Such contextualist objectivism grants that neutral standards may not be ahistorical or acultural, yet within delimited historical, social contexts, neutral standards or perspectives are available.

The nonobjectivist conception questions appeal to neutral standards as either necessary or sufficient for the rational resolution of any particular dispute about ethical norms. To be clear, the claim is not that there are no standards that are in some significant sense neutral. Laws of logic such as noncontradiction would be candidates for standards that could be used to judge the rationality of a community's ethical standards and that could be deemed neutral to any particular community.[13] Nor is the claim made that such logical standards are in general dispensable in critical inquiry. However, such standards are typically insufficient for carrying out critical ethical reflection to adequate depth. The central issue of critical ethical inquiry, at least so far as I am conceiving that task here, concerns the goodness of the form of life of a community, the rightness of its principles and values; and principles of logic have a limited role in informing that inquiry. Furthermore, such neutral standards as noncontradiction are not necessary to the rational resolution of disputes arising out of critical inquiry. While noncontradiction *must* be operative in the language of any community if there is to be the possibility of argument at all,[14] when it is the substance of nonneutral standards that is in dispute, the dispute can be rationally resolved on the basis of these nonneutral standards without appeal to some further neutral adjudicating standards.[15]

We have made a number of claims here. It is necessary to examine these more closely. We should first be clear about what sort of norms we are discussing and how they are nonneutral. The work of Thomas Kuhn in the history and philosophy of science has done a great deal to inspire the nonobjectivist view, and I turn to him to explicate this position. First, we should be clear that to claim that vital standards are not neutral to particular communities is not to say that these standards cannot be *shared* by different communities. However, even in the case that standards are shared, these may be *applied* differently.16 Kuhn writes that scientists may share standards for theory choice such as accuracy, simplicity, and fruitfulness, but these

> function as values and...they can thus be differently applied, individually and collectively, by men who concur in honoring them. If two men disagree, for example, about the relative fruit-fulness of their theories, or if they agree about that but disagree about the relative importance of fruitfulness and, say, scope in reaching a choice, neither can be convicted of a mistake....There is no neutral algorithm for theory-choice, no systematic decision procedure which, properly applied, must lead each individual in the group to the same decision.[17]

Kuhn argues that basic scientific norms are shared across scientific communities, and this is significant, for such shared norms prevent science from being merely arbitrary. Nevertheless, such shared norms rationally underdetermine theory-choices. At the level of generality of which these standards are shared, these standards cannot perform the critical function of resolving disputes between competing interpretations of the standards. Nor is it to say that these general standards lack all discriminatory power; it may be possible to distinguish broad sets of simple theories from nonsimple theories, say.[18] However, in the sort of disputes Kuhn has in mind, where it is "the question of which aims, values, and problems *ought* to dominate and define a certain domain of activity,"[19] the general standard does not have the requisite discrimi-natory power. At the level of specificity required for the critical application of standards to instances of choice, the standards are interpreted from particular perspectives in which views as to what are the *central* aims, values, and purposes of scientific activity will differ. These interpretations may differ without any interpretation being rationally mistaken. There is no recourse to neutral standards that will resolve these differences in interpretation.[20]

This point is at the core of Kuhn's thesis of incommensurability.[21] This thesis has generated considerable controversy, one prominent criticism being that Kuhn's thesis implies that incommensurable forms of life cannot be compared.[22] If this is so, the argument about scientific values can only be relativistic. However, incommensurability does not imply that such forms of life cannot be objectively compared and evaluated. What it does imply is that these forms of life cannot be straightforwardly compared point-by-point against each other.[23] Even if there was agreement on what points these forms of life should be judged (which likely will not be the case), judgments as to how the forms of life compare in reference to specific points, and as to what the relative significance of the specific comparisons might be, may legitimately differ. This is because comparison of incommensurable forms of life will be at least partially in terms of standards as these are interpreted and applied by the particular communities attempting the comparison. The attempt to examine one's scientific way of life objectively by means of comparing it to alternative ways of life must be carried on, at least in part, in terms of standards constitutive of particular ways of scientific life.

In what way does this go beyond relativism, then? In this sort of comparison, are we not condemned to argumentation that is merely circular? We must acknowledge that inquiry into forms of life must be circular in some sense. Indeed, Hans-Georg Gadamer suggests that we must begin inquiry from our "prejudices."[24] Critique must begin from where we are and not from some neutral place; "[w]hat we prepare to welcome is never without some resonance in ourselves."[25] But the circularity is not vicious, for one's prejudices need not be blind; they can and must be "suspended,"[26] critically examined in light of feedback from the object of study and from alternative understandings of that object. There is a hermeneutic circle of interaction between what is familiar and what is unfamiliar such that one's initial prejudices can be transformed. Through this interaction, disputes over values can be brought to rational closure as consensus about interpretation of standards is built through argument, even if these arguments are not compelling in the manner of proofs.[27]

So, in disputes about the relative importance of fruitfulness, for instance, consensus as to the importance of that standard can be built. The debate will typically go beyond that value strictly to involve such issues as the relative importance of other standards and what "fruits" of particular theories are to be deemed worthwhile. But this discussion will not be resolved by appeal to some neutral conception of fruitfulness of some other neutral standard(s). The debate must be resolved on the basis of the standards in dispute; the task is to "hammer out" (to use Richard Bernstein's phrase) consensus as to the proper interpretation of the disputed values themselves.

The Role of Community

In this hermeneutic argumentation, community plays a key role in the quest for objectivity. Kuhn emphasizes that scientific activity is significantly guided by the "prejudices" of the scientific community into which one is initiated. Scientists must view the world from *some* perspective. But to say that scientists must begin from some perspective is not to say that these perspectives are arbitrary and without rational warrant. Kuhn characterizes the elements of scientific knowledge as a *group* possession, the "tested and shared possessions of the members of a successful group."[28]

This is a significant point in that it places community prejudices on a nonarbitrary ground. Still, it does not answer the charge of relativism. Community plays a key role in the nonobjectivist response to this also. The contention is that a theory held by a particular community can be critically examined, but this examination is typically prompted and conducted in light of a rival theory. Thus, science does not progress by offering theories whose adequacy is finally determined by direct comparison with nature. Such a comparison is not decisive. Rather, the comparison is made with nature and alternative interpretations of nature.[29] Thus we see the vital role played by communities of scientists in developing differing theories that permit critical reflection on the adequacy of any particular theory.

Having spent some time wandering among the trees of philosophy of science, it is perhaps helpful to pause and take stock here lest we lose sight of the forest of critical thinking. The foregoing discussion has attempted to show that a significant part of scientific endeavor involves critical thought of the sort we are trying to consider, namely, thought about what aims, values, and purposes should guide scientific efforts. This critical thought can be rationally and objectively conducted. It is based on reasons, on appeal to standards that have rational warrant and which give scientific thought a nonrelativistic basis. However, the "ought" question cannot be rationally resolved by appeal to broad standards or to some other set of standards that can be deemed neutral. It is through the clash of divergent views that a resolution might be "hammered out."

There are parallels between critical thought in science and in ethics. The concern of critical ethical thought is to discern what aims, values, and purposes should be the fundamental guides to our personal and social lives. Critical thought in the ethical domain shares the essential features of the sort of critical thought in science that we have considered. This is a theme emphasized by Richard Rorty, Gerald Doppelt, and Bernstein. Rorty argues that "the lines between disciplines, subject matters, parts of culture" may become blurred.[30]   He sees Kuhn as pointing out the similarities of the deliberative process in science and other areas. Doppelt contends that Kuhn shows that "conflict between scientific theories becomes much more like conflicts in ethical and political life than the absolute distinction between scientific and normative discourse advanced by classical positivism allows."[31] Bernstein links rational thought in ethics and science through Aristotle's notion of *phronesis*. Bernstein argues that in science and ethics, particular judgments about what one ought to do (in the sense of what action to take or what scientific theory to be committed to) take the form of *phronesis*.[32]

Thus, while there are differences between scientific and ethical inquiry, for example, in the role of empirical evidence in those forms of inquiry, there are significant similarities in the critical, deliberative task of reaching good judgments about what aims and values ought to guide thought and action. One aspect of this should be emphasized. In each domain of inquiry, confronting divergent views is essential for a critical perspective. In science, a critical perspective is attained in the clash of rival theoretical positions. A critical ethical perspective is pursued through encounters with cultures whose ethical perspectives differ from one's own. Bernstein argues, "It is precisely in and through an understanding of alien cultures that we can come to a more sensitive and critical understanding of our own culture and of those prejudices that may lie hidden from us."[33] Peter Winch suggests that in encounters with alien cultures we are confronted "with new possibilities of good and evil in relation to which men may come to terms with life."[34]

It is the quest for understanding of such possibilities that takes us beyond objectivism and relativism. It is crucial that we understand what this sort of understanding involves. The task is to understand alien cultures, and, from our nonobjectivist standpoint, this involves a particular conception of social inquiry. In the quest for understanding, the characteristics of an adequate understanding cannot be fully stated beforehand.   The quest for understanding involves a hermeneutic process. The researcher aims to give a "reading" of the culture, but the adequacy of any reading must ultimately be evaluated vis-à-vis other readings, not some neutral framework.[35]

Thus, critical social inquiry is acknowledged to be a value-laden activity. Here lie both the opportunity and challenge of the conception of social inquiry as hermeneutic. It is an opportunity, for it presses upon the researcher the need for reflection upon herself as a moral being. Charles Taylor writes, "In the sciences of man insofar as they are hermeneutical there can be a valid response to 'I don't understand' that takes the form, not only 'develop your intuitions,' but more radically 'change yourself.'...A study of the science of man is inseparable from an examination of the options between which men must choose."[36]

In the objectivist conception of social science, failure to achieve understanding, that is, failure to meet supposedly neutral standards of understanding, implies that the researcher must look for more data or a better research procedure.[37] This fails to recognize the fundamental importance of examining the normative assumptions that are brought to the research. Failing to do that, one misses the opportunity for more profound self-understanding gained through critical reflection on those norms.

Of course, with the opportunity comes significant challenges. Bernstein emphasizes the clash of *alien* cultures. This highlights the challenge of confronting the incommensurability of conceptions of life, the fact that to some extent these different communities operate in different worlds. Critics of Kuhn's incommensurability thesis have suggested that Kuhn makes understanding impossible. This is a misunderstanding of his position. Rather than showing understanding to be impossible, what Kuhn and others show is that understanding must be pursued in a certain way, through a hermeneutic process.

Educational Implications

The philosophical work we have considered offers us invaluable insights into the possibility and challenges of critical thought within our social context. If a nonobjectivist orientation to critical thinking is correct, we must see critical thinking as something rooted in community and in which we cannot appeal to neutral standards to offer us security amid the many complexities that must be encountered. A critical perspective is developed as people struggle to understand forms of life that present them with "new possibilities of good and evil," new possibilities for the conduct of their personal and professional lives.

This work indicates the possibility of critical thought in a social context, and we should be firm in our commitment to that possibility. But, at the same time, we must recognize that there are psychological and political obstacles to the realization of that possibility, obstacles to openness to divergent views. We cannot do justice to all the issues involved in this, but by way of closing remarks I wish to offer a few brief reflections on what our nonobjectivist conception of critical thought implies for attempts to teach critical thought, attempts that would be part of the process of overcoming the psychological and political problems mentioned. Particularly, I wish to consider how the educational process might differ from one guided by objectivist assumptions.

Our nonobjectivist view emphasizes the need for community if critical thought is to flourish. An objectivist view would not necessarily deny all importance to community, yet the importance would be understood differently. Essentially, an objectivist view implies a "monological" approach to critical reflection, reflection "which may be practiced by [for example] an individual moral reasoner in isolation," where "intersubjective communication is not theoretically recognized to contribute in any special way to the quest for impartiality."[38] Thus, for example, Mill's defense of freedom of opinion and of expression of opinion in his "On Liberty" certainly places value on community for the pursuit of knowledge. Yet the community is only contingently necessary in Mill's view. Community helps us guard against our fallibility, but, in principle, knowledge can be pursued in isolation provided the individual is talented and honest enough.

In contrast, the nonobjectivist view is that community is necessary in that standards of judgment and critical judgments themselves are community products ultimately. Community does not merely help us reach or properly apply a neutral perspective or procedure, which is the ultimate guide for critical thought. Rather, it is the community itself which is the guide. We must "accept our inheritance from, and our conversation with, our fellow-humans as our only source of guidance."[39]

A very basic implication of this is that education aimed at critical thinking must be concerned with developing a particular content and context as opposed to focusing merely on skills. Skills certainly have their place. But while there may be techniques or skills *in* critical thinking, there can be no technique of critical thinking. Critical thought is a dynamic, ultimately social process requiring judgment and deliberation on the part of people. As such it cannot be formalized. This is not to say that skills of critical thought cannot or should not be taught. But such teaching would typically take the form of facilitation, coaching, and dialogue as opposed to being didactic. This is not to say that an objectivist orientation relies exclusively on a skills approach. But it would be able to legitimate a curriculum that separates the practice of skills from the dialogue in which those skills are utilized and tested.

Our nonobjectivist view emphasizes that beyond skills there needs to be a particular sort of content for critical thinking curricula. A critical perspective develops through encounters with divergent views. In attempting to teach critical thought in science or ethics or literature or music, teachers must expose students to differing views as to what aims, values, and purposes should guide activities in those areas. These should include differing views not only from within our own contemporary culture but also from other cultures and time periods as well. Thus historical and cultural studies are an important groundwork for critical inquiry. While some students do engage in such studies, we would do well to wonder whether the link between these studies and critical thought is often made. Making the link is vital, for it puts these studies on a different level. It shows that these studies are more than sources of information; they are sources of fundamental questions as to how we should conceive our personal and social projects and aspirations.

This issue of content needs to be pressed further, though. While this principle of broad experience with divergent views is important, we must make it more determinate if it is to represent a really critical experience. Following Doppelt's criticism of Michael Sandel's communitarianism, we must be wary that our conception of experience may be "too loose and abstract a notion to sustain any determinate epistemological conception of *critical* reflection."[40] Following Doppelt further, we may say that focusing reflection upon the particular traditions of our culture does something to provide the concreteness needed for critical inquiry. Hence, so far as the content of critical inquiry is concerned, examination and criticism of the relevant traditions of our own culture provide a focus.[41]

Again, this is not to say that an objectivist could not have similar concerns about content, although it is rather unlikely that such concerns would have the central place that they have in a nonobjectivist approach. However, even if such content was central for the objectivist, critical inquiry would still be construed to be monological. The content and the questions it might raise could be, in principle, adequately dealt with by individuals in isolation.

Our nonobjectivist view emphasizes the necessity of dialogue. As important as skills and content may be, critical thought of the sort we are considering depends ultimately upon a social context where divergent views can be honestly expressed and examined. Teachers concerned to develop such critical thought must work to establish, in their classrooms and beyond, communities where people can engage in critical dialogue and work to hammer out understandings of social norms.

This leads to one final observation I wish to make. It is that a commitment to a nonobjectivist conception of critical thought entails certain ethical commitments; it is not itself an ethically neutral conception of intellectual and social life. The full realization of critical thought[42] depends upon the existence of communities of inquirers and honest and forthright communication within and among these communities. Needed is a commitment to the existence of a "communication-community."[43] This implies a commitment to democracy in Dewey's sense of an association of people who share interests among themselves and with other communities.[44] If this sharing is to be honest and undistorted, it must be guided by values such as freedom and equality of people. Thus, an essential part of initiation into critical thought is the development of a commitment to these ethical values of community, democracy, freedom, and equality that are essential for the full realization of critical thought.[45] This may be the most significant insight for education that comes out of the nonobjectivist conception of critical thinking.[46] It highlights what may be the greatest challenge to educators who wish to promote critical thought.

Notes

This is a revised version of a paper presented at the conference "Critical Thinking: Focus on Social and Cultural Inquiry," Montclair State College, Upper Montclair, New Jersey, 19 October 1989, under the title, "The Social Context of Critical Thinking." My thanks to that audience, my colleagues in the Qualitative Studies Group at the University of Nebraska, and Tom Deeds for their questions, comments, and criticisms. Inadequacies that persist are solely my responsibility.

1. My discussion draws extensively from Richard Bernstein's *Beyond Objectivism and Relativism* (Philadelphia: University of Pennsylvania Press, 1983).

2. Donald Schon, *The Reflective Practitioner* (New York: Basic Books, 1983). Schon offers further examples of occupations that require critical thought of the same sort.

3. For the idea that Kant intended the Categorical Imperative as a test of maxims, see Onora O'Neill, *Acting on Principle* (New York: Columbia University Press, 1975); and Barbara Herman, "The Practice of Moral Judgment," *The Journal of Philosophy* 82, no. 8 (1985): 414–36. The Categorical Imperative may indeed have value as such a test and capture an important dimension of critical moral reflection. However, it cannot be considered to be a neutral standard, nor one that in itself fully captures the essence of the task of critical thought about the ethical value of social norms, values, and purposes.

4. Onora O'Neill, "Kant after Virtue," *Inquiry* 26, no. 4 (1983): 392–97.

5. See John Rawls, *A Theory of Justice* (Cambridge, Mass.: Harvard University Press, 1971). This charge of objectivism is accurate so long as Rawls is interpreted to offer the Original Position as a neutral perspective for evaluating different forms of life. He does appear to suggest this in his notion of the veil of ignorance and the sort of impartiality that notion demands. For a criticism of Rawls's idea of impartiality in rational ethical deliberation, see Bernard Williams, Persons, Character and Morality," in *The Identities of Persons*, ed. Amelie Rorty (Berkeley: University of California Press, 1976), 197–216; and Marilyn Friedman, "The Impracticality of Impartiality," *The Journal of Philosophy* 86, no. 11 (1989): 645–56. On a more generous reading, though, the Original Position is consistent with a nonobjectivist view, the key being that the commitment is to conditions where dialogue can occur but without supposing that participants must be ignorant of those particular values or projects that give meaning to their lives, and without supposing that the conclusions that emerge from the dialogue can serve as neutral arbiters in ethical disputes. It is through that dialogue, not through the operation of some neutral procedure, that different beliefs are evaluated. Consider Bernstein's summary of Hannah Arendt's argument that "[t]here is no test for the adequacy of an opinion, no authority for judging it, other than the force of the better public argument. The formulation of opinions therefore requires a political community of equals and a willingness to submit to public exposure and debate." See Bernstein, *Beyond Objectivism*, 216.

Recently, Rawls has modified his views about the Original Position to acknowledge the particular social context in which we must understand it to operate. See Friedman, "Impracticality of Impartiality," 653; and Gerald Doppelt, "Beyond Liberalism and Communitarianism: Towards a Critical Theory of Social Justice," *Philosophy and Social Criticism* 14, nos. 3–4 (1988): 277. It still is not clear, though, that Rawls's modified liberalism can provide an adequate critical perspective on issues of justice. See Doppelt, "Beyond Liberalism," 284–91.

6. Friedman, "Impracticality of Impartiality," 649.

7. This view holds an ethic of duty to be superior to an ethic of virtue for the reason that the latter does not do justice to the notion of autonomy. See Marcia Baron, "The Ethics of Duty/Ethics of Virtue Debate and Its Relevance to Educational Theory," *Educational Theory* 35, no. 2 (1985): 147.

8. This charge of relativism is a common one leveled against Thomas Kuhn, whom I take to be a representative of the nonobjectivist view.

9. This possibility is the central theme of Bernstein's book.

10. Imre Lakatos, "Falsification and the Methodology of the Scientific Research Programmes," in *Criticism and the Growth of Knowledge*, ed. Imre

Lakatos and Alan Musgrave (Cambridge, England: Cambridge University Press, 1970), 91–195.

11.   Harvey Siegel, *Relativism Refuted* (Dordrecht, The Netherlands: D. Reidel, 1987), 10, emphasis added. To reiterate, our objection is not to objectivity but to the idea that objectivity and neutrality necessarily are conjoined.

12.   Doppelt, "Beyond Liberalism," 291.

13.   On this issue of the role of standards of logic in inquiry, see Steven Lukes, "Some Problems about Rationality," in *Rationality*, ed. Bryan Wilson (Oxford, England: Basil Blackwell, 1970), 194–213.   Lukes refers to these standards as "universal" criteria (as opposed to "context-dependent" criteria), whereas I refer to them as neutral criteria. I suggest that there is an important distinction to be made between universal and neutral criteria. I comment on this below (note 20).

14.   Ibid., 209.

15.   As a practical matter, it may be possible and desirable for disputants to move to a ground that is "neutral enough" (to use Larmore's phrase), to in some sense distance themselves from beliefs that are in dispute and to move to places of more agreement, for the sake of keeping conversation going and perhaps resolving the dispute. See Charles Larmore, *Patterns of Moral Complexity* (Cambridge, England: Cambridge University Press, 1987), 53–55. Our claim is not that there can be no such level of agreement. There may be broader and narrower understandings of particular standards, understandings that command more or less consensus. However, the fact that people may share certain standards does not imply that these standards are neutral. More on this below.

16.   I want to be careful about this notion of application. Gadamer argues that speaking of "application" of a standard such as we are considering is problematic.   Such a standard, like a law, "is always general and can never address itself to all the concrete complexities of a particular case." See Hans-Georg Gadamer, "The Problem of Historical Consciousness," in *Interpretive Social Science*, ed. Paul Rabinow and William Sullivan (Berkeley: University of California Press, 1979), 141. Thus, in "applying" such standards, we cannot consider them to be neutral and fixed.   Part of the "application" involves working out an understanding of the standard that is appropriate to the particular context.

17.   Thomas Kuhn, *The Structure of Scientific Revolutions*, 2d ed. (Chicago: University of Chicago Press, 1970), 199–200.

18.   See ibid., 186, for Kuhn's claim that "shared values can be important determinants of group behavior even though the members of the group do not all apply them in the same way."

19.   Gerald Doppelt, "Kuhn's Epistemological Relativism: An Interpretation and Defense," *Inquiry* 21, no. 1 (1978): 41, emphasis in the original.

20. Here let me attempt to summarize and clarify the notion of neutral standards that is developing in our discussion. First, there is a distinction between neutral standards and universal standards. The law of noncontradiction may be deemed a universal standard, following Lukes, and it is also a neutral standard in that judgments as to its proper application are essentially free from influence of community-specific criteria. Of course, it may be difficult to determine for a particular community what the content of the "p and not-p" relation is, but having determined the relevant content, judgments about the logical relation of the relevant entities is not "dependent on social relations between men" (Lukes, "Problems about Rationality," 210).

However, I suggest the possiblity that there are standards that are universally shared but that are not neutral. (Kuhn talks about standards universal to the community of scientists. I would go beyond that to suggest that there may be values or traits universal to human beings.) Kuhn suggests that theoretical fruitfulness is a universal scientific value, but this is not a neutral standard in that judgments about fruitfulness are dependent upon social relations in a way that judgments about self-contradiction are not.

Another point: It might seem that I am myself advocating a self-contradictory thesis, namely that these values such as fruitfulness are shared but not *really* shared. Taylor's distinction between common meanings and consensus is helpful here. See Charles Taylor, "Interpretation and the Sciences of Man," in *Knowledge and Values in Social and Educational Research*, ed. Eric Bredo and Walter Feinberg (Philadelphia: Temple University Press, 1982), 153–86. Taylor writes: "We could…say that common meanings are quite other than consensus, for they can subsist with a high degree of cleavage; this is what happens when a common meaning comes to be lived and understood differently by different groups in a society. It remains a common meaning, because there is the reference point which is the common purpose, aspiration, celebration… .But this common meaning is differently articulated by different groups." (p. 176)

Thus I suggest that values can be shared in the manner of common meanings without the "articulation" or application of those values being shared. In that sense, these values cannot be considered standards neutral to disputes among different groups.

Finally, I have used "neutrality" as a blanket term that encompasses positions that differ to some degree. For example, I have questioned the necessity of neutrality conceived as radical impartiality to one's own personal projects. I have questioned the necessity of neutral standards conceived as standards whose application is not influenced by community-specific understandings of those standards. The common thread in these notions of neutrality is that we can and must reach a perspective where, at least in principle, particular personal or community views exert no significant influence over the articulation or application of shared standards by which we critically examine our thought and activities.

21. For discussions of Kuhn's incommensurability thesis see Bernstein, *Beyond Objectivism*; Doppelt, "Kuhn's Epistemological Relativism"; Kuhn, *Structure of Scientific Revolutions*; and Siegel, *Relativism Refuted*.

22. For example, see Siegel's suggestion that "incommensurability signified precisely the in-principle impossibility of such [rational] debate and comparison" (p. 83). See Bernstein, *Beyond Objectivism*, 84–86, for a discussion of incommensurability and comparability and the claim that these are not mutually exclusive.

23. Contrary to what Siegel suggests (p. 61), there is a substantive difference between comparison and point-by-point comparison. See Bernstein, *Beyond Objectivism*, 86, for a discussion.

24. See Bernstein's discussion of Gadamer's notion of prejudice and its place in the hermeneutic circle, *Beyond Objectivism*, 126–39. For other discussions of the hermeneutic circle see Gadamer, "The Problem of Historical Consciousness" and Taylor, "Interpretation."

25. Gadamer, "The Problem of Historical Consciousness," 134.

26. Ibid., 108.

27. See Kuhn, *Structure of Scientific Revolutions*, 144–59, for his discussion of the resolution of scientific disputes.

28. Ibid., 191.

29. This is one point on which Lakatos and Kuhn agree. For example, see Lakatos, "Falsification," 130; and ibid., 77.

30. Richard Rorty, *Philosophy and the Mirror of Nature* (Princeton, N.J.: Princeton University Press, 1979), 329.

31. Doppelt, "Kuhn's Epistemological Relativism," 41.

32. Bernstein, *Beyond Objectivism*, 54 and passim.

33. Ibid., 36.

34. Quoted in ibid.

35. Taylor, "Interpretation," 156.

36. Ibid., 182.

37. Ibid., 181.

38. Friedman, "Impracticality of Impartiality," 649.

39. Richard Rorty, *The Consequences of Pragmatism* (Minneapolis: University of Minnesota Press, 1982), 166.

40. Doppelt, "Beyond Liberalism," 283, emphasis in the original.

41. However, we should be careful to recognize the proper scope of such criticism. As Rorty remarks, "The hermeneutic point of view...is possible only if we once stood at another point of view. Education has to start from acculturation...[W]e cannot be educated without finding out a lot about the descriptions of the world offered by our culture." See *Philosophy and the Mirror of Nature*, 365. Rorty makes a similar point in his "The Dangers of Over-Philosophication," *Educational Theory* 40, no. 1 (1990): 41–44.

42. I do not suggest that no legitimate sort of critical thinking can occur in the absence of such community.

43. Karl-Otto Apel, "Types of Rationality Today: The Continuum of Reason between Science and Ethics," in *Rationality To-Day*, ed. Theodore Geraets (Ottawa, Ont.: University of Ottawa Press, 1979), 307–40.

44. John Dewey, *Democracy and Education* (1916; New York: Macmillan, The Free Press, 1966), 83.

45. A great deal more needs to be said about how we are to secure the possibility of communication-communities, how we are to achieve a situation where people are truly free and equal. Bernstein discusses this issue in parts 3 and 4 of his book. I only make some brief comments here. Friedman ("Impracticality of Impartiality," 655–56) suggests that the strategy should not be to try to eliminate undue biases en masse, contrary to what objectivists would seem to suggest, but rather that the process should be one of eliminating particular distorting biases as these are identified. This would seem to be in keeping with our nonobjectivist orientation in that identification of distorting biases must itself be a task of the hermeneutic process.

In the abstract of his reply to Friedman, McGary charges that "Friedman needs a criterion for identifying forms of partiality that negatively impact on critical moral thinking," for while with her method "we can eliminate some forms of recognizable partiality...she does not provide a means for determining how many biases still remain and the role these remaining biases might play in our critical moral thinking." Thus her method can be criticized as being impractical. See Howard McGary, "Friedman on Impartiality and Practicality," *The Journal of Philosophy* 86, no. 11 (1989): 658. It is true that criteria for identifying forms of partiality must be developed if distorting biases and their role are to be identified. The hermeneutic process is aimed at this. In this process certain distorting biases may remain operative yet hidden. Does that make the method impractical? Only if we hold an inflated notion of the sort of objectivity we are seeking. In the hermeneutic process we aim to suspend our prejudices, but we must also realize that we will likely achieve only partial success. This does not entail that judgments reached in that process cannot be deemed objective, although it must be said that this is a different conception of objectivity than what McGary would appear to have in mind.

46. This is not to say that an objectivist cannot believe in the values of community, democracy, freedom, and equality. What would distinguish a nonobjectivist view is how these values are articulated and how they are emphasized as requirements for critical thought. For example, a liberal understanding of such values would be "detached from rethinking the good and reconstructing established moral-political right and social justice" since liberal conceptions of right are considered to be independent of particular conceptions of good and/or are considered to be uncontroversial. See Doppelt, "Beyond Liberalism," 290–91. Such detachment is unacceptable to the communitarian view advocated here.

9

Critical Thinking and Feminism

Karen J. Warren

Introduction: Critical Thinking and Feminism

What does feminism have to do with critical thinking? What can a political movement, feminism, contribute to an understanding of a reflective activity, critical thinking? If critical thinking is a feminist issue, what makes it so?

In this paper I suggest answers to these questions by raising two sorts of worries about current conceptions of critical thinking from a feminist perspective. The first and primary worry concerns the nature of critical thinking and the critical thinker. The second concerns the learning/teaching of critical thinking. Underlying this twofold worry is the view that an adequate understanding of critical thinking—both what it is and how it is taught—must involve a recognition of the importance of *conceptual frameworks*. I argue that since critical thinking always occurs within a conceptual framework, what is needed is a *contextual* understanding of critical thinking, i.e., one which acknowledges the ways in which conceptual frameworks affect the sort of thinking we do. Furthermore, I argue that insofar as a given conceptual framework is biased, the critical thinking that grows out of and reflects it will inherit this bias. Just as *patriarchy* is the special interest of feminists, it is *patriarchal conceptual frameworks* and the bias they generate that is of special interest to a feminist critique of critical thinking.

The Nature of Critical Thinking

While there is no single definition of critical thinking that is accepted by all specialists,[1] it is sufficient for our purposes to use the term as it is frequently used in the literature and as it has been used by Robert Ennis: Critical thinking is *reasonable reflective thinking that is focused on deciding what to believe or do.*[2]

Critical thinking so defined involves both abilities (or skills) and dispositions (or tendencies). Setting aside taxonomical questions about classification, a typical list of critical thinking abilities and dispositions includes several of special interest in this paper: the abilities of deducing and assessing deductions, inducing and assessing inductions, identifying and assessing assumptions, observing and assessing observation reports, identifying and assessing the credibility of a source, detecting and avoiding unnecessary and avoidable bias, identifying and assessing generalizations, and identifying and assessing causal claims, as well as the dispositions of open-mindedness and interpersonal sensitivity.[3]

Notice that this broad definition of critical thinking in terms of both abilities and dispositional aspects allows that creative thinking, passion, and empathy may play important roles in "reasonable reflection" about what to do or believe.[4] Critical thinkers are those who exercise such skills and display such dispositions. This broad definition also allows for the important role knowledge, especially background or prior knowledge, plays in one's ability to think critically.

Feminism and Patriarchal Conceptual Frameworks

Although there are important differences among the variety of feminisms (e.g., liberal feminism, traditional Marxist feminism, radical feminism, socialist feminism, black and Third World feminism, ecological feminism), all feminists agree that feminism is (at least) *the movement to end sexist oppression.*[5] All feminists agree that sexism exists, that it is wrong, and that it must be eliminated. As such, all feminists are opposed to patriarchy, i.e., the systematic domination of women by men.

Contemporary feminists claim that, whether we know it or not, each of us operates out of a historically and socially constructed "frame of reference," "world view," or what I am calling *"conceptual framework,"* i.e., a set of *basic* beliefs, values, attitudes, and assumptions which explain, shape, and reflect our view of ourselves and our world. Conceptual frameworks are influenced by such factors as sex/gender, class, race/ethnicity, age, affectional preference, and nationality. Although one's conceptual framework can change, all individuals perceive and construct what they perceive, know, and value through some conceptual framework. At any given time, a conceptual framework functions for an individual as a finite lens, a "field of vision," in and through which information and experiences are filtered. As such, conceptual frameworks set boundaries on what one "sees."

Some conceptual frameworks are *oppressive*. For our purposes, there are three typical features of oppressive conceptual frameworks, at least in Western societies, for an understanding of women's oppression.[6] First, an oppressive conceptual framework typically is characterized by *value-hierarchical thinking*. As I am using the expression, value-hierarchical thinking (as distinguished from "hierarchical thinking") is "a perception of diversity which is so organized by a spatial metaphor (Up-and-Down) that greater value is always attributed to that which is higher."[7] Value-hierarchical thinking has put men "up" and women "down," culture "up" and nature "down," minds "up" and bodies "down," reason or intellect "up" and emotion "down."[8]

Second, an oppressive conceptual framework typically supports the sort of "either-or" thinking that posits inappropriate or misleading or harmful *value dualisms*, i.e., either-or pairs in which the disjunctive terms are seen as exclusive (rather than inclusive) and oppositional (rather than complementary), and where higher value is attributed to one disjunct than the other. Value perceives and describes reality (viz., evaluatively dualistically); they also conceptually separate as opposite aspects of reality that may in fact be inseparable or complementary, e.g., reason and emotion.[9] As will be illustrated, such uses of value dualisms may be inappropriate, misleading, or harmful.

The third and most important feature of an oppressive conceptual framework is that it gives rise to a *logic of domination*, i.e. a structure of argumentation which explains, justifies, and maintains the subordination of an "inferior" group by a "superior" group *on the grounds* of the (alleged) superiority and inferiority of the respective groups. Since it is the logic of domination that supplies the missing assumption that *superiority justifies subordination*, it is the logic of domination that gives the final moral stamp of approval to the "justified" subordination of that which is deemed lower or less valuable.[10]

Many contemporary feminists are interested in oppressive conceptual frameworks that are *patriarchal*, i.e., ones in which historically or traditionally male gender-identified beliefs, values, attitudes, and assumptions are taken as the only, or the standard, or the more highly valued ones than female gender-identified ones.[11] *Historically*, a patriarchal conceptual framework has assigned greater value, status, or prestige to that which traditionally has been identified as "male" than to that which traditionally has been identified as "female," or carves out different spheres (e.g., the "public" sphere of the polls and the "private" sphere of the home) and gives value to what is female-identified only within that female-identified and relatively lower status sphere.[12]

Conceptually, a patriarchal conceptual framework functions to maintain the subordination of women.[13]

It is by understanding the nature and power of conceptual frameworks, particularly oppressive and patriarchal ones, that one can see the respects in which critical thinking is a feminist issue. It is to this topic that I now turn.

Critical Thinking as a Feminist Issue

Any issue is or could be a feminist issue. What makes any issue a feminist issue is that an understanding of it contributes in some way to an understanding of the oppression of women. Lack of comparable pay for comparable work is a feminist issue wherever and whenever an understanding of it bears on an understanding of the oppression of women. Carrying water is a feminist issue if, in a given culture, it is the women who spend several hours a day carrying water and that activity contributes to their unequal, inferior, or subordinate status.

Critical thinking is a feminist issue because there are important ways in which an understanding of critical thinking bears on an understanding of the subordination of women. The basic link or connection provided in this paper between the two—critical thinking and feminism—is located in the nature of conceptual frameworks, especially oppressive patriarchal ones.[14]

Critical thinking does not occur in a vacuum; it *always* occurs within some conceptual framework. Stated differently, when one does the sorts of things critical thinkers do, e.g. observe, infer, generalize, predict, define, make assumptions, give causal explanations, there is always *some* point of view that is the point of view of the critical thinker. The so-called ideal of a "neutral observer," i.e., one who has *no* point of view is, at best, an ideal, and at worst, an "ideological prejudice."[15]

Recent feminist scholarship in two different areas—science and ethics—reveal the importance of conceptual frameworks. Consider ways in which feminist challenges in these two areas bear on an understanding of what makes critical thinking a feminist issue.[16]

Feminist Science. In her book *Science and Gender*, neurophysiologist Ruth Bleier argues that "science is *not* the neutral, dispassionate, value-free pursuit of Truth."[17] According to Bleier, traditional or dominant science occurs within an androcentric conceptual framework and inherits the androcentric bias of that framework.[18] Bleier and other feminist scientists have defended their charge that male gender-bias arises in two areas of scientific research in which important critical thinking skills are used: so-called "sex differences" research between men and women and primatology.

"Sex Differences" Research. Suppose an assumption of a given conceptual framework is that there is a meaningful distinction between "pure biology" and "environment" (or "culture"). Within such a framework, the question "Are there genetic sex-based differences in men's and women's behaviors?" makes sense. Research projects and methodologies aimed at isolating sex-linked differences in brain structure, hemispheric lateralization, hormones, or genes to explain behavior differences between "the sexes" (e.g., in verbal fluency, mathematical skill, visual-spatial information processing skills, or cognitive abilities) are countenanced, and conclusions about purely biological bases for male superiority in certain activities are offered as empirically verified or verifiable.

However, what if the initial assumption about the dichotomy between pure biology and environment is false or conceptually flawed? Then the controversy about purely genetic, inherited, sex-based behavior traits itself, including the questions asked, the research projects undertaken, the methodologies employed, and the answers given, is also conceptually flawed.

This is what feminist scientists like Ruth Bleier argue. They claim that the question "Are there biological sex differences between men and women?" is conceptually flawed, since it is not possible to separate off any "pure" biology from culture in the requisite way.[19] Stated differently, in order for the question to be meaningfully raised at all, one must presuppose the legitimacy of the very biology/culture dualism that feminist scientists like Bleier deny. Furthermore, if the question "Are there biological sex differences between men and women?" is conceptually flawed, then so is any conceptual framework that countenances a debate over sex differences, since it will also mistakenly assume that it *does* make sense to talk of a "pure" biology separate from culture, that one *can* measure how much of human behavior can be attributed to pure biology and how much to environment and learning, and that any differences in *behaviors* between men and women—socially constructed gender categories—is based in pure biology. This is especially important to notice since, historically, assumptions about "sex differences" have functioned to explain and justify the alleged "natural" or "innate" inferiority of "the female sex" and the biological basis of women's oppression in her childbearing and childrearing roles.

If the views of feminist scientists such as Ruth Bleier are correct (no attempt is made to defend them here) and "sex difference" research is *conceptually* flawed, then so is any conceptual framework that sanctions, maintains, or gives rise to the meaningfulness of such research. The point here is not whether the distinction between "pure biology" and "environment" is patriarchally motivated or causally linked to a patriarchal conceptual framework; establishing that would be a different task. The point here is that the sort of conceptual framework that sanctions, maintains, or gives rise to such value-laden "either-or" thinking is flawed. Since feminist scientists claim that "sex-differences research" is comfortably housed in dominant science, and that dominant science reflects a patriarchal conceptual framework, then, if they are correct, "sex-differences research" is comfortably housed within a patriarchal conceptual framework—one that has historically functioned to value as inferior or lower-status whatever is genetically or biologically linked with "the female sex," or has historically sanctioned "sex difference" conclusions about superior male abilities and behavior over female abilities and behavior. Understood in this way, the feminist objection to "sex differences research" *done from within* an oppressive conceptual framework is that it takes as meaningful and tenable the either-or (and not both) distinction between "pure genetics" and "environment" and mistakenly assumes that information about genetics alone will explain human behavior. The feminist position that biology is both genetic and cultured, both determined and conditioned, is never entertained. For feminist scientists, it isn't so-called "biological differences" (whatever they are) between males and females that is really at issue, but the values, beliefs, attitudes, and assumptions *about* biological differences and *about* the relevance of such differences for how men and women are viewed and treated that is at issue. And to get at *that* issue is to get at the nature and significance of conceptual frameworks.

Primatology. Feminist primatologists such as Donna Haraway and Sarah Hrdy[20] have challenged traditional androcentric observational and explanatory models for primate social organization. The assumption of such models was that primate social organization was structured around "male dominance hierarchies." If any attention was focused on observing female primate behavior, females were cast in passive and primarily nurturing roles, while males were cast in culturally stereotyped and sanctioned active, courting, and promiscuous roles. Assumptions of "male dominance hierarchies" prevented primatologists from seeing "the full extent of female choice, initiative and aggressivity or its polyandrous expression," and from seeing that dominance hierarchies are neither universal nor always male.[21] It prevented researchers from seeing, for example, that it is usually estrous females that select mating partners, that in some species (e.g., Japanese macaques, rhesus macaques, and vervets) species dominance is matrilineal, and that no evidence supports the view that dominant males have more frequent access to females than less dominant males in baboon troops.[22] As Bleier writes,

> In the absence of knowledge about female primates based on observations of their behavior, primatologists then felt free to speculate (that is, to construct) female primates in ways that allowed their imagined behaviors and characteristics to fit existing male-centered theories of human cultural evolution and thus to embellish, naturalize, and reinforce the social construction of human female and male genders and of relations of dominance and subordination.[23]

Again, *if* this view is correct (and I do not attempt here to defend the view that it is), then the basic beliefs, values, attitudes, and assumptions, which describe a patriarchal conceptual framework blinded these researchers from raising and addressing crucially relevant issues about "male dominance hierarchies" and female primate behavior. The "point of view" of these researchers does not permit such issues to get raised at all.   (More is said about this in connection with the discussion of assumptions, below.)

Feminist Ethics. One target of feminist criticisms of gender bias in contemporary Western philosophy is the dominant *"rights/rules ethic,"* i.e., an ethical framework for assessing moral conduct in terms of alleged rights of relevant parties and/or in terms of governing rules or principles, appeal to which provides a decision-procedure for resolving conflicts among rights. This ethical framework is essentially hierarchical or "pyramidal," where the "authority" of a right or rule is given from the top of the hierarchy.

Judith Thomson's discussion of abortion in her well-known article, "A Defense of Abortion"[24] is characteristic of a discussion within a rights/rules framework. Thomson critiques the argument that since a fetus' right to life overrides a pregnant woman's right to decide what shall happen in and to her body, abortion is wrong. She does so *not* by challenging the rights/rules framework in which that argument occurs, but by challenging the truth of the claim that a fetus' right to life overrides a pregnant woman's right to decide.

Feminist philosophers like Kathryn Addelson raise several objections to "the Thomson tradition" approach to discussions of abortion.[25]

First, it represents moral situations in a value-hierarchical way that conceals that "the point of view" from the top of the hierarchy is an invisible, unmarked, and hence privileged point of view of the dominant group (historically white males), while the point of view of the "other" (women, blacks) functions as a value-laden, biased, or marked point of view. A judge is a judge unless she is female or black. A philosopher is a philosopher unless she is feminist; then she is a feminist philosopher. And the Western philosophical tradition is just that until it is critiqued by feminists who insist on marking it as "the white male dominant Western philosophical tradition." It is not, as traditional philosophers have assumed, an ungendered, unraced, or unclassed point of view.

Addelson argues that the sort of bias that infects the Thomson approach to abortion "allows moral problems to be defined from the top of various hierarchies of authority in such a way that the existence of the authority is concealed."[26] By concealing the authority (e.g. of traditional academic philosophers), the point of view from the top of the hierarchy *appears* to be impartial when it is not. Furthermore, according to Addelson, since the Thomson tradition systematically ignores discussions of hierarchy, dominance, and subordination, it does not provide an adequate conception of ethics from the point of the experiences of women (including poor, pregnant women) in subordinate positions.

Second, a rights/rules approach to abortion incorrectly assumes that talk of rights adequately captures all the morally relevant features of abortion. Other morally relevant data, e.g., what Jane Martin calls the "3 C's of caring, concern, and connection,"[27] either do not get included at all, or, if they do, get included only insofar as they can be unpacked in terms of the relevant moral categories of property, rules, and rights of moral agents.

For these two sorts of reasons, feminists like Addelson object that a rights/rules approach to abortion incorrectly assumes that a rights/ rules framework provides an objective, impartial, and universalizable decision-procedure for resolving moral conflicts such as abortion; what (they claim) it really provides is a decision-procedure that grows out of a value-hierarchical, historically well-entrenched system of social relationships, which assumes that "authority" (objectivity, impartiality, universalizability) is given from the top of the hierarchy—the dominant group.[28]

As with the preceding discussion of feminist science, the point here is neither to defend the feminist positions given by Addelson and others nor to establish some sort of logical entailment relation between a "rights/rules ethic" and male-dominance value-hierarchies (even if such an entailment relationship could be shown to exist). Rather, the point is to suggest that if the view of feminists like Addelson is correct, viz., that a rights/rules ethic within a hierarchical social system of male dominance, *whatever else its virtues or strengths*, has historically functioned as if it were an observer-neutral position when it is not and has not been, then use of a rights/rules ethic within a patriarchal conceptual framework serves to explain, maintain, and justify the point of view of those "on top" as an unmarked and unprivileged point of view (e.g., of the "rational," or "objective," or "detached and impartial," or "neutral observer") when it is not. Calling attention to the nature and power of historically constructed patriarchal conceptual frameworks is part of what makes this historical and contemporary feature of a rights/rules ethic visible.

Feminist Science, Feminist Ethics, and Critical Thinking

If what I have said so far is plausible, then critical thinking in and about science and critical thinking in and about ethics requires recognition of the ways in which the exercise of important critical thinking skills and dispositions is not always easy to do, and is sometimes impossible to do, within a patriarchal conceptual framework. A consideration of a few such selected skills and dispositions will show why this is so.

1. Recognizing and assessing an assumption. When an assumption is basic to a conceptual framework, it may not always be possible to challenge or revise the assumption and yet remain within that framework. It is *impossible* when the framework itself presupposes the truth of the claim one is denying. In such a case, the framework itself must be changed; no reformist moves from within the framework (e.g., changing the meanings of some terms or altering other-than-basic assumptions) will remedy the defect.

This issue, the "reform or revolution" issue—change from within or change from without—arises in all areas of contemporary feminist scholarship. For example, it arises in "feminist curricular transformation projects," i.e., feminist discussions of ways to change the traditional or "mainstream" curriculum to make it more inclusive of women. There, the "reform or revolution" issue often arises in connection with the "add women and stir approach" to curriculum development. As one "adds" women—particularly feminist women—to traditional science or ethics courses, for instance, one soon realizes that the inclusion of women begins to challenge the way in which science and ethics are conceived, the way each is taught and practiced, and which issues get labeled as bona fide "scientific" or "ethical" issues. This is because, in the words of Elizabeth Minnick, one cannot simply add the idea that the world is round to the idea that the world is flat. Some ideas or assumptions simply don't mix. When they do not, the result one gets is more like an explosion than a mixture. The idea that there is no clear conceptual distinction between biology and culture *cannot* simply be added to the idea that there is a clear conceptual distinction between biology and culture. The idea that animal dominance hierarchies are neither universal nor male *cannot* be added to the idea that they are. The ideas that there is androcentric bias in science and ethics (even if "only" a historical bias rather than one "in the nature of things") and that there currently is no value-neutral, objective, and impartial view in science or in ethics *cannot* simply be added to the ideas that there is no such bias or that there is a value-neutral, objective, and impartial point of view in science and ethics. In each of these cases, to adopt a feminist-identified stance is to deny some of the main assumptions of traditional science and ethics, and thereby to abandon, at least on these issues, the conceptual framework that gives rise to them.

2. *Observing and judging observation reports.* As has been suggested already, what an author notices or fails to notice, what she takes as "given" in what she observes, or what she considers relevant or credible or a reason is ultimately affected by the conceptual framework through which she does the observing and assessing. Feminist neurophysiologists looking at a cluster of cells under a microscope may take very different observations than traditional scientists engaged in observing cells. Feminist scientists like Ruth Bleier who assume that there is no "pure" biology separate from environment or "culture," that cells are "cultured," look for interconnections among cells when observing cells.[29] Any generalizations, predictions, correlations, or causal claims offered based on those observations will stress the complex interconnections among multiple (not single or "linear") biological mechanisms and environmental factors.[30] Single-cause theories will be highly unlikely, if not impossible, to give.

Similarly, feminist primatologists will reject as unwarranted extrapolations from observations about rodents and primates to generalizations, predictions, or causal explanations about purely biological explanations of human behaviors, because "rodent or monkey behavior is not basic behavior minus culture."[31] The basic assumption on which such extrapolations are based is flawed. And feminist ethicists will insist on including observations based on women's felt experiences of abortion among the morally relevant data of ethical theory-building and conflict resolution regarding abortion.

3. *Identifying and assessing causal claims.* One helpful test for assessing causal claims is given by Mary Anne Wolff's acronym "CPROOF": To assess the adequacy of a causal claim, establish a Correlation between events to be explained, Precedence of some events relative to others, and then Rule Out Other Factors. How would one apply "CPROOF" to the "sex-difference research" on human and primate behaviors that is conducted from *within* a patriarchal conceptual framework? It is difficult, if not impossible, to apply the test since included among the crucial factors that need to be ruled out is the very assumption that is necessary to generate the research in the first place, viz., that it is possible to conduct biological sex-based research "uncontaminated" by the culture. Unless *that* assumption gets challenged, any explanations or causal claims based on it will be highly suspect, if not simply wrongheaded and ill-conceived.[32] This is worth noticing because the CPROOF test is a perfectly good test. It is just that it is not a test one cannot effectively or adequately use *within* a patriarchal conceptual framework by one who subscribes to that framework when that very conceptual framework is characterized by basic assumptions, the falsity of which would have to be challenged in order to adequately apply the CPROOF test. To do so one needs to challenge the patriarchal conceptual framework *itself*—an activity that those who subscribe to it for as long as they subscribe to it cannot consistently undertake.

The influence of patriarchal conceptual frameworks is not limited to critical thinking skills. There are also conceptually-bound limits on one's ability to exercise important critical thinking dispositions as well. Consider a mainstay disposition, "openmindedness."

4. *Openmindedness.* It is difficult, if not impossible, to consider seriously other points of view than one's own if one is not aware that there *are* other points of view. Suppose, for instance, that a fundamental and invisible assumption of one's conceptual framework is that science is objective or value-neutral or that there is a basic distinction between "innate" biology and learned culture. It then will be extremely difficult, if not impossible, to take seriously the view that science is androcentric, that there are no innate biological differences between men and women (even if there are some between males and females), or that women's childbearing and childrearing roles are not an inevitable consequence of her anatomy.[33]

One thing this shows is that the extent of one's willingness and ability to be openminded about issues is significantly affected by the conceptual framework out of which one operates. *Openmindedness is a disposition that persons do or do not exercise within a given conceptual framework.* This is the *essentially contextual* nature of openmindedness: it is always exercised from within a (some) conceptual framework. Notice that this view of openmindedness does not conflict with the view that openmindedness includes being receptive ("open") to points of view different than one's own on a given topic or issue. In some conceptual frameworks, the basic beliefs, values, attitudes, and assumptions of the framework might make being "open" to different points of view quite easy, e.g., a conceptual framework in which a basic belief is that one must always be open to differing point of view. Whether such a conceptual framework is a desirable one or not, of course, is a separate and, as I suggest shortly, a debatable issue.

Suppose this view of the contextual nature of openmindedness is correct. What, then, is required of persons in order for them properly to be said to be openminded? *From within* a given conceptual framework, certain positions, claims, or points of view may be viewed as *undeserving* of serious and equal consideration. Consider, for example, a *feminist conceptual framework*, one that views women as equal to men, views the subordination of women as wrong, and rejects any claim to a biological "innateness" of gender differences. From *within* that framework, the claim that women are innately inferior to men not only will not get "equal treatment;" it *cannot* be raised for two related reasons: first, none of the assumptions necessary to give rise to the claim are included within the conceptual framework; second, and more importantly, the assumptions necessary to give rise to the claim are *logically incompatible* with the basic and defining assumptions of the feminist conceptual framework and so cannot consistently be added to it. It is a variation of the "add women and stir" problem again. Feminists who take the time to address such arguments may do so because such arguments are taken seriously in a patriarchal conceptual framework, or because they want to defeat such arguments. Since the successes of feminism involved the defeat or undermining of patriarchal conceptual frameworks, it is important that *someone* defeat or undermine such arguments. Still, given the sorts of beliefs, attitudes, and value commitments that characterize his world view as "feminist" and given the fact of finite time, resources, and energy, he may choose to pay them no heed.

Is a feminist who chooses not to take seriously arguments for the conclusion that women are innately inferior to men failing to be openminded? Or, is a feminist who chooses not to take seriously arguments for the genetic inferiority of black people to whites failing to be open-minded? The answer is "Yes" *only if* one assumes (as I do not) that openmindedness requires "considering seriously other points of view than one's own" *without regard for the truth, bias, or prejudice* of those points of view. But the answer is "No" if one assumes otherwise and recognizes that openmindedness *always* takes place within some conceptual framework. From a *feminist* point of view, some conceptual frameworks are better than others, and not all positions are worthy of equal consideration. From a *feminist* point of view, being openminded does not necessarily require that *all* points of view be given equal consideration; some points of view simply may not warrant such consideration. From a *feminist* point of view, contemporary Western society is thoroughly structured by race, class, and sex/gender factors; as such, in contemporary Western society at least, there is no currently available value-neutral conceptual framework *within which* the trait of openmindedness can be exercised. From a *feminist* point of view, then, a feminist who chooses not to take seriously arguments for the innate inferiority of women or people of color is not being "closeminded."[34]

At this point a critic might object as follows: Feminists who choose not to take seriously nonfeminist or antifeminist viewpoints are "partial" or "biased." Since such bias or partiality is incompatible with open-mindedness, feminists who take such a stand fail to be openminded. By extension, since openmindedness is an important critical thinking disposition, feminists who take such a stand also fail to be critical thinkers (or good critical thinkers).

A feminist could respond to this objection in either of two ways. She could argue *either* that a feminist view is *not* biased *or* that it *is* biased but a better bias than the alternatives. Which response is most appropriate depends on what counts as bias. In one sense of "bias," the charge of bias attaches to such items as assumptions, reasons, conclusions, or conceptual frameworks that are based on *false or faulty generalizations* (a common conception of bias).[35] In this sense of "bias," feminist bias arises in the same sort of way that bias arises in generalizations generally, viz., through stereotyping too small a sample size, a skewed sample that is not representative of the total population, or a generalization from one case only. One determines bias by assessing the reasons or evidence offered.

A patriarchal conceptual framework is biased (in this sense) insofar as the sorts of reasons or evidence it offers or countenances, the assumptions on which it is based, and the conclusions it warrants produce false or faulty generalizations (e.g., about biologically based sex-differences between men and women, or male dominance in primate societies). Is a feminist conceptual framework biased? Insofar as it rejects *as* false claims those that *are* indeed false, or rejects *as* conceptually flawed distinctions those that *are* indeed conceptually flawed, or does not seriously consider reasons, arguments, or data based on such false or flawed claims, it is *not biased*, or not biased in the way in which patriarchal conceptual frameworks are biased.

However, a feminist point of view may be "biased" or "partial" in a different sense, a sense in which *all* conceptual frameworks, *all* points of view, are "biased" or "partial." In this second sense of "bias," a claim, position, or conceptual framework is biased if it is not value-neutral or objective. Since a conceptual framework is, by definition, based on certain beliefs, values, attitudes, and assumptions that permit certain sorts of reasons and omit others, it is biased (in this second sense). This sort of bias makes certain claims *from within* a given conceptual framework resistant to certain new evidence (especially logically incompatible evidence). Feminists who, from within a feminist conceptual framework, dismiss as unworthy of equal and serious consideration arguments for the biological inevitability of patriarchy would then be correctly described as "biased" in this second sense, i.e., as not offering a value-neutral, ahistorical, or noncontextual objectivity. In this sense, bias is a matter of degree as well as kind.

Given this second sense of "bias," the proper question is *not* whether a feminist view is biased, but whether a feminist bias is a *better bias* than a patriarchal or androcentric bias. Feminists who argue that it *is* a better bias do so precisely because it is *more inclusive* and *less partial*. To be impartial on an issue is not to have no opinion or feelings about it. Nor is it to take some "value-neutral" stance outside *any* given conceptual framework, since (I have claimed) no such stance is possible. Impartiality, like the critical thinking dispositions of openmindedness and interpersonal sensititivity, is always exercised from within some conceptual framework.

From a feminist point of view, impartiality consists partly in listening to points of view of those in subordinate positions, of those without established authority within the dominant culture, of those at the bottom of the hierarchy. It involves being sure that the felt experiences of women, however diverse those experiences may be, are part of theory building. From a feminist point of view, *impartiality requires inclusiveness*. A patriarchal conceptual framework that supports or fails to challenge assumptions, beliefs, values, and attitudes; that serve to reinforce male domination; and that omits the felt experiences, contributions, and perspectives of women is *more partial because it is less inclusive* than one (e.g., a feminist conceptual framework) that does not. A feminist conceptual framework thereby provides a better bias ("bias" in the second sense).

Furthermore, since a feminist conceptual framework which is more inclusive of the realities of more people provides a *better database* from which to make generalizations, it helps to ensure that the generalizations one makes are not biased in the first sense. That is, the bias ("bias" in the second sense) of a feminist conceptual framework contributes to its being less biased (in the first sense).

From a feminist point of view, then, a commitment to feminism *is* a commitment to impartiality and openmindedness (properly understood), *and* a commitment to impartiality and openmindedness (properly understood) *is* a commitment to feminism. Alison Jaggar expresses this viewpoint succinctly in her article "Teaching Sedition: Some Dilemmas of Feminist Pedagogy:"

> Indeed, feminists believe that a genuinely impartial consideration of contemporary social life must generate inevitably a commitment to feminism....From the feminist point of view, it is not feminism that is irrational or biased, but rather positions that ignore or discount the specific interests of women. Far from constituting a disqualifying bias, feminist commitment is a defense against one very common and damaging form of bias. Impartiality is not undermined by feminism; instead, feminist commitment helps to safeguard impartiality.[36]

If what I have said is correct, a "proper understanding" of "openmindedness" requires an understanding of the nature and power of conceptual frameworks, particularly patriarchal ones.

Teaching/Learning Critical Thinking: Some Feminist Considerations

I have argued that critical thinking is always contextual in that it always occurs within a given conceptual framework. Current research on critical thinking suggests that critical thinking is extremely sensitive to context in other ways as well. According to Stephen Norris,

> This is true for two reasons. First, the inferences and appraisals of inferences that a person can justify making depend on the back-

ground assumptions, level of sophistication, and concept of the task. Inferences that do not agree with those sanctioned by a test or with those a teacher might make do not necessarily indicate a critical thinking deficiency.... Second, critical thinking is sensitive to context because context can dramatically affect the quality of one's performance. This is a highly confirmed result in the area of deductive logical reasoning (Evans, 1982). Deductive logical reasoning is based on the form rather than on its content.... Despite this, people reason better deductively when dealing with thematic contexts, with contexts that relate to their personal experience, and when they do not have presumptions about the truth of the conclusion. In addition, deductive reasoning performance is lowered in contexts involving threats or promises.[37]

According to Norris, both the inferences one can justify making and the quality of one's ability to make inferences is sensitive to context, e.g., to the "background assumptions, level of sophistication, and concept of the task" as well as to whether the environment feels safe. Some inferences may be justified against one background set of assumptions but not others, or within one conceptual framework but not another. If, as Norris claims, "people reason better deductively when dealing with thematic contexts, with contexts that relate to their personal experience, and when they do not have presumptions about the truth of the conclusion," then a person's ability to reason well deductively is affected by conceptual frameworks.

The element of contextual sensitivity is also important to the effective teaching/learning of critical thinking.[38] It raises the problem of the "*transfer*" of critical thinking to domains other than those in which the skill was originally taught. A discussion of the problem of transfer must attend to various levels of transfer: transfer *within* a restricted field of study to new examples within that field, transfer *across* disciplinary boundaries, and transfer *into* the thinking practices in which we engage in our everyday lives.[39] An attention to the problems of transfer is an attention to context: the learner's background knowledge, assumptions, and experiences and the nature of her "everyday life." One who manifests such *contextual sensitivity* manifests an important critical thinking disposition.

According to Norris, this general need for contextual (including *interpersonal*) sensitivity and for "teaching critical thinking for transfer" is confirmed, even if there is as yet little detailed knowledge about what specifically makes students who have had direct instruction in critical thinking better thinkers or how to accomplish the desired transfer.[40] To achieve this contextual sensitivity, teachers/learners must eventually come to recognize their own conceptual frameworks, see alternative conceptual frameworks, and, where possible, conduct discussions across conceptual frameworks.

It is because critical thinking is extremely sensitive to context that both the teaching and assessments of critical thinking abilities and performance must seek *explicit* indications of people's reasons for their conclusions. Otherwise, one will be unable to "differentiate between deficiencies in thinking abilities and differences in background assumptions and beliefs between the examiner and examinee."[41]

Robert Swartz may be correct that, as a rule of inference, "Modus ponens is the same in science as in history."[42] But, if Norris's research conclusions are correct, then a person's ability to *learn* and *use* modus ponens may be very different in different contexts, including the contexts provided by science and history. One implication of Norris's view is that the ability to recognize, use, and assess inferences based on modus ponens will be affected by both the "safety" of the environment and the inferer's own prior knowledge. A learner's critical thinking performance and abilities may be significantly affected if the examples used and conclusions drawn are given from a very different conceptual framework. Failure to take seriously one's own conceptual framework ("point of view") as well as the learner's could also incline an evaluator to conclude, prematurely if not incorrectly, that the learner is not very good at deductive reasoning.

Conclusion

In this paper I have argued that an adequate conception of critical thinking must involve the recognition that critical thinking always takes place within *some* conceptual framework. In this respect, critical thinking must be understood as *essentially contextual*, i.e., sensitive to the conceptual framework in which it is conceived, practiced and learned or taught. What makes this contribution distinctively *feminist* is that it makes visible the ways in which patriarchal conceptual frameworks are relevant to the theory and practice of critical thinking.

Feminism changes the agenda of critical thinking by problematicizing old issues in new ways. If what I have said in this paper is correct or even plausible, then the link between critical thinking and feminism is much deeper and potentially more liberating than the current scholarship on critical thinking would suggest. The aims of each are interrelated and mutually reinforcing. It may be, then, that critical thinking is not *simply* a feminist issue. It may be that critical thinking *must* be feminist if it is truly to be what it purports to be, viz., reasonable and reflective activity aimed at deciding what to do or believe.

Notes

1. I do not take up directly the debate over the proper definition of critical thinking in this paper. Nor do I debate the related issues of the proper taxonomy of "critical thinking skills," whether critical thinking is "subject-area specific," or the most effective ways of teaching critical thinking. For a discussion of various views on critical thinking, see Barry K. Beyer's "Critical Thinking: What Is It?" *Social Education* (April, 1985): 270–76.

2. Robert H. Ennis, "Rational Thinking and Educational Practice," in *Philosophy of Education* (80th yearbook of the National Society for the Study of Education, Vol. 1), ed. by J. F. Soltis (Chicago: The National Society for the Study of Education, 1981), and more recently, "A Logical Basis for Measuring Critical Thinking Skills," *Educational Leadership* 43 (October, 1985): 44–48, and "A Taxonomy of Critical Thinking Dispositions and Abilities," in *Teaching Thinking Skills: Theory and Practice*, ed. by Joan B. Baron and Robert J. Sternberg (New York: W. H. Freeman and Company, 1987), pp. 9–26. This definition is "sufficient for our purposes" because the position advanced in this paper would not change substantially even if some other definition of critical thinking currently in use is preferable.

3. For a more complete listing of critical thinking abilities and dispositions, see Ennis, "A Taxonomy of Critical Thinking Abilities and Dispositions," ibid. It is worth noting that according to current research, having a "critical spirit" (or "critical disposition") is as important in critical thinking as having certain skills: Stephen P. Norris, "Synthesis of Research on Critical Thinking," *Educational Leadership* 42 (May, 1985): 44.

4. Richard Paul, for instance, argues that since "emotions and beliefs are always inseparably wedded together," empathy and passions are important in critical thinking. See Paul, "Dialogical Thinking: Critical Thinking Essential to the Acquisition of Rational Knowledge and Passions," in *Teaching Thinking Skills*, ibid., 127–48. This broad definition seems to have two distinct advantages: it accommodates narrower definitions in terms of skills, while also being attractive from a feminist point of view. The latter is so because, as I argue in the paper, exclusive and oppositional dualisms (e.g., critical vs. creative thinking, reason vs. emotion) are viewed with extreme suspicion by many feminists.

5. Alison Jaggar provides a thorough analysis of the first four leading conceptions of feminism in her book, *Feminist Politics and Human Nature*

(Totowa, N.J.: Rowman & Allanheld, 1983), and a discussion of black and Third World feminism in *Feminist Frameworks*: 2nd Edition, eds. Alison M. Jaggar and Paula S. Rothenberg (New York: McGraw-Hill, 1984). A discussion of ecological feminism vis-à-vis the other feminisms can be found in Karen J. Warren, "Feminism and Ecology: Making Connections," *Environmental Ethics* (Spring, 1987): 3–0.

6. This discussion of oppressive conceptual frameworks is a revised version of what I offered in my "Feminism and Ecology: Making Connections," ibid.

7. Elizabeth Dodson Gray, *Green Paradise Lost* (Wellesley, Mass.: Roundtable Press, 1981), p. 20.

8. Although I do not argue for these claims here, arguments for ways in which Western culture, particularly Western philosophy, has sanctioned such value-hierarchical thinking can be found, for example, in: Susan Bordo, *The Flight to Objectivity: Essays on Cartesianism and Culture* (Albany: SUNY Press, 1987); Genevieve Lloyd, *The Man of Reason: "Male" and "Female" in Western Philosophy* (Minneapolis: University of Minnesota Press, 1984); Carolyn Merchant, *The Death of Nature: Women, Ecology, and The Scientific Revolution* (San Francisco: Harper & Row, 1980).

9. See Jaggar, ibid., p. 96.

10. I discuss this point with regard to ecological feminism in my piece "The Power and Promise of Ecological Feminism," read at the American Philosophical Association Eastern Division Meetings, Dec. 27–30, 1987.

11. Although many feminists argue that all the dominant cultures of Western history have been patriarchal, whether enlightened, reformed, feudal, capitalist, or socialist, I leave open here the question whether that is true.

12. In Western culture at least, women are presumed to be the ones to do so-called "women's work" (e.g., raising children, attending to domestic responsibilities, caregiving), work relegated primarily to the "private" sphere. So, while that work may have some status or value, typically it is status or value within a sphere generally taken to be of less seriousness, significance, or political importance than the "public sphere" of man's work.

13. Notice that calling a conceptual framework "patriarchal" does not mean that it is one held by all, or by only, males. To the extent that both males and females in contemporary culture are raised within a patriarchal conceptual framework, they will both be affected by that framework, even if, as men and women, they are affected by it in different ways and to different extents.

14. Other approaches to showing the link between critical thinking and feminism also could be used. For instance, one could show the ways in which

understanding how the college and precollege climate is "chilly for women" bears on understanding women students' abilities or dispositions to think critically, or how testing situations and measurements fail to use examples or situations that draw on the particular or cultural experiences of women. See Roberta M. Hall and Bernice R. Sadler, "The Classroom Climate: A Chilly One for Women?" *Project for the Status and Education of WOMEN,* Association of American Colleges, 1818 R. Street NW, Washington, DC 20009.

15. For a helpful discussion of bias, and the unavoidable but potentially dangerous bias of a "point of view," see J. Anthony Blair's "What is Bias?" in *Selected Issues in Logic and Communication,* ed. Trudy Govier (Belmont, Calif.: Wadsworth Publishing, 1988): 93–103.

16. The examples are chosen from science and ethics because these two fields represent a wide range of issues concerning the making and assessing of so-called factual and value claims which are central to discussions of critical thinking. They thereby illustrate both the *breadth* and *depth* of feminist concerns about the nature and teaching of critical thinking.

17. Ruth Bleier, *Science and Gender: A Critique of Biology and its Theories on Women* (New York: Pergamon Press, 1984).

18. Bleier, "Introduction," in *Feminist Approaches to Science,* edited by Ruth Bleier (New York: Pergamon Press, 1986), p. 2. I do not intend to defend Bleier's views here, or any of the other views given by the feminist scientists and feminist ethicists cited. My objective is simply to use their views to show why and how the way critical thinking is conceived and practiced within patriarchal conceptual frameworks is a feminist issue.

19. Sherry B. Ortner was one of the first to address a similar question of interests to ecological feminists: "Are women closer to nature than men?": Ortner, "Is Female to Male as Nature Is to Culture?" in Michelle Rosaldo and Louise Lamphere, eds., *Woman, Culture, and Society* (Stanford: Stanford University Press, 1974), pp. 67–68. Ecological feminists raise the same sort of objection to this question "Are women closer to nature than men?" that I have raised here to the question "Are there biological differences between men and women?" For example, Joan Griscom argues that "the question is itself flawed" since "we are all part of nature, and since all of us, biology and culture alike, is part of nature": Joan Griscom, "On Healing the Nature/Culture Split in Feminist Thought," *Heresies 13: Feminism and Ecology* 4 (1981): 9.

20. See Donna Haraway, "Primatology is Politics by Other Means" and Sarah Blaffer Hrdy, "Empathy, Polyandry, and the Myth of the Coy Female," in *Feminist Approaches to Science,* ibid., pp. 77–118 and 119–46, respectively.

21. Bleier, "Introduction," *Feminist Approaches to Science,* p. 8.

22. Bleier, *Science and Gender,* p. 29.

23. Ibid., p. 9.

24. Judith Jarvis Thomson, "A Defense of Abortion," *Philosophy and Public Affairs* 1 (September, 1971): 47–66.

25. See Kathryn Adelson, "Moral Revolution," in *Women and Values: Readings in Recent Feminist Philosophy*, ed. Marilyn Persall (Belmont, Calif.: Wadsworth, 1986): 291–309.

26. Ibid., p. 306.

27. Jane Roland Martin, *Reclaiming a Conversation: The Ideal of the Educated Women* (New Haven, Conn.: Yale University Press, 1985), p. 197.

28. As in the preceding section on feminist science, my purpose here is not to resolve this important issue about bias in ethics. Nor is it to suggest that whatever bias exists in ethics requires revolutionary, rather than reformist, changes to remedy (as Addelson claims). Rather, it is to use recent feminist discussions in ethics to illustrate ways in which the charge of bias arises in ethics and what the bias has to do with conceptual frameworks.

29. Compare Evelyn Fox Keller's discussion of cytogeneticist Barbara McClintock's approach to her research of the maize plant. According to Keller, McClintock urges scientists to "let the material speak to you [the material in McClintock's case is the corn plant" by developing a "feeling for the organism." Evelyn Fox Keller, "Women, Science, and Popular Mythology," in *Machina Ex Dea: Feminist Perspectives on Technology*, ed. Joan Rothschild (New York: Pergamon Press, 1983), p. 141. For a complete discussion of Keller's treatment of McClintock's work, see Keller, *A Feeling for the Organism: The Life and Work of Barbara McClintock* (San Francisco: W. H. Freeman, 1983).

30. Bleier, *Science and Gender*, p. 107.

31. Ibid.

32. Such considerations have led many feminist scientists to conclude that there is no single correct scientific methodology and that scientific methodology cannot protect research and its conclusions from the investigator's biases, values and beliefs. See Bleier, *Science and Gender*. pp. 4–5.

33. Similarly, if one operates from within a racist conceptual framework, which assumes that nonwhites are genetically inferior to whites, it will be very difficult to take seriously the points of view that there are no relevant genetic differences between whites and nonwhites, that whites and blacks are equal, that "white supremacy" is a piece of ideology. It will be impossible to take these opposing views seriously if one continues to adhere to the basic assumptions of the racist conceptual framework.

34. Notice that I have not argued here for the view that only a feminist point of view is an "openminded" view. What I have claimed is that from a feminist point of view, openmindedness does not require taking seriously all points of view, since some points of view (e.g., that women ought to be treated as inferior to men) do not warrant serious consideration.

35. This is the notion of bias that Michael Scriven offers in his book *Reasoning* (New York: McGraw-Hill, 1976): 208.

36. Alison M. Jaggar, "Teaching Sedition: Some Dilemmas of Feminist Pedagogy," *Report from the Center for Philosophy and Public Policy*, pp. 8–9.

37. Norris, ibid., p. 42. The reference is to J. St. B. T. Evans, *The Psychology of Deductive Reasoning* (London: Routledge and Kegan Paul, 1982).

38. Space does not permit me to discuss the relevance of research on "feminist pedagogy" in this paper. For a discussion of such issues, see the journal *Feminist Teacher*; Mary Anne Wolff's "According to Whom? Helping Students Analyze Contrasting Views of Reality," *Educational Leadership* (October, 1986): 36–41; Charlotte Bunch and Sandra Pollack, eds. *Learning Our Way: Essays in Feminist Education* (Trumansburg, N.Y.: Crossing Press, 1983); Margo Culley and Catherine Portugues, eds. *Gendered Subjects: The Dynamics of Feminist Teaching* (Boston: Routledge and Kegan Paul, 1985); Bernice Fisher, "What Is Feminist Pedagogy?" in *Radical Teacher* 18 (1981): 20–24; Henry A. Giroux, *Theory and Resistance in Education: A Pedagogy for the Opposition* (South Hadley, Mass.: Bergin and Garvey, 1983); Nancy Hoffman, "White Woman, Black Woman: Inventing an Adequate Pedagogy," in *Women's Studies Newsletter* 1–2 (1977): 21–24; Nancy Porter, "Liberating Teaching," in *Women's Studies Quarterly* X (1982): 19–24.

39. Robert J. Swartz, "Critical Thinking, the Curriculum, and the Problem of Transfer," in *Thinking: Progress in Research and Teaching.* ed. David N. Perkins et al. (Hillsdale, N.J.: Erlbaum, 1987), p. 283.

40. Norris, ibid., p. 44.

41. Ibid., p. 42.

42. Swartz, ibid., p. 270.

III.

Critical Thinking and Emancipation

Instruction in thinking skills should do more than simply teach students the nuts-and-bolts of logical analysis. As we've seen, such an abstract approach both decontextualizes the process of thinking and depersonalizes the thinker. Instruction in thinking skills should not only improve a student's ability to fairly and reasonably investigate knowledge claims and arguments. It should also provide the student with strategies for personal emancipation from biases and predispositions that blinker her thinking. It should encourage in her a sense of wonderment and curiosity that prompts her to explore both her own fundamental beliefs and the (often opposing) fundamental beliefs of others. And it should serve, in some small way, as a vehicle for her personal enlightenment. The essays in this concluding section all speak to this ideal.

Richard Paul's essay, first published in 1982 but rewritten especially for this volume, opens the discussion. There is probably no other single article that has been as influential as Paul's in prompting non-logicistic explorations of critical thinking. In it, Paul distinguishes between critical thinking in the "weak" and "strong" senses. The former concentrates primarily upon schooling students in the basics of logical analysis by having them focus on isolated, discrete arguments. But this sort of "atomistic" analysis tends to leave untouched the basic world-view assumptions of the students themselves, and instead directs their critical skills to the arguments and beliefs of others. As an alternative method, Paul advocates critical thinking in the strong sense, which encourages students to focus on their own deep-seated assumptions and biases as well as the arguments of others, to encourage them to see that rational thinking is an emancipatory as well as a critical tool. In rewriting his now-classic defense of strong sense critical thinking, Paul also responds to criticisms of his position raised in the last ten years.

Henry Giroux argues in his contribution that mainstream critical thinking comes out of the positivist tradition and is characterized by its emphasis on the "Internal Consistency position": that being a good thinker means analyzing arguments in terms of their formal, logical patterns of consistency. But such an abstract approach clearly misses the obvious points that (1) theory and facts are related and (2) knowledge is inseparable from values, norms, and interests. In order to overcome these reifications and to invite students to understand the significance in their own lives of good thinking, thinking skills pedagogy needs to stress the contextualization of information as well as help students to examine social institutions and relationships—including those of the classroom—that influence the ways in which they think and what they think about.

Laura Duhan Kaplan, influenced (like Giroux) by the Brazilian philosopher of education Paolo Freire, argues in her essay that conventional critical thinking fails in one of its stated goals: to train students for responsible citizenship. Instead, she argues, it schools them in passivity by pedagogically focusing on analyses of given, ready-to-hand arguments rather than shifting attention to the social structures and relations that give rise to them. Appealing to the spirit of Freire's "critical pedagogy," Kaplan argues for a critical thinking that stresses reflective emancipation from existing models and the envisioning of new, alternative ones. As Kaplan says, "The [mainstream] critical thinking movement teaches students to provide criticism of arguments, while the critical pedagogy movement teaches students to provide critique as a foundation for criticism of the world around them."

In his essay, Thomas Warren asserts that there's something "fundamentally wrong" with the way critical thinking is conventionally conceived and taught. Drawing upon a distinction defended by Hannah Arendt, Warren argues that mainstream critical thinking in fact emphasizes "reasoning" at the expense of "thinking." To reason is to "measure," to calculate, to discursively analyze with the aim of arriving at answers. But to think is to search not so much for answers as for meaning and to do so in a manner that cannot be reduced to analytic modes. Thinking encourages wonder, while reasoning tends to stifle it by concentrating on immediately solvable problems. Critical thinking, then, at least as it's currently taught, may well enable individuals to calculate more efficiently, but it does very little to encourage self-examination and enlightenment.

Similarly, Lenore Langsdorf worries about the conventional tendency in critical thinking instruction to focus on what she calls "instrumental reason" at the expense of "judgment." The former enables us to calculate means and ends, but the latter is necessary to examine those means and ends in light of human needs and goals. Taking her cue from Richard Paul's defense of a "strong sense" critical thinking, which encourages students to forego egocentric biases in the examination of their own worldviews, Langsdorf, following Paul Ricoeur, argues for a conception of critical thinking that encourages individuals to submit to a "concrete dialectic of confrontation with opposite points of view." Such a dialogue of selves, she concludes, encourages imagination as well as critical analysis and serves as a force for personal and social enlightenment.

10

Teaching Critical Thinking in the Strong Sense: A Focus on Self-Deception, World Views, and a Dialectical Mode of Analysis

Richard W. Paul

"…no abstract or analytic point exists out of all connection with historical thought: …every thought belongs, not just somewhere, but to someone, and is at home in a context of other thoughts, a context which is not purely formally prescribed. Thoughts…are something to be known and understood in these concrete terms."

—Isaiah Berlin, *Concepts and Categories*, xii

Introduction

When I first wrote this paper I was concerned to underscore the way in which our reasoning on any given occasion tends to be of a piece with our reasoning on many other occasions and tends over time to congeal into a complete system of thought, and, ultimately, into a system as grand as a full-scale worldview. I was also thinking in terms of a self-contained course in critical thinking and not in terms of an overall design for education across the curriculum and grades. Some misunderstandings of my views emerged as a result. For one, some persons erroneously took me to be opposed to teaching critical thinking across the curriculum. For another, some erroneously took me to be advocating a "political" approach to the teaching of critical thinking, because the example I focused on could in a broad sense be considered "political." Finally, because I emphasized that a person's view of the world is often lurking in the background, I was erroneously taken to mean or be committed to the view that one is somehow "trapped" in whatever worldview one has, as if a reasoner had no chance of getting out of the dominance of one worldview without falling into the dominance of another. I apparently did not adequately underscore the fact that critical thinking, in my conception, is to be understood as a way of holding a point of view, a way of entering into a frame of reference, a way of participating in a worldview, a way that, in the fullest sense, frees one from dominance by the views, the frames of reference, the worldviews in which one becomes critically literate.

Such critical empowerment is not a matter to be achieved over-night in one course, certainly. If students are to learn to think critically in a strong sense, they must be exposed to it over an extended period of time, over years not months. To think critically in a strong sense is to become a certain kind of person. It is to develop particular values and traits of mind in addition to particular skills and abilities. If we are committed to critical thinking, we must then be committed to major reform of education, for most schooling is didactic in nature and discourages rather than encourages critical thinking and the values and dispositions essential to it.

Critical thinking, at least as I conceive it, is defined in the strong sense as inescapably connected with discovering both that one thinks within "systems" and that one continually needs to strive to transcend any given "system" in which one is presently thinking. Critical thinking as such is therefore thinking that routinely takes charge of itself and of its relation to the ideas embedded in it. Surely there is a difference between using an idea and being dominated by it. Surely there is a difference between using a system of ideas and thinking that there is no other system that one could use or that the system one uses is descriptive in some univocal way of reality in itself. Surely there are also degrees of scope in the systems one might use. Consider, for example, the following distinction between points of view (narrow scope), frames of reference (wider scope), and worldviews (widest scope). We can use these phrases to mark three distinct possibilities of shifts of thinking which should not be conflated.

a. Our point of view, in the narrowest sense, may continually shift, in certain respects, from circumstance to circumstance. One and the same person typically functions in different roles, experiences changing moods, tackles widely different problems, even comes at the same problem from different vantage points at different moments or within different situations. Hence, two professional car buyers, who share the same economic frame of reference, not only may have different views of the world (in the grand sense) but may have different points of view on a given purchase and its implications for their company. They might in fact consider a given purchase from a number of different points of view (all within the same economic frame of reference), such as turnaround time, effect on tax situation, and so on.

b. Everyone is capable of functioning within somewhat different frames of reference (some, of course, better than others) and so shift the system in which we are thinking in a larger way than in the example above. One might shift the frame of reference, for example, from economics to morality. One of the two car buyers above may ask that the other consider not only the economics of a buy but the ethics of it. This frame of reference shift is a larger shift than that involved in a consideration from a variety of economic angles. We all think in a wide variety of frames (e.g., we may at times think mathematically, at other times historically, at still other times, biologically, or sociologically, or politically…).

c. Finally, not only is it possible, it is inevitable in the chaos of the modern world that we all internalize at least fragments of different worldviews, not to speak of the differences between the views of the world we articulate and those we "live." Furthermore, we can all learn to throw ourselves into strikingly different worldviews from our own both by reading—in great literature, philosophy, history of ideas—and by rich experience—living in other societies, speaking with persons who have a very different worldview. We need not be "captive" of any one view, frame of reference, or worldview, and in some sense no one completely is. Our views need not be an intellectual straitjacket, but depend, rather, on how we hold them, whether, in a phrase, we control them or they control us.

Critical thinkers are not to be defined by the worldview(s) they hold, but by the way they hold it (them), by their awareness of radically different worldviews and by a common discovery that they, like everyone else, are at times capable of being not only wrong but also of thinking irrationally, narrowly, unclearly, imprecisely, superficially, irrelevantly, and inconsistently. They share a real commitment to monitor their thinking to minimize these pathologies of thought. They respect their minds as students of physical fitness respect the structure, the inherent capacities and limitations, of their bodies, as capacities that must be understood in order to be developed. Let us now consider a case for teaching critical thinking, in a strong sense.

Critical Thinking in the Weak Sense: Dangers and Pitfalls

To teach a critical thinking course is to make important and often frustrating decisions about what to include and exclude, what to conceive as one's primary and secondary goals, and how to tie all of what one includes into a coherent relationship to one's goals. There have been considerable and important debates on the value of a "symbolic" versus a "nonsymbolic" approach, the appropriate definition and classification of fallacies, appropriate analysis of extended and nonextended arguments, and so forth. There has been little discussion and, as far as I know, virtually no debate, on how to avoid the fundamental dangers in teaching such a course: that of "sophistry" on the one hand (inadvertently teaching students to use critical concepts and techniques to maintain their most deep-seated prejudices and irrational habits of thought by making them appear more rational and putting their opponents on the defensive), and that of "dismissal" (the student rejects the subject either as sophistry or in favor of some supposed alternative—feeling, intuition, faith, higher consciousness,...).

Students, much as we might sometimes wish it, do not come to us as "blank slates" upon which we can inscribe the inference-drawing patterns, analytic skills, and truth-facing motivations we value. Students studying critical thinking at the university level have highly developed belief systems buttressed by deep-seated uncritical, egocentric, and sociocentric habits of thought by which they interpret and process their experiences, whether academic or not, and place them into some larger perspective. Consequently, most students find it easy to question *only* those beliefs, assumptions, and inferences they have already "rejected," and very difficult, often traumatic, to question those in which they have a personal, egocentric investment.

I know of no way of teaching critical thinking so that the student who learns to recognize questionable assumptions and inferences only in "egocentrically neutral" cases, *automatically* transfers those skills to the egocentric and sociocentric ones. Indeed, I think the opposite more commonly occurs. Those students who already have sets of biased assumptions, stereotypes, egocentric and sociocentric beliefs, been taught to recognize "bad" reasoning in "neutral" cases (or in the case of the "opposition") become *more* sophistic rather than less so, more skilled in rationalizing and intellectualizing their biases. They are then *less* rather than *more* likely to abandon them if they later meet someone who questions them. Like the religious believer who studies apologetics, they now have a variety of critical moves to use in defense of their a priori egocentric belief systems.

This is not the effect, of course, we wish our teaching to have. Virtually all teachers of critical thinking want their teaching to have a global "Socratic" effect, making major inroads into the everyday reasoning of the student, enhancing to some degree that healthy, practical, and skilled skepticism one naturally and rightly associates with the *rational* person. Therefore, students need experience in seriously questioning previously held beliefs and assumptions and in identifying contradictions and inconsistencies in personal and social life. When we think along these lines and get glimpses into the everyday lives and habits of our students, most of us probably experience moments of frustration and cynicism.

I don't think the situation is hopeless, but I do believe the time has come to raise serious questions about how we now teach critical thinking. Current methods, as I conceive them, often inadvertently encourage critical thinking in the "weak" sense. The most fundamental and questionable assumption of these approaches (whether formal or informal) is that critical thinking can be successfully taught as a battery of technical skills that can be mastered more or less one-by-one without giving serious attention to self-deception, background logic, and multi-categorical ethical issues.

The usual scenario runs something like this. One begins with some general pep talk on the importance of critical thinking in personal and social life. In this pep talk one reminds students of the large-scale social problems created by prejudice, irrationality, and sophistic manipulation. Then one launches into a discussion of the difference between arguments and nonarguments and students are led to believe that, without any further knowledge of contextual or background considerations, they can learn to analyze and evaluate arguments by parsing them into, and examining the relation between, "premises" and "conclusions." (The "nonarguments" presumably do not need critical appraisal.) To examine that relationship, students look for formal or informal fallacies, conceived as atomically identifiable and correctable "mistakes." Irrationality is implied thereby to be reducible to complex combinations of atomic mistakes. One roots it out, presumably, by rooting out the atomic mistakes, one-by-one.

Models of this kind do not effectively teach critical thinking. This atomistic "weak sense" approach and the questionable assumptions underlying it should be replaced by an alternative approach specifically designed to avoid its pitfalls.

This alternative view rejects the idea that critical thinking can be taught as a battery of atomic technical skills independent of egocentric beliefs and commitments. Instead of "atomic arguments" (a set of premises and a conclusion) it emphasizes argument *networks* (points of view, frames of reference, worldviews, systems of thought); instead of merely teaching evaluation of atomic arguments it emphasizes a more dialectical and dialogical approach. Arguments need to be appraised in relation to counter-arguments. One can make moves that are very difficult to defend or ones that strengthen one's position. An atomic argument is merely a limited set of moves that are very difficult to defend or ones that strengthen one's position. An atomic argument is merely a limited set of moves with a more complex set of moves reflecting a variety of logically significant engagements in the world. Argument exchanges are means by which contesting points of view, frames of reference, or worldviews are brought into rational conflict. A line of reasoning can rarely be refuted by an individual charge of fallacy, however well supported. The charge of fallacy is a move, however, it is rarely logically compelling; it virtually never refutes an organized way of looking at things. We typically begin with a way of seeing something. We then argue when we find someone who sees things differently. Both of us, in all likelihood, took some time to come to our way of seeing, and, in all likelihood, it will take us some time to become persuaded of another way. This approach more accurately reflects our own and the student's experience of argument exchanges.

By immediately introducing students to these deeper, more "global" problems in the analysis and evaluation of reasoning, we help them to see how rich reasoning really is, that we reason from a point of view, within a frame of reference, and with a worldview in the background. They see, from the beginning, the relationship between reasoning and human engagements and interests. They also begin to see the difference between what is at stake and what is at issue, how the unexpressed as well as the expressed may be significant, the difficulties of judging credibility, and the ethical dimension in most important and complex human problems.

One should not assume, of course, that the human mind is ever homogenized into one, totally self-consistent or univocal system of thought. Indeed, even one's native language, or any other natural language, provides for the possibility of conceiving an unlimited set of divergent patterns of thought. For example, it is possible in one and the same natural language—say, English—to think like a Marxist, like a capitalist, like a Buddhist, like a Christian, even like a Russian or a Chinese. Hence, a student in China may learn to speak fluent English and yet not think, as a result, like an Englishman or American or

Australian. It follows that natural languages do not force the user to operate within the worldview found in any particular culture that uses the language.

Some Basic Theory: World Views, Forms of Life

Here are some basic theoretical underpinnings for a "strong sense" approach to critical thinking:

1. As humans we are—first, last, and always—engaged in interrelated life projects, which, taken as a whole, define our personal "form of life" in relation to broader social forms. Because we are engaged in some projects rather than others, we organize or conceptualize the world and our place in it in somewhat different terms than others do. We have somewhat different *interests*, somewhat different *stakes*, and somewhat different *perceptions* of what is so. We make somewhat different assumptions and reason somewhat differently from them.

2. We also express to ourselves and others a more articulated view of how we see things, a view at best only partially consistent with itself and with the view presupposed by and reflected in our behavior. We have, then, *at least two* worldviews overlapping each other, one implicit in our activity and engagements, another implicit in how we describe our behavior, each with its own contradictions and tensions. One must recognize contradictions between conflicting views to develop as a critical thinker and as a person in good faith with one's self. Both traits are measured by the degree to which we can articulate what we live and live what we articulate.

3. Reasoning is an essential and defining operation presupposed by all human acts. To reason is to use elements in a logical system to generate conclusions. Conclusions may be explicit in words or implicit in behavior. Sometimes reasoning is explicitly cast into the form of an argument, sometimes not. However, since reasoning presupposes a system or systems of which it is a manifestation, the full implications of reasoning are rarely (if ever) exhausted or displayed in the arguments in which they are cast. Arguments presuppose questions at issue. Questions at issue presuppose a purpose or interests at stake. Different points of view frequently differ, not simply in answers to questions but in the appropriate formulations of questions themselves.

4. When we, including those of us who are logicians, analyze and evaluate arguments important to us (this includes all arguments

that, if accepted, would strengthen or weaken beliefs to which we have committed ourselves in word or deed), we do so in relationship to prior belief-commitments and particular ways of seeing things. The best we can do to move toward increased objectivity is to bring to the surface the set of beliefs, assumptions, inferences, and ways of seeing things from which our analysis proceeds and to see explicitly the dialectical nature of our task, the critical moves we might make at various points, and the various possible counter-moves to them.

5. Skill in analyzing and evaluating reasoning requires skill in reciprocity, the ability to reason within more than one point of view, or frame of reference, or world view, understanding strengths and weaknesses through comprehending the objections that could be raised at various points in the arguments by alternative perspectives.

6. Laying out elements of reasoning in deductive form is useful, not principally to see whether a "mistake" had been made but to see critical moves one might make to determine the strengths and weaknesses of the reasoning in relation to alternatives.

7. Since vested interest and other forms of bias typically influence perceptions, assumptions, reasoning in general, and specific conclusions, we must become aware of the nature of our own and others' engagements to begin to recognize strengths and weaknesses in reasoning.

    a. As we recognize that a given argument reflects or, if justified, would serve a given interest we can, by imaginatively entertaining competing interests, construct opposing points of view and so opposing arguments or sets of arguments. By developing a range of arguments dialectically, we can begin to see their strengths and weaknesses.

    b. Arguments are not things-in-themselves but constructions of specific people who must further interpret and develop them, for example, to answer objections. By recognizing the interests typically correlated with given arguments, we can often challenge the credibility of others' premises by alluding to discrepancies between what they say and what they do. In doing so we force them to critique their own behavior in line with the implications of their arguments, or to abandon the line of argument. There are a variety of critical moves they may make upon being so challenged.

    c. By reflecting on interests and purposes as implicit in behavior, one can often much more effectively construct the assumptions most favorable to those interests and purposes. Once formulated, one can begin to formulate alternative competing assumptions. Both can then be more effectively questioned, and arguments for and against them can then be entertained.

8. The total set of factual claims that buttress a well-supported worldview, hence the various arguments generated in favor of it, is usually indefinitely large and often involves shifting conceptual problems and implicit judgments of value (including shifts in how to formulate the "facts"). The credibility of an individual claim often depends on the credibility of many other claims; very often the claims themselves are very difficult to verify "directly" and atomically. Very often then, to analyze an argument, we must judge relative credibility. These judgments are more plausible if they take into account the vested interests and the track records of the sources. Of course, it is rare that any one mind thinks exclusively within one worldview. There are often at least fragments of conflicting views present in most persons' thinking and a variety of contradictions that result from same. On one occasion a person may talk as if she accepted a "hard-cruel-world" philosophy, while on others, as if she accepted a "romantic" or "religious" worldview.

9. The terms in which an argument is cast often reflect the biased interests or purposes of the person who formulated it. Calling into question the very concepts used or the use to which they are put is an important critical move. To become adept at this, we must practice recognizing how articulate individuals and social groups systematically and selectively move back and forth between usage in keeping with the logic of ordinary language and that which accords with a well-developed personal philosophy or the ideological commitments implicit in it (and so conflicts with ordinary use). Consider the ways many people use key terms in international debate—say, "freedom fighter," "liberator," "revolutionary," "guerrilla," "terrorist"—and reflect on:

a. what is implied by the *logic* of the terms apart from the usage of any particular social group (say U.S. citizens, Germans, Israelis, Japanese);

b. what is implied by the usage of a particular group with vested interests (say, U.S. citizens, Germans, Israelis, Japanese); and

c. the various historical examples that suggest inconsistency in the use of these by that group, and how this inconsistency depends on fundamental, typically unexpressed, assumptions. Through such disciplined reflection, one can identify predictable, self-serving inconsistencies.

Multi-Dimensional Ethical Issues

Teaching critical thinking in the strong sense helps students develop reasoning skills precisely in those areas where they are most likely to have egocentric and sociocentric biases. Such biases exist most profoundly in areas of their identities and vested interests. Their identities and interests are often linked in turn to their unarticulated worldviews. One's unarticulated predominant worldview or views represents the person that one *is* (the views implicit in the principles used to *justify* one's actions). Excepting honest mistakes, the contradictions or inconsistencies between and within these two represent the degree to which one reasons and acts in bad faith or self-deceptively.

Multidimensional issues involving proposed ethical justifications for behavior are ideal for teaching critical thinking. Most political, social, and personal issues that most concern us and students are of this type— abortion, nuclear energy, nuclear arms, the nature of national security, poverty, social injustices of various kinds, revolution and intervention, socialized medicine, government regulation, sexism, racism, problems of love and friendship, jealousy, rights to private property, rights to world resources, faith and intuition versus reason, and so forth.

Obviously one can cover only a few such issues, and I believe that the advantages lie in covering fewer of them deeply and intensively. I am certainly unsympathetic to inundating the student with an array of truncated arguments set up to "illustrate" atomic fallacies.

Since I teach in the United States and since the media here as everywhere else in the world reflects, and most students have internalized, a profoundly nationalistic bias, I have often focused one segment of my course on identifying national bias in the news. In doing this, students must face issues that, to be approached dialectically, require them to discover that mainstream "American" reasoning and the mainstream "American" perspective on world issues is not the only dialectical possibility. I identify as mainstream American views any that have significant support with the Democratic and Republican parties. This segment of the course serves a number of purposes:

1. Though most students have internalized much media "propaganda" so that their egos are partly identified with it, they are neither totally taken in by that propaganda nor incapable of beginning to systematically question it.

2. The students become more adept at constructing and more empathetic toward alternative lines of reasoning as the *sociocentric*

assumptions of mainstream media coverage come more and more to
the surface—for example, the assumptions that:

   a.   the U.S. government, compared to other governments, is
more committed to ideals;

   b.   U.S. citizens have more energy, more practical know-how,
and more common sense than others;

   c.   the world as a whole would be better off (freer, safer, more
just) if the U.S. had *more* power;

   d.   U.S. citizens are less greedy and self-deceived than other
peoples;

   e.   U.S. lives are more important than the lives of other peoples.

3.   Explicitly addressing and constructing dialectical alternatives to
political and national as well as professional and religious "party
lines" and exploring their contradictions enables students to draw
parallels to their personal and their peer groups' "party lines" and
the myriad contradictions in their talk and behavior. Such "dis-
coveries" explicitly and dramatically forge the beginnings of a commitment to developing the "critical spirit," the foundation for
"strong sense" skills and insights.

A Sample Assignment and Results

   It is useful to provide one sample assignment to indicate how my
concerns and objectives can be translated into assignments. The following was assigned in a 1982 class as a take-home midterm examination, approximately six weeks into the semester. The students were
allowed three weeks to complete it.

   "The objective of this mid-term is to determine the extent to which
you understand and can effectively use the basic concepts of the course:
world view, assumptions, concepts (personal, social, implicit in
language, technical), evidence (empirical claims), implications, consistency, conclusions, premises, questions-at-issue.

   You are to view and critically and sympathetically analyze two
films: *Attack on the Americas* (a right-wing think-tank film alleging Communist control of Central American revolutionaries) and *Revolution or
Death* (a World Council of Church's film defending the rebels in El
Salvador). Two incompatible world views are presented in those films.
After analyzing the films and consulting whatever background material
you deem necessary to understand the two world views, construct a
dialogue between two of the most intelligent defenders of each
perspective. They should each demonstrate skills in explicating the basic

assumptions, the questionable claims, ideas, inferences, values, and conclusions of the other side. Both should be able to make some concessions to the other point of view without conceding their basic positions. Each should be able to summarize some of the inferences of the other side and raise questions about those inferences (e.g., 'You appear to me to be arguing in the following way. You assume that...You ignore that...And then you conclude that...').

In the second part of your paper, write a third-person commentary on the debate, indicating which point of view is in the logically strongest position in your view. Argue for your position; do not simply assert it. Give good reasons for rejecting or accepting whatever aspects of the two world views you reject or accept. Make clear to the reader how your position reflects your world view. The dialogue should have at least 14 exchanges (28 entries) and the commentary should be at least 4 type-written pages."

A variety of background materials were made available, including the U.S. State Department "White Paper," an open letter from the late Archbishop of San Salvador, a copy of the platform of the El Salvador rebels, and numerous current newspaper and magazine articles and editorials on the issue. The students were encouraged to discuss and debate the issue outside of class (which they did). The students were expected to document how the major newspapers were covering the story (e.g., that accounts favorable to the State Department position tended to be given front page coverage while accounts critical of the State Department position, say from Amnesty International, were de-emphasized on pages 9 through 17). There was also discussion of internal inconsistencies within the accounts.

Many of the students came to see one or more of the following points:

1. That in a conflict such as this the two sides disagree not only on conclusions but even about how the issue ought to be put. One side will put the issue, for example, in terms of the dangers of a communist takeover, the other in terms of the need for people to overthrow a repressive regime. One will see the fundamental problem as caused by Cuban and Soviet intervention, the other side by U.S. intervention. Each side will see the other as begging the essential question.

2. That a debate on how to word the issue will often become a debate on a series of factual questions. This debate will be extended into a series of historical questions. Each side will typically see the other

as suppressing evidence. Those favorable to the Duarte regime, for example, will see the other side as suppressing evidence of the extent of communist involvement in El Salvador. Those favorable to the rebels will see the other side as suppressing evidence of government complicity in terrorist acts of the right. There will be disagreement about which side is committing most of the violent acts.

3. That these factual disagreements will at some point or another lead to a shifting of ground to *conceptual disagreements*: which acts should be called "terrorist," which "revolutionary," and which "acts of liberation." This debate will at some point become a debate about *values*, about which acts are reprehensible or justified. Very often the acts that from one perspective seem required by circumstances will be morally condemned by the other.

4. That at various points in the discussion the debate will become "philosophical" or "anthropological," involving broad issues concerning "the nature of man" and "the nature of human society." The side supporting the government tends to take a philosophical position that plays down the capacity of "mass man" to make rational and appropriate judgments in its own behalf, at least when under the influence of outside agitators and subversives. The other side tends to be more favorable to "mass man" and suspicious of our government's capacity or right to make what appear to them to be decisions that should be left to the people. Each side thinks the other begs important questions, suppresses evidence, stereotypes, uses unjustified analogies, uses faulty causal reasoning, misuses concepts, and so forth.

Such assignments help students appreciate the kinds of moves that typically occur in everyday argument, put them into perspective, and construct alternative arguments, precisely because they more clearly see how arguments develop in relation to each other and so in relation to a broader perspective. They give students more practical insight into the motivated nature of argument "flaws" than the traditional approach. They are therefore better able to anticipate them and more sensitive to the special probing moves that need to be made. Finally, they are much more sensitive (than I believe they would be under most "weak sense" approaches) to the profound ethical consequences of ego-serving reasoning, and to the ease with which we can fall prey to it. If we can indeed accomplish something like these results, then there is much to be said for further work and development of "strong sense" approaches. What I have described here is, I hope, the beginning of such work.

Caveat

I would like to emphasize that the use of a "political" issue is only one approach to the teaching of strong sense critical thinking, and it is emphasized only in one section of the course and only in one of many ways I have taught the course. Teaching critical thinking shouldn't be a goal simply for one course, as I suggested above and as I have frequently written, but a way of teaching any course, a way of teaching any subject, and, finally, a way of thinking and living in the everyday world. In every case, education should be problem- and issue-based, and students should reason their way to knowledge in every domain, having continual opportunities to voice and pursue their own points of view within divergent frames of reference. Their personal worldviews should continually be expanded and enriched as a result. They should learn in time to think within many points of view, many frames of reference, and many worldviews. Only to the extent that they do, do they become liberally educated persons, for only to the extent that we can use our thinking to transcend our thinking are we free.

Is Critical Thinking Itself a World View?

Before I close, I would like to respond to a particularly important misconception, and that is that critical thinking is itself to be considered a world view. Suppose someone objected to critical thinking, saying:

"Clearly, critical thinking itself is a worldview, on a par with, but not superior to, other competing worldviews and to be chosen, ultimately, for the same subjective and personal reasons. Critical thinkers see the world as filled with irrational, uncritical thought. They aspire to a particular value—rationality—and a particular, rational way of life. They choose this value for personal reasons of their own. Why should anyone else be bound by their subjective choice? Let everyone freely choose their own worldviews for themselves. Let us not assume the values of one particular worldview in judging the values of another."

There are a number of reasons why this objection misses the mark. We can illustrate with a variety of examples. First:

Suppose we raised a child so that she uncritically accepted the views—however you might define them—of a critical thinker. (I hold, of course, that there is no one worldview that all critical thinkers hold.) The child would then learn to see the world in a particular way no doubt—would learn to use the language of critical thinking, no doubt. But, since the child came to hold these views in an uncritical manner, since she was, in effect, indoctrinated into "conclusions" without being taught how to reason to those conclusions from premises she critically examined, since she did not notice the assumptions she was making nor the assumptions she was in effect rejecting, since she failed to recognize the concepts she was using as concepts, since she took her "concepts" to be embedded in reality itself, she would not, in fact, be a critical thinker.

Let us change the example:

> Instead of indoctrinating the child into someone's conception of the "views" common to critical thinkers (so that she ended up holding them uncritically), suppose we taught her a variety of critical thinking skills but all in such a way as to imply that those abilities were to be used only in defense of the worldview in which we raised her. We might even teach her "apologetics," namely, how to anticipate objections to her views from other perspectives, with plenty of practice in "refuting" those objections. She would then have a range of critical thinking skills, and in this sense be a critical thinker, but she would still not be a critical thinker in the strongest sense of the term, for she would lack the traits of mind that elevate the holding of a worldview to the higher levels of criticality. She would have an uncritical dimension to her criticality, namely, the inability to enter empathically into other worldviews, the inability to grow beyond her worldview to a yet richer one.

We could of course also come at this from another direction:

> Take any worldview of your choice (one you take to be antithetical to critical thinking). It can be demonstrated that this worldview, and any and all others, can be held in qualitatively different ways. Suppose, for example, you identified the worldview of some modern "stone age" culture to be antithetical to critical thinking. A person could be raised in this view in three qualitatively different ways: (1) without any intellectual skills, (2) with the skills but without the dispositions to use them in a self-reflective way, or (3) with both skills and dispositions. Imagine, for example, a person raised in an uncritical manner in this worldview who left her home culture, at the age of eighteen, to study at a modern university, and

while there, discovered persons with worldviews different from her own. She could either continue to "uncritically" assume that her original views are correct and those which conflict with them are wrong, or she could begin to question and probe into the possibility of her own views being, in part, mistaken, namely, begin to think critically about not only her views but the views of others. Once again it is not the substance of one's views per se that make one a critical thinker but the manner in which one holds those views.

Consider yet another way to illuminate the mistake in considering critical thinking a worldview:

> If I—given any worldview that you might choose to attribute to me—meet someone with a different worldview and that other person asks me to consider the possibility that something I was assuming to be true might not be true or asks me to consider the implications of what I was saying or to clarify what I thought the issue was that we were discussing, would it be fair of me to say that merely in asking these questions, the person was trying to force me to accept her worldview? Clearly not. Yet it is precisely the asking of questions such as these, and the taking of these questions seriously, that defines critical thinking. It is not defined in terms of the conclusions someone may come to in asking the questions. To determine whether you are a critical thinker I do not ask *what* you think but how—in what manner—you think.

A final example will, I hope, nail the point down. It is one that makes the connection—quite a parallel one—between the manner in which one comes to hold one's view of the world and the manner in which one learns an academic subject, like chemistry, physics, sociology, history, anthropology, or philosophy. In each case one can "learn" a frame of reference in an uncritical or critical manner. If one's learning is uncritical, then the learning is superficial because by definition one cannot then reason within the discipline. This is, unfortunately of course, the way most students learn disciplines, not as a system of concepts within which one reasons but as a set of pronouncements that one atomically memorizes. On the other hand, one might be taught to reason within the discipline—for example, to reason historically, or sociologically, and so on—but not to reason beyond the discipline, not to reason so as to question the assumptions of the discipline.

To sum up. No matter what views one might possibly adopt, there is always an independent question to be raised as to the manner in which one comes to hold those views. There will always be the possibility of learning them critically and therefore with some perspective on their logical components: their assumptions, their information sources, their concepts, their way of making inferences about the world. As soon as one questions, as soon as one begins to probe into the structure of one's views, one begins to conceive of the possibility of alternative structures, one begins to gain some critical distance, a greater measure of objectivity, a greater sense of the logical structures one is in fact using.

One final point. It is important not to confuse the empirical fact that most people hold to their worldviews uncritically or merely in a weak sense with the logically untenable point that it is not possible to broaden one's views or to transcend one's views as a result of strong critical thinking. Not everyone need be the kind of person that Galsworthy describes Clauda Fresnay, Viscount Harbinger, to be in his novel *The Patrician* (New York: Charles Scribner's Sons, 1911, pp. 168–69):

It would have been unfair to call his enthusiasm for social reform spurious. It was real enough in its way, and did certainly testify that he was not altogether lacking either in imagination or good-heartedness. But it was over and overlaid with the public-school habit, so powerful and beguiling that it becomes a second nature stronger than the first—of relating everything in the Universe to the standards and prejudices of a single class. Since practically all his intimate associates were immersed in it, he was naturally not in the least conscious of this habit; indeed there was nothing he deprecated so much in politics as the narrow and prejudiced out-look, such as he had observed in the Nonconformist, or labour politician. He would never have admitted for a moment that certain doors had been banged-to at his birth, bolted when he went to Eton, and padlocked at Cambridge. No one would have denied that there was much that was valuable in his standards—a high level of honesty, candour, sportsmanship, personal cleanliness, and self-reliance, together with a dislike of such cruelty as had been officially (so to speak) recognized as cruelty, and a sense of public service to a State run by and for the public schools; but it would have required far more originality than he possessed ever to look at Life from any other point of view than that from which he had been born and bred to watch Her. To fully understand Harbinger, one must, and with unprejudiced eyes and brain, have attended one of those great cricket matches in which he had figured conspicuously as a boy, and looking down from some high impartial spot watched the ground at lunch time covered from rope to rope and stand to stand with a marvellous swarm, all walking in precisely the same manner, with precisely the same expression on their faces, under precisely the same hats—a swarm enshrining the greatest identity of creed and habit ever known since the world began.

11

Toward a Pedagogy of Critical Thinking

Henry A. Giroux

For the sake of clarification, I want to stress that it is not my purpose to provide an in-depth treatment of what constitutes critical thinking. Such a task remains for another time. In the account that follows, I simply want to suggest a few theoretical components that I think constitute a good starting point for a pedagogy of critical thinking.

I want to begin by commenting in general terms on the problems that continue to shape social studies teaching. These problems are important, I believe, because they reflect a pedagogical misunderstanding on the part of educators over what constitutes critical thinking in both general and specific terms. First, most of what students acquire in school is a systematic exposure of selected aspects of human history and culture. Yet, the normative nature of the material selected is presented as both unproblematic and value free. In the name of objectivity, a large part of our social studies curricula universalizes dominant norms, values, and perspectives that represent interpretive and normative perspectives on social reality.¹ The latter approach to social studies might be aptly characterized as the pedagogy of the "immaculate perception." Second, the pedagogy of the "immaculate perception" represents an approach to learning that not only sanctions dominant categories of knowledge and values but also reinforces a theoretical and undialectical approach to structuring one's perception of the world. Students are not taught to look at curricula knowledge, the facts, within a wider context of learning. Moreover, the relationship between theory and "facts" is often ignored, thus making it all too difficult for students to develop a conceptual apparatus for investigating the ideological and epistemological nature of what constitutes a "fact" in the first place. Lastly, the pedagogy of the "immaculate perception" both creates and reproduces classroom social relationships that are not only boring for most students but also, more importantly, mystifying. Rather than developing actively critical thinkers, such a pedagogy produces students who are either afraid or unable to think critically.[2]

Before examining the nature of critical thinking, a short comment should be made about the source of the pedagogical ills that are gnawing at North American schools and the social studies field in particular. If the social studies field, particularly at the secondary education level, is in part characterized by a pedagogy that inveighs against critical thinking, who in the final analysis is responsible for such a default? Any conclusive answer to such a question would have to begin with the recognition that it is too simpleminded a response to lay the blame exclusively on either teachers or students. Such a perspective ignores that the essence of schooling lies in its relationship to the larger socio-economic reality, particularly the institutions of work. Schools appear to have little to do with the Kantian notion that they should function to educate students for a "better future condition of the human race, that is, for the idea of humanity."[3] The real business of schools appears to be to socialize students into accepting and reproducing the existing society.[4] While teachers cannot be blamed in the long run for many of the ills that plague North American education, they can examine the commonsense assumptions behind their approaches to teaching. This means they would have to reshape and restructure their pedagogy in accordance with the categorical dictum once voiced by Nietzsche, "A great truth wants to be criticized, not idolized."[5] This leads us directly to the thorny issue of defining the concept of critical thinking in both theoretical and programmatic terms.

Traditional views on the nature of critical thinking have failed to support Nietzsche's call for a critical search for the truth. This is true, not only because textbooks and pedagogical approaches in the social studies have objectified prevailing norms, beliefs, and attitudes, but also because of the very way in which critical thinking has been defined. The most powerful, yet limited, definition of critical thinking comes out of the positivist tradition in the applied sciences and suffers from what I call the Internal Consistency position.[6] According to the adherents of the Internal Consistency position, critical thinking refers primarily to teaching students how to analyze and develop reading and writing assignments from the perspective of formal, logical patterns of consistency. In this case, the student is taught to examine the logical development of a theme, "advance organizers," systematic argument, the validity of evidence, and how to determine whether a conclusion flows from the data under study. While all of the latter learning skills are important, their limitations as a whole lie in what is excluded, and it is with respect to what is missing that the ideology of such an approach is revealed.

At the core of what we call critical thinking, there are two major assumptions that are missing. First, there is a relationship between theory and facts; second, knowledge cannot be separated from human interests, norms, and values. Despite a seeming oversimplification, it is within the context of these two assumptions that further assumptions can be developed and a theoretical, programmatic groundwork can be created for a pedagogical approach to teaching students how to think critically.

Alvin Gouldner has stressed the importance of acknowledging the relationship between theory and facts, a relationship that raises fundamental questions about the fragile nature of knowledge. "[Critical thinking]...is here construed as the capacity to make problematic what had hitherto been treated as given; to bring into reflection what before had only been used...to examine critically the life we lead. This view of rationality situates it in the capacity to think about our thinking."[7] Translated pedagogically, this means that facts, issues, and events in any social studies should be presented problematically to students. Knowledge in this case demands constant searching, invention, and reinvention. Knowledge is not the end of thinking, as Paulo Freire claims, but rather the mediating link between students and teachers. The latter suggests not only a very different approach to classroom social relationships as compared to those that have prevailed traditionally, but it also suggests that a great deal of time should be spent teaching students about the notion of frame of reference and its use as a theoretical/ conceptual interpretive tool. By looking at similar information through different frames of reference, students can *begin* to treat knowledge as problematic, and thus, as an object of inquiry.

The connection between theory and facts throws into high relief another fundamental component of a critical thinking pedagogy: the relationships between facts and values. How information is selected, arranged, and sequenced to construct a picture of contemporary or historical reality is more than a cognitive operation; it is also a process intimately connected to the beliefs and values that guide one's life. Implicit in the reordering of knowledge are ideological assumptions about how one views the world, assumptions that constitute a distinction between the essential and the nonessential, the important and the nonimportant. The point here is that any concept of frame of reference has to be presented to students as more than an epistemological framework, it also has to include an axiomatic dimension. Moreover, to separate facts from values is to run the risk of teaching students how to deal with means divorced from the question of ends.

Related to the two major assumptions about critical thinking is a procedural issue that centers around what might be called the contextualization of information. Students need to learn how to be able to move outside of their own frame of reference so that they can question the legitimacy of a given fact, concept, or issue. They also have to learn how to perceive the very essence of what they are examining by placing it critically within a system of relationships that give it meaning. In other words, students must be taught to think dialectically rather than in an isolated and compartmentalized fashion. Fredric Jameson, while pointing out the limitations of an undialectical approach to thinking, presents a fitting comment on the need for a more dialectical approach to the latter: "[t]he antispeculative bias of that tradition, its emphasis on the individual fact or item at the expense of the network of relationships in which the item may be embedded, continue to encourage submission to what is by preventing its followers from making connections, and in particular, from drawing the otherwise unavoidable conclusions on the political level."[8]

In addition to the contextualization of information, the form and content of classroom social relations have to be considered in any pedagogy that concerns itself with critical thinking. Any pedagogy of critical thinking that ignores the social relations of the classroom runs the risk of being mystifying and incomplete. Sartre has captured the latter point with his comment that knowledge is a form of praxis.[9] In other words, knowledge is not studied for its own sake but is seen as a mediation between the individual and the larger social reality. Within the context of such a pedagogy, students become subjects in the act of learning. Under such circumstances, students must be able to examine the content and the structure of the classroom relationships that provide the boundaries for their own learning. The important point here is that if educational knowledge is to be a study in ideology, the question of what constitutes legitimate knowledge must be undertaken amidst classroom social relations that encourage such an approach. Any approach to critical thinking, regardless of how progressive it might be, will vitiate its own possibilities if it operates out of a web of classroom social relationships that are authoritatively hierarchical and promote passivity, docility, and silence. Social relations in the classroom that glorify the teacher as the expert, the dispenser of knowledge, end up crippling student imagination and creativity; in addition, such approaches teach students more about the legitimacy of passivity than about the need to examine critically the lives they lead.[10]

Crucial to the development of progressive classroom social relationships is the opening of channels of communication in which students use the linguistic and cultural capacity they bring to the classroom. If students are subjected to a language as well as a belief and value setting whose implicit message suggests that they are culturally illiterate, students will learn very little about critical thinking and a great deal about what Paulo Freire has called the "culture of silence."[11]

Bourdieu and others have unveiled the essence of the "culture of silence" pedagogy by pointing out that classroom knowledge, far from being the "outcome of negotiated meanings between students and teachers," is often the imposition of a literacy and cultural style "that is specific to the language socialization of the privileged classes."[12] In short, if knowledge is to be used by students to give meaning to their existence, educators will have to use the students' values, beliefs, and knowledge as an important part of the learning process before, as Maxine Greene points out, "a leap to the theoretical" can be attempted.[13]

Notes

1. For an excellent comment on the relationship between knowledge and values, see Michael F. D. Young, ed., *Knowledge and Control* (London: Collier-Macmillan, 1971). Michael Apple has written extensively on the latter subject, and his article, "The Hidden Curriculum and the Nature of Conflict," *Interchange* 2 (1971): 2740, deals directly with the social studies field. See also Jonathon Kozol, *The Night Is Dark and I Am Far from Home* (Boston: Houghton Mifflin, 1975), pp. 63–73.

2. For an excellent description of this type of pedagogy, see Paulo Freire, *Pedagogy of the Oppressed* (New York: Seabury Press, 1973), and Henry A. Giroux and Anthony N. Penna, "Social Education in the Classroom: The Dynamics of the Hidden Curriculum," *Theory and Research in Social Education* 7 (Spring 1979): 21–42.

3. Herbert Marcuse, *Counter-Revolution and Revolt* (Boston: Beacon Press, 1972), p. 27.

4. There are many sources that treat this position seriously. One of the best is Samuel Bowles and Herbert Gintis, *Schooling in Capitalist America* (New York: Basic Books, 1976). See also Martin Carnoy and Henry M. Levin, *The Limits of Educational Reform* (New York: David McKay, 1976), pp. 52–82, 219–44.

5. Martin Jay, *The Dialectical Imagination* (Boston: Little, Brown, 1973), p. 65.

6. This approach has been widely popularized through the works of Hilda Taba, *Teacher's Handbook for Elementary Social Studies* (Reading, Mass.: Addison-Wesley, 1967); J. Richard Suchman, *Inquiry Box: Teacher's Handbook* (Chicago: Science Research Associates, 1967); Joseph J. Schwab, *Biology Teacher's Handbook* (New York: Wiley, 1965).

7. Alvin J. Gouldner, *The Dialectic of Ideology and Technology* (New York: Seabury Press, 1976), p. 49.

8. Fredric Jameson, *Marxism and Form* (Princeton, N.J.: Princeton University Press, 1971). p. xx.

9. Jean-Paul Sartre, *Literature and Existentialism*, 3rd ed. (New York: Citadel Press, 1965).

10. See Michael W. Apple and Nancy King, "What Do Schools Teach?" *Humanistic Education*, Richard Weller, ed., (Berkeley, Calif.: McCutchan Publishing, 1977), pp. 29–63 and Bowles and Gintis, *Schooling in Capitalist America*. A decent collection of articles can be found in Norman Overly, ed., *The Unstudied Curriculum* (Washington, D.C.: Association of Curriculum and Supervision, 1970).

11. Paulo Freire, *Education for Critical Consciousness* (New York: Seabury Press, 1973).

12. See David Swartz, "Pierre Bourdieu: The Cultural Transmission of Social Inequality," *Harvard Educational Review* 47 (Nov. 1977): 545–55; Pierre Bourdieu and Jean-Claude Passeron, *Reproduction in Education, Society, and Culture* (Beverly Hills, Calif.: Sage, 1977); Basil Bernstein, *Class, Codes, and Control*, vol. 3 (London: Routledge & Kegan Paul, 1977), pp. 85–156. For a good general study on the politics of language, see Claus Mueller, *The Politics of Communication* (New York: Oxford University Press, 1973).

13. Maxine Greene, "Curriculum and Consciousness," in William F. Pinar, ed., *Curriculum Theorizing: The Reconceptualists* (Berkeley, Calif.: McCutchan Publishing, 1975), p. 304.

12

Teaching Intellectual Autonomy:
The Failure of the Critical Thinking Movement

Laura Duhan Kaplan

Introduction

The currently popular courses in critical thinking offered at the college level are advertised as courses that prepare students for the intellectual autonomy required for political autonomy. However, according to the criteria set forth by the critical pedagogy movement, the critical thinking course tends to teach political conformity rather than political autonomy. Against the expressed intention of teachers and textbook authors, critical thinking courses may encourage students to accept without question certain political perspectives and discourage students from asking questions about the genesis of these perspectives.

Two Approaches to Developing Intellectual Autonomy

The Practice of Teaching Critical Thinking As It Originated in Philosophy Departments

Philosophers in the United States have seized the opportunity to respond simultaneously to two educational trends: the demand for college graduates who can think critically and declining enrollments in philosophy courses. The response has taken the form of a course titled "critical thinking" offered in philosophy departments across the country, with particular frequency in public universities. In theoretical contexts, i.e., learned journals, defenders of the involvement of philosophers in teaching critical thinking define critical thinking as variously as "proficiency in correctly assessing statements plus the tendency to exercise that proficiency";[1] "the ability to recognize the world views in which arguments are embedded";[2] and "being appropriately moved by reasons."[3] Authors argue eloquently about the need for each of these talents in a democracy peopled by intellectually and politically autonomous human beings. In practical contexts, i.e., documents addressed to university administrators and state legislators, philosophers justify their involvement in teaching critical thinking by appealing to their expertise in logic and argumentation and suggesting that a course in logic and argumentation develops the above-listed skills. Consequently, courses in critical thinking taught by philosophers have taken the form of courses in informal logic, i.e., the application of the concepts of logic to the analysis and evaluation of arguments occurring in the English language.

A typical course in critical thinking teaches students two skills: (1) to identify arguments and (2) to evaluate arguments. The first skill is developed through drill and practice in a particular type of textual analysis that may be called "argument analysis." Early in the course students practice reading paragraphs with an eye to identifying arguments. They learn to identify the claim being made (the conclusion of the argument) and the reasons offered in support of the claim (the argument's premises). Later in the course students have the opportunity to apply logical analysis to article-length texts.

The second skill is developed by teaching students rules for evaluating the reasons presented in support of claims. This is a delicate matter, as reasons are contextual. What may be a good reason in a bar room conversation may be a poor reason in a formal labor negotiation. Courses in critical thinking typically simplify the matter by presenting students with a list of reasons that do not adequately support claims in any context. These insufficient reasons are summarized in a list of "informal fallacies." The informal fallacies include such mistakes as "appeal to authority," "appeal to pity," and "inconsistency." Too often, students check arguments against the list of fallacies and immediately reject any argument that contains one.

The critical thinking model now in use aims to teach students valuable skills in logical analysis and, in my opinion, succeeds. However, the actual practice of teaching critical thinking does not fulfill the promise of education for autonomy articulated by the theoretical defenders of teaching critical thinking. Below I attempt to support my claim by revealing some of the beliefs about autonomy, curriculum, and reading that inform the model of teaching critical thinking and that are taught to students along with the skills of logical analysis.

The Basis for a Critique: Critical Thinking and Critical Pedagogy

My analysis of the critical thinking model now in use is informed by the perspective of the critical pedagogy movement. In order to avoid confusion between the similar names of the two dissimilar movements, I shall distinguish between the use each makes of the word "critical." The adjective "critical" can be related to the noun "critique" or to the noun "criticism." When someone provides a criticism of my work she or he is giving me information about what is wrong with it, perhaps with the aim of helping me to improve it. When someone provides a critique of my work she or he is giving me information on dimensions of meaning in the work of which previously I might not have been aware. She or he gleans this information by reading with a theory of how meaning is encoded in texts. The critical thinking movement teaches students to provide criticism of arguments, while the critical pedagogy movement teaches students to provide critique as a foundation for criticism of the world around them.

Critical pedagogy borrows the word "critical" from "critical theory," a sociological perspective developed largely by German intellectuals in the early to middle part of this century. Critical theory is a synthesis of Marxism, phenomenology, and psychoanalysis. From Marxism comes an orientation toward maximizing human freedom from political and economic domination. From phenomenology comes an emphasis on observing and articulating the structures of lived experience. From psychoanalysis comes a push to decode cultural forms. Critical theory provides a critique of lived social and political realities with the aim of changing those realities to allow greater freedom of thought and action.

Critical pedagogy applies the tools of critical theory to a critique of educational institutions, guided by the belief that all education should aim at maximizing human freedom. Maxine Greene suggests that literature be taught as a means of awakening the student's awareness that the world contains unrealized possibilities for thought and action.[4] David Purpel attempts to articulate the structures of lived experience by calling the attention of teachers and students to the "hidden curriculum," i.e., lessons implicit in the organization of school life.[5] Michael Apple attempts to decode cultural forms that distort the aims of education through a study of the ways in which schools reinforce economic structures by training students to meet the economic needs of large corporations.[6] Other members of the movement work on a number of levels, attempting to introduce change into educational institutions through the agency of students, teachers, and intellectuals. For example,

Henry Giroux invites teachers to examine their institutional roles and to redefine themselves as "critical intellectuals."[7]

The critical pedagogy movement identifies its roots in the work of Paulo Freire. Freire's famous book *Pedagogy of the Oppressed* is a manifesto and guidebook for radical educators who wish to raise the consciousness of members of the working class.[8] Freire's basic principle says that education that aims at the creation of autonomous political actors must constitute its students as such throughout the learning process. He defines education for liberation in opposition to what he calls "the banking concept of education," in which "education...becomes an act of depositing, in which the students are the depositories and the teacher is the depositor."[9] The banking concept of education is built on an image of students as absolutely ignorant and teachers as absolutely knowledgeable. Teachers are the active subjects of education and students are the passive objects. Because the banking concept of education does not constitute students as autonomous actors, educational programs modeled on the banking concept cannot successfully mold autonomous actors.

Freire notes that radical educators typically fall into the trap of the banking model of education in three ways: by substituting radical slogans for conservative ones; by interpreting the students' social reality for them; and by presenting students with a menu of possible political actions from which they can choose. Each of these educational activities leaves students free only to classify and organize the information deposited with them. A radical educator who wishes genuinely to raise the consciousness of his or her students should inspire them to examine actively the "themes" that characterize their identity in the world. In order to avoid the pitfalls of the banking concept of education, the radical educator should study her or his students' social world, present situations drawn from that actual social world for students to analyze and decode, and lead students in a process of shared inquiry that aims at understanding and evaluating their social reality. For the members of the critical pedagogy movement, variations on Freire's model of education have the potential to prepare students for intellectual and political autonomy.

Educational Deficiencies of the Critical Thinking Model

Critical Thinking's Failure to Address Intellectual Autonomy

Some clarification of the ideal of autonomy is in order. The critical thinking movement seeks to prepare students to exercise the most accessible political right guaranteed by the constitution: the right to vote. The critical pedagogy movement seeks to prepare students to access other political rights and expand the freedoms available to citizens.

Philosopher of education Harvey Siegel defines critical thinking as operationalized rationality: demanding, giving, and evaluating reasons. Critical thinking, he argues, is essential for citizens in a democracy. Citizens must demand and be able to evaluate reasons given in support of the actions of legislators, judges, and executives. Citizens must be able to choose between the competing claims of lobbyists and political candidates.[10] Unfortunately, choosing between prepackaged claims is the level of political responsibility taken by most citizens in our country. In this sense, courses in critical thinking prepare students to assume the responsibilities of autonomous political actors.

Critical pedagogues would argue that an educational program that aims to reproduce this level of responsibility rests on a narrow interpretation of political freedom. In a free society, political actors ought to be able to create alternatives, not merely to choose between them. Political actors ought to share leadership, not merely ask for convincing reasons from leaders. Critical thinking courses fail to introduce students to autonomy at this level.

An analysis of the introductory sections of three widely used college-level critical thinking texts shows that each text falls into one of the traps of the banking model of education that Freire says radical educators must avoid. The banking model of education constitutes students as relatively passive, allowing them to contribute to their education by storing and organizing information. By making use of the banking model, the teaching of critical thinking communicates to students a limited picture of what it means to be an active participant in a significant social institution. The first text I examine defines critical thinking as the ability to select rationally among competing options. A course based on this text conveys the message that citizens who make an informed choice between options outlined by authorities have fully exercised their critical capacities. The second text implicitly defines the critical thinker as a political liberal who has rejected conservative attempts at domination. A course based on this text conveys the message that the acceptance of the right slogans is an adequate substitute for the critical analysis of those slogans. The third text defines a critical thinker as one who can argue appropriately (i.e., as shown in the text) in the different social settings of courtroom, classroom, and business. A course based on this text conveys the message that critical thinking is primarily valuable as a means of adapting to situations rather than as a means of changing them.

The Model of Rational Selection Between Alternatives. Most of David Kelley's *The Art of Reasoning* introduces traditional concepts of logic and applies them to the analysis of brief texts written in English.[11] Because Kelley has the weight of tradition behind his approach, it is not surprising that he is unequivocal about the purpose of his book. He states, "this is a book about thinking. It's a book about *how* to think,"[12] and he tells the reader, also unequivocally, about the characteristics of thinking: thinking is distinct from "our emotional responses to things" and thinking "aims at a goal."[13] "It differs from activities such as daydreaming and fantasizing, in which we simply let our minds wander where they will."[14] Thinking, then, is dispassionate inquiry aimed at a goal.

Students may wonder in what situations they would aim at goals about which they are dispassionate. Therefore Kelley presents examples of such situations: discussing free will and determinism in a philosophy class, interpreting Hamlet in a literature class, understanding a scientific theory. In these situations, students "are presented with competing ideas or theories and asked to discuss them critically."[15] If critical thinking is confined to discussing the relative merits of options presented by a teacher, it is easy to see why Kelley describes thinking as "dispassionate."

Kelley tries to make it clear that critical thinking has a place outside of the classroom:

> In our own personal lives, finally, we all have choices to make, major ones or minor, and here too we need to weigh the reasons on each side and try to consider all the relevant issues.[16]

Kelley interprets the word "choice" narrowly, as a selection made from a small number of competing options. Unfortunately most major and many minor life choices do not present themselves as opportunities to select among clear-cut options. More frequently there is no clear option, and we are forced to create one. An adult's personal life is not modelled on the typical classroom where a higher authority presents clear-cut options to be accepted or rejected. The skills we have learned in Kelley's critical thinking text will not help us here.

A perspective offered by the critical theorist Friedrich Pollock leads to the observation that Kelley's conception of critical thinking reinforces citizen passivity. An analogy between Kelley's notion of choosing between competing ideas in the classroom and Pollack's analysis of choosing between items on a public opinion poll may help to clarify this claim. In an age where enormous amounts of information are disseminated through printed and electronic media, the average citizen has "neither the time, the energy nor the education to put together the data necessary to form a personal opinion" on many topics.[17] The pressure to inform oneself on issues is relieved when the citizen has the opportunity to choose between a small set of stereotyped opinions. Kelley's course reinforces the illusion that informed choice between options presented by an authority is an adequate substitute for an analysis of the issue that aims at understanding the genesis of the choices offered. Kelley's critical thinkers could fall prey to what Pollock identifies as the domination of citizens by public opinion polls. By presenting respondents with a list of "acceptable" beliefs from which to choose, public opinion polls tend to create rather than to measure public opinion.[18]

The Model of Political Liberalism. Kahane, author of *Logic and Contemporary Rhetoric,* wants to avoid precisely this sort of indoctrination but fails.[19] In the preface to his text, Kahane celebrates "citizens who can think critically" as the "foundation of any society that wants to remain truly free."[20] Kahane does not define explicitly the term "critical thinking," but his book suggests that it involves the full-scale rejection of conservative slogans. Unfortunately, it seems not to involve the parallel examination of liberal slogans.

In his preface, Kahane comments on the apolitical intention behind his book:

> The intent is not to move students to the right or left on the social/political spectrum but to help them move *up* on the scale of rational sophistication.[21]

Yet nearly all of Kahane's examples of fallacies come from the mouths of conservative Republican politicians, and most of the cartoons he reprints are by liberal political cartoonists, such as Garry Trudeau and Jules Feiffer. In this way, the book implies that conservative political slogans should be scrutinized with the tool of fallacy identification while liberal political slogans are immune. Acceptance of this implication is dangerous to clear thinking in politics even if one is committed to liberal ideals. In real-world political discourse conservative programs are often packaged in the language of liberalism. For at least this reason, students should be encouraged to analyze critically all political slogans.

Although Kahane explicitly says that critical thinkers must reject indoctrination,[22] in many places he clearly does tell students what critical thinkers should believe. I will present two examples. At one point, he tells students that they should desire to visit the country from which their great-grandparents came and would be able to afford it if they didn't spend so much money on the marginal needs pushed by advertisers.[23] At another point, he explains that old United States history texts "gave you a distorted view of history, your country and the world." Now, "because of changing American attitudes towards blacks and other minority groups," our texts:

> slant history and how our system works much less than they used to...some of the recent public school history and social studies texts are the best of their kind in history, anywhere.[24]

We may evaulate Kahane's claim using the questions he teaches students to ask of conservative politicians. Is the achievement of the goal of pluralism, currently an urgent need in the United States, the only criterion for a good textbook? Has Kahane read history texts from other countries and other eras? If not, his statement seems like "puffery" (which he explicitly says it is not),[25] crass provincialism, or—worse— propaganda.

The Model of Situational Accommodation. Stephen Toulmin, Richard Rieke, and Allan Janik, authors of *An Introduction to Reasoning*, introduce reasoning as a social practice.

> Evidently reasoning—or at least the giving of reasons—is pervasive in our society. The practice of providing reasons for what we do, or think, or tell others we believe is built firmly into our accepted patterns of behavior.[26]

Reinforcing the point that engaging in reasoning is a matter of con- forming to social norms, the authors write:

> there are plenty of situations in which that demand is set aside. And there are familiar and accepted ways of brushing aside the demand for reasons in such cases, with a noncommittal response— with a "I can't say" or "I don't know," a "No special reason," or whatever.[27]

We learn that this book is designed to teach students how to assess the demand for reasons in a particular context and how to supply reasons in a variety of contexts.

The trains of reasoning that it is appropriate to use vary from situation to situation. As we move from the lunch counter to the executive conference table, from the science laboratory to the law courts, the "forum" of discussion changes profoundly.[28]

This book teaches reasoning in the sense that we say the Sophists in ancient Athens taught reasoning. The Sophists taught young citizens the social skill of how to get along in law courts and other public forums. Implicit in this type of tuition is an interpretation of and an attitude toward the socially acceptable: what is socially acceptable is the foundation of human behavior and therefore of human education. One should learn how to conform and how to get the better of the situation.

But this approach to critical thinking does not encourage students to submit the social context to any type of critical analysis. For example, students preparing to be managers must learn to justify their hiring decisions. Toulmin's course in critical thinking will help them in this regard. They will sharpen their skills in assessing a regional and organizational climate to determine what can be stated publicly as justifications for hiring decisions. In some northern U.S. cities one may be able to say "I hired him because he is black," affirming a commitment to affirmative action. In those cities it may well be unacceptable to say "I chose not to hire him because he is black." In some southern U.S. cities it may be acceptable to say "When I found out he was black I decided not to hire him," thereby espousing a commitment to give whites first choice at certain jobs. The "critical thinker" trained by Toulmin, et at., will not be encouraged to ask why certain chains of reasoning are taboo—particularly if it is a subject, such as race relations in the southern United States, on which there is a strong social pressure to brush aside any demand for reasons.

A perspective on education taken from the critical pedagogue Svi Shapiro provides an economic interpretation of the significance of training students to meet the social demand for reasons.[29] Shapiro presents the thesis articulated by Nicos Poulantzas that American schooling sorts those who are destined to do manual labor from those who are destined to engage in mental labor. Those who are channeled into manual labor learn little in the way of job skills at school. Instead they learn discipline and respect for authority. Those who are channeled into mental labor are taught "a series of rituals, secrets and symbolisms"[30] that are not so much identified with any particular technical skill but rather qualify one to enter the "culture" of mental labor.[31]

Shapiro identifies those who engage in manual labor as the working class and those who engage in mental labor as the:

> new petty bourgeoisie—that massive and ever expanding group of salaried workers who are involved in tertiary-sector and white-collar work. These include civil servants, human services and education workers, and those employed in commercial, insurance, accounting and banking concerns.[32]

(In the vernacular, members of this group are called "yuppies.") However, Shapiro notes that this group engages not so much in mental labor, but in professions that make use of many of the symbols of mental labor, including "paperwork," emphasis on the ability "to write and to present ideas," and "a certain use of speech."[33]

A course in critical thinking may provide some initiation into the "rituals, secrets and symbolisms" of mental labor including information on speaking and writing in ritual ways. The terse logical style taught in critical thinking classes is the standard for contemporary business writing. The names of fallacies are symbolic tokens that declare that their pronouncers are well-educated people. Critical thinking may be, as Toulmin suggests, a social ritual; it involves knowing what sorts of reasons to provide and to demand for every situation. One must know how to behave in the courtroom, the health spa, the realtor's office, and the office party in order to be accepted as a member of the petty bourgeoisie. On this interpretation, the critical thinking model now in use is a step in the creation of well-behaved white-collar workers.

From the perspective of critical theory, Kelley's emphasis on critically evaluating competing options is a piece in the creation of a passive electorate. From the perspective of critical pedagogy, Toulmin's emphasis on learning to satisfy the social demand for reasons is a step in the creation of, or at least the maintenance of, yuppie culture. Popular opinion evaluates yuppies as politically passive, content to choose between the platforms offered by Republican and Democratic candidates. The critical thinking model now appears as a piece of an educational program that creates and maintains many facets of a particular social class.

Critical Thinking and Reading

In the practice of teaching critical thinking, logical analysis often is used as a model of college-level reading. Below I argue that this model of reading may preclude the asking of certain types of politically significant questions about a text.

Maxine Greene identifies two approaches to reading championed by two sets of literary theorists. The first approach has been articulated by British and American literary critics. These theorists understand a text

> in relative isolation from the writer's personal biography and undistorted by associations brought to the work from the reader's own daily life.[34]

A text may bring up associations for each of its readers, but readers must carefully distinguish their lives from what the text actually says. The text may inspire readers to change ideas or institutions, but, again, that inspiration is a part of the reader's life, not the text. An approach to reading that isolates a text from its readers' conscious experience has the virtue of inviting a certain kind of "close reading."[35] However, Greene says the danger of such an approach is the tendency to see the text "as a language game insulated from life and essential human concerns."

The second approach to reading, which Greene favors, has been articulated by continental literary critics. For these theorists:

> Literature is viewed as a genesis, a conscious effort on the part of an individual artist to understand his own experience by framing it in language. The reader who encounters the work must recreate it in terms of his consciousness.[36]

On this view, a text is not distorted by a reader's experience. Instead, it is illuminated by a reader's experience. Greene quotes Sartre's statement that a text is "only a collection of signs" until it is lent meaning by the experiences of a reader.[37] A text is viewed in relation to human thought and action, rather than in isolation from them. The writer's activity has given her or him occasion to write. The reader's activity gives her or him the tools to breathe life into a text. The text mediates between the two, stimulating the reader to participate in the experience of the writer. In so doing, the reader will reframe both the writer's experience and her or his own.

Of the two approaches to reading, the critical thinking model now in use favors the first. A prerequisite for careful argument analysis is the student's ability to separate her or his preconceptions and reactions to the text from what is written in the text. But if argument analysis becomes an end in itself, attempts to understand the writer's experience that can genuinely illuminate the meaning of a text may be excluded.

The following excerpt from a letter to the editor, which appeared in The Charlotte Observer on 15 July 1990, will serve as an example.

Harvey Gantt's credentials don't make him the perfect candidate for anything....Gantt also spoke at a National Abortion Rights Action League rally in Raleigh on July 3. NARAL supports legalized child-killing for any reason—from convenience to sex selection.[38]

The author's argument may be summarized as follows. The conclusion or claim is, "Harvey Gantt is not a good candidate." The premise or reason offered in support of the conclusion is, "Gantt speaks to groups who advocate child-killing." The argument is fairly easy to discredit by referring to the list of fallacies typically taught in critical thinking courses. The adequacy of the premise that supports the conclusion could be challenged. The author rejects Gantt as a viable political candidate because she rejects some of the political views of the groups who invited Gantt to speak. She could be charged with committing the fallacy of "guilt by association." The logic that led the author to formulate her premise could also be challenged. From the fact that NARAL supports abortion, she draws the conclusion that NARAL would support any kind of child-killing. The author could be charged with committing the fallacy of "slippery slope."

In most critical thinking classes, the analysis of the argument would end in the identification of the fallacies and the rejection of the argument. In keeping with what Greene calls the British and American approach to literary criticism, the text's message is revealed plainly in the argument. The reader's only task is to reject or accept the message. Some teachers would push their students farther and require them to strengthen the argument by correcting the author's mistakes. But because of their emphasis on teaching logical skills, few teachers would hint that the more interesting dimensions of the editorial are revealed in the places where the author's logic fails. Few students would be encouraged to ask *why* the author's logic breaks down. At these points the argument's message becomes unclear. In order to understand it, students must bring in information about the writer's biography or, if it is not available, their own associations.

If the above letter to the editor were analyzed in a typical critical thinking course, it is unlikely that the identification of the fallacy would lead the class to consider the question,"What or who makes the abortion issue so powerful that this writer would base her entire voting decision on it alone?" This sort of question could lead to a critique of the letter, enabling the reader to analyze some of the forces that have shaped the author's experience and to explore some of the forces shaping her or his own political views. The class would also be unlikely to try to understand why the author commits the fallacy of "guilt by association" by asking "Why does Gantt's appearance before pro-choice groups appear to the author as sufficient grounds for her inferences about his views?" Exploration of this question could reveal some of the forces that have shaped the author's ways of reasoning about political issues and could enable the reader to reflect on the forces that have shaped her or his reasoning patterns.

The latter question is dangerous to the entire list of fallacies. Another way of asking it is, "If 'guilt by association' is a fallacy, why do we usually use it successfully to make decisions?" This question leads to further questions. Why is an inference that works in everyday life labeled "irrational" in the critical thinking course? Why is critical thinking defined in opposition to common sense? Henry Giroux and Roger Simon provide part of an answer in their conclusion to *Popular Culture, Schooling and Everyday Life*. Educational policymakers identify popular culture with lower-class culture, while the American educational system is designed to elevate and perpetuate bourgeois culture.[39] Critical thinking is part of this educational program. Earlier I applied Shapiro's discussion of schooling's role in the development of a culture of mental labor to the critical thinking model. Here again, I suggest that the critical thinking course plays a role in the development of class consciousness. In this case, the development of class consciousness involves the development of a trained unconsciousness to certain aspects of experience.

Conclusion

It should be clear that my aim is not to discredit the ideal of critical thinking. Rather, I question whether the practice of teaching critical thinking at the college level as it has evolved into the practice of teaching informal logic is sufficient for actualizing the ideal. I have argued that it is not sufficient, if "critical thinking" includes the ability to decode the political nature of events and institutions, and if it includes the ability to envision alternative events and institutions. Speaking broadly, I have offered two sorts of reasons for my thesis. First, the raising of certain critical questions may escape the net of strict logical analysis. Second, recognizing who is being educated in a college critical thinking course, and why, help explain why certain critical questions fail to be raised.

Notes

1. Harvey Siegel, *Educating Reason* (New York: Routledge, 1988), 18–28, describing Ennis's theory of critical thinking.

2. Ibid., 5–10, describing Paul's theory of critical thinking.

3. Ibid. See also Harvey Siegel, "Why Be Rational? On Thinking Critically about Critical Thinking," in *Philosophy of Education 1989: Proceedings of the Forty-fifth Annual Meeting of The Philosophy of Education Society*, ed. Ralph Page (Normal, Ill.: Philosophy of Education Society, 1990), 392–401.

4. Maxine Greene, "The Humanities and Emancipatory Possibility" in *The Hidden Curriculum and Moral Education*, ed. Henry Giroux and David Purpel (Berkeley: McCutchan, 1983), 384–402 (hereafter cited as *Hidden Curriculum*).

5. David Purpel and Kevin Ryan, "It Comes With the Territory: The Inevitability of Moral Education in the Schools" in *Hidden Curriculum*, 267–75.

6. Michael Apple, "Is the New Technology Part of the Solution or Part of the Problem in Education?" in *Teachers and Texts* (New York: Routledge and Kegan Paul, 1986). See also Michael Apple and Nancy King, "What Do Schools Teach?" in *Hidden Curriculum*, 82–99.

7. Henry A. Giroux, *Teachers as Intellectuals* (Granby, Mass.: Bergin and Garvey, 1988).

8. Paulo Freire, *Pedagogy of the Oppressed*, trans. Myra Bergman Ramos (New York: Herder and Herder, 1970).

9. Ibid., 58.

10. Siegel, Educating Reason, 60–61.

11. David Kelley, *The Art of Reasoning* (New York: Norton, 1988).

12. Ibid., 1.

13. Ibid.

14. Ibid.

15. Ibid., 3.

16. Ibid.

17. Friedrich Pollock, "Empirical Research into Public Opinion" in *Critical Sociology* ed. Paul Connerton (New York: Penguin Books, 1976), 229.

18. Ibid.

19. Howard Kahane, *Logic and Contemporary Rhetoric*, 5th ed. (Belmont, Calif.: Wadsworth, 1988).

20. Ibid., xv.

21. Ibid., xiii.

22. Ibid., xv.

23. Ibid., 216.

24. Ibid., 275.

25. Ibid.

26. Stephen Toulmin, Richard Rieke and Allan Janik, *An Introduction to Reasoning*, 4.

27. Ibid., 5.

28. Ibid.

29. Svi Shapiro, "Education and the Unequal Society: The Quest for Moral 'Excellence'" in *Schools and Meaning*, ed. David E. Purpel and Svi Shapiro (Lanham, Md.: University Press of America, 1985), 27–49.

30. Nicos Poulantzas, *Classes in Contemporary Capitalism* (London: New Left Books, 1975), 258; quoted in Shapiro, "Education and the Unequal Society," 34.

31. Ibid.

32. Ibid., 33.

33. Ibid.

34. Maxine Greene, "Curriculum and Consciousness" in *Hidden Curriculum*, 169.

35. Terry Eagleton, *Literary Theory* (Minneapolis: University of Minnesota Press, 1983), 45.

36. Greene, "Curriculum and Consciousness," 169.

37. Jean-Paul Sartre, *Literature and Existentialism*, 3rd ed. (New York: Citadel Press, 1965), 45; quoted in Greene, "Curriculum and Consciousness," 170.

38. Sheryl Chandler, "I Won't Vote for Gantt," *The Charlotte Observer*, 15 July 1990.

39. Henry A. Giroux and Roger I. Simon, "Schooling, Popular Culture, and a Pedagogy of Possibility" in *Popular Culture, Schooling and Everyday Life*, ed. Henry Giroux, Roger Simon et al. (Granby, Mass.: Bergin and Garvey, 1989), 219–53.

13

Critical Thinking Beyond Reasoning: Restoring Virtue to Thought[1]

Thomas H. Warren

Introduction

There is something fundamentally wrong with the "critical thinking" (CT) movement that has gained so much momentum in American education over the last decade. In this essay I shall argue (1) that the general content of CT pedagogy is not truly centered on human *thinking* at all, but on some *other* vital, but radically different, mental faculty that might better be called "reasoning;" and (2) that the development of the capacity for true thinking, and *not* merely reasoning, is profoundly important and may even be the crucial condition for the development of individual moral consciousness. Thus, the so-called CT movement, while intending in part to develop moral insight or knowledge, may actually be self-restricting in this regard.

In distinguishing thinking from reasoning, this essay endeavors to restore virtue to the activity of thinking, virtue in the sense of essential nature, as well as in the sense of moral worth.

Reasoning vs. Thinking

In developing the distinction between "reasoning" and "thinking" one might first consider the etymology of the two terms. (I am consulting the *American Heritage Dictionary of the English Language*). While acknowledging some lexical commonality, it is apparent that the two have radically different semantic origins. "To reason" means primarily "to fit together," and this involves primarily the skills of rationality (logic) and calculation (e.g., quantitative analysis, argumentation, conceptual analysis, fallacy recognition, syllogistic reasoning, symbolic logic, statistics, "information processing," and so on).

"Thinking," on the other hand, is characterized essentially by reflection, "ponderment," or "feeling." Thinking involves the activities of wonderment and perplexity. *Reasoning is bent on measuring; thinking is a quest for meaning.* The impulse behind reasoning is "how much?" and "does it follow?" The impulse behind thinking is "why?" (as justification) and "what is the significance?" Reasoning "counts"; thinking "contemplates." Reasoning is strict reckoning; thinking is "feeling," not, obviously, in the physical sense, but in the sense of having "impressions" or intuitions. Finally (and most curiously), thinking is "thanking," about which more will be said at the end of the essay.

In her *Life of the Mind: Thinking,*[2] Hannah Arendt sheds further light on the distinction I am making between thinking and reasoning. Following Kant, Arendt recognizes "two altogether different mental activities, thinking and knowing, and two altogether different concerns, meaning in the first category, and cognition in the second."[3] She writes that one of the greatest "metaphysical fallacies" is to confuse the "'urgent need' to think and the 'desire to know.'"[4] For Arendt the faculty of knowing or cognition is motivated by the desire for *truth,* "which is located in the evidence of the senses." "But," she goes on,

> that is by no means the case with meaning and the faculty of thought, which searches for it; the latter does not ask what something is or whether it exists at all—its existence is always taken for granted—*but what it means for it to be.*[5]

It seems clear that my notion of reasoning resides principally in the activities of knowing, cognition, and truth-fixing that Arendt describes.

The difference I have in mind (between thinking and reasoning) appears to be the very one elaborated in the upper part of Plato's "Divided Line," namely, the difference between "Level C" *dianoia* (mathematical or other analytical understanding, or truth), and "Level D" *noesis* (thinking or intuition guided by the method of dialectic). My own formulation is to identify the content of *dianoia* as "reasoning," and the content of *noesis* as "thinking."[6]

The primary trouble with the CT pedagogy is *that its scope is almost entirely limited to "Level C" reasoning, logical, or truth-fixing skills to the exclusion of the profoundly important activity of thinking ("Level D")*—a "thinking" that both Arendt and I comprehend as the human quest for meaning and its characteristics of wonderment, contemplation, and reflection.

I wish next to develop further this *noetic* concept of thinking and to show how several key characteristics of that concept are at variance with, or ignored by, various influential writers currently involved in the CT movement.

Thinking is Non-Utilitarian. Arendt writes that thinking implies "withdrawal from the world," and that it is "good for nothing in the ordinary course of human affairs."[7] She contends that this non-useful or purposeless quality of thinking is the central characteristic of Socratic thought: "The first thing that strikes us in Plato's Socratic dialogues is that they are all aporetic. The argument either leads nowhere or goes around in circles."[8] She writes that there is no more of a practical answer to the question "Why do we think?" than there is an answer to the question "Why do we live?" Or to Heidegger's question "Why is there anything, and not, rather, nothing?" She further acknowledges Heidegger who wrote:

> Thinking does not bring knowledge as to the sciences. Thinking does not produce usable practical wisdom. Thinking does not solve the riddles of the universe. Thinking does not endow us directly with the power to act.[9]

This functionally nonpurposeful conception of thinking is in sharp contrast to the views of various prominent writers on the subject of critical thinking. Robert H. Ennis, for example, has defined critical thinking as "reasonable reflective thinking that is focused on deciding what to believe or do."[10] For John McPeck, critical thinking is an essentially "epistemological" enterprise that entails the "understanding of various kinds of reasons [which] involves understanding complex meanings of field-dependent concepts and evidence."[11] In McPeck's "open textured" view of CT the concern is not so much with logical validity as it is "about the truth of the putative evidence."[12] According to my *noetic* theory of CT, issues of conceptual "field dependency" and evidence are not vital. Again, my (and Arendt's) conception is thoroughly incompatible with Michael Scriven's contention that critical thinking is essential for "survival" in a world in which "the wrong decision can mean injury or long term commitment to a disastrous form of life such as addiction, or criminality or resented parenthood."[13]

Socrates is an Ideal Thinker. In Socrates we may identify three striking features of thinking:

a. Thinking is inherently sociable, or convivial. Socrates, the gadfly, was *compelled* to arouse the activity of thinking in others, an activity without which "life is not worth living." This compulsion is suggestive of "being in love" wherein lovers are driven to share with others their joy. It does not seem to me that the activity of reasoning or rationality possesses this convivial power.

b.   The thinker does not claim knowledge. Here, Socrates the "midwife" recognizes he is sterile (of knowledge) and can at best merely deliver others of their thoughts or wonderments.

c.   Thinking is not teachable. It is doubtful (contra Robert Ennis, Harvey Siegel, and most other CT theorists) that there exists a body of thinking "skills and dispositions" that may be "taught." Socrates, the "stingray," says in the *Meno* (and this is a superb example of the nature of thinking):

> As for myself, if the stingray paralyzes others only through being paralyzed itself, then the comparison [to myself] is just....It isn't that knowing the answers myself I perplex other people. The truth is rather that I infect them also with the perplexity I feel myself.[14]

"Perplexity" (as a hallmark of thinking) is not teachable.

Thinking is Always "Out of Order". As Arendt puts it, genuine thinking

> interrupts any doing, any ordinary activities no matter what they happen to be. All thinking demands a *stop* and think....It is indeed as though thinking paralyzes me in much the same way as an excess of consciousness may paralyze the automatism of my bodily functions....This striking observation...insists on an antagonism between being and thinking which we can trace back to Plato's famous saying that only the philosopher's [i.e., thinker's] body...still inhabits the city of men, as though by thinking, men removed themselves from the world of the living.[15]

Thus, the activity of thinking must be seen as inherently "radical" and even dangerous—witness the careers of thinking's most famous practitioners, e.g., Socrates, Christ, or Gandhi (as well as note the absolute appropriateness of the military motto, "Yours is not to 'reason' why, yours is but to do and die"). I have yet to see this "disobedient" aspect of thinking adequately dealt with in the CT literature.

Thinking is Inherently "Critical". Insofar as the quality of criticism arises out of a sense of *crisis*, or the impulse to get to the *crux* of the matter, then, thinking is necessarily critical. One can no more conceive of "uncritical" thinking than one can conceive of "unmeasured" harmony, or "unmoral" responsibility. This redundancy does not appear to obtain in the case of "critical reasoning."

Thinking is Dialectical. Thinking is a "soundless dialogue" ultimately between "you and yourself," but does not exclude a dialogue between yourself and others. In pursuit of essential Reality it is a dialogue fundamentally between your *conscious* ego and your *conscience.* Writes Arendt: "It is this duality of myself with myself that makes thinking a true activity, in which I am both the one who asks and the one who answers."[16]

Thinking Abhors Contradiction. Arendt writes that "the dialogue of thought can be carried out only between friends, and its basic criterion, its supreme law, as it were, says: 'Do not contradict yourself.'"[17] It would appear that on this point—contradiction—thinking and reasoning surely intersect.

Thinking is the Aspiration of Eros. Arendt explains that *eros*, or love, can be described as a need: "It desires what it has not." Thinking's quest for meaning is the same as love's quest. Furthermore, "because thought's quest is a kind of desirous love, the objects of thinking can only be lovable things—beauty, wisdom, justice, and so on."[18] More will be said about this connection shortly.

Thinking is not "Strong Sense" CT. Obviously Richard Paul's "strong sense" CT abilities are extremely important traits, viz., overcoming egocenteredness, striving for empathy, recognizing different frames of reference, sensitivity to the universalization of one's principles, fairmindedness, and the willingness to live one's principles.[19] Any conscientious teacher knows well the indispensable value of these intellectual qualities and also knows how sorely deficient all of us— students and teachers—are in understanding and practicing them.

At the same time, however, I am not convinced that teaching these general intellectual qualities, these "passions for accuracy, clarity, and fairmindedness" (as Paul puts it), will *in itself* fire the passion of thinking as I have construed it. Analogously, mastering the skills and dispositions of good writing does not necessarily make a *poet*; nor does possessing all the attributes of good scholarship and intellectual and theoretical rigor necessarily produce a scientist, and so on.

Thinking and Moral Consciousness

One of the most startling implications of my inquiry into the virtue of thinking is the recognition of the quite novel possibility that moral knowledge and behavior are an *exclusive property of human thinking* (and *not* some other mental faculty such as reasoning, believing, willing, judging, etc.).

In her *Eichmann in Jerusalem*[20] Arendt concluded that Adolf Eichmann (one of the convicted WWII Nazi war criminals) "was neither demonic nor monstrous." She observed that "it was not stupidity but *thoughtlessness*" that explained Eichmann's murderous acts.[21] (It was from this insight that she developed her well known thesis of the "banality of evil"). In her *Thinking* she poses this provocative question:

> Might the problem of good and evil, our faculty of telling right from wrong, be connected with our faculty of thought? To be sure, not in the sense that thinking would ever be able to produce the good deed as a result, as though 'virtue could be taught'...[but in the sense that] this activity could be among the conditions that make men abstain from evil doing or even actually 'condition' them against it?[22]

I would like to set forth my interpretation of Arendt's idea regarding this special relationship between thinking and moral insight and conduct.

1. It is apparent that our consideration here is more with the process of thinking, or the activity itself, rather than the epistemological "objects" of thinking.
2. Thinking, as a quest for meaning, is a "need" expressed in terms of *eros* ("it desires what it has not"). As noted earlier, thinking as desirous love can pursue only lovable things, such as beauty or goodness (and here is thinking's epistemic aspect). Notes Arendt:

> Ugliness and evil are almost by definition excluded from the thinking concern....If thinking dissolves positive concepts into their original meaning, then the same process must dissolve these 'negative' concepts into their original meaninglessness, i.e., *nothing* for the thinking ego. That is why Socrates believed no one could do evil voluntarily—because of, as we would say, its ontological status: it consists in an absence, in something that is not.[23]

A practical illustration of thinking's "positive" ontological status may be offered here. Consider the concept of an absolutely perfect "straight line" versus the notion of an absolutely perfect "crooked line." The thinker will immediately discern that while it is possible to comprehend a notion of an "absolutely perfect 'straight line,'" it is not possible to comprehend, however far one may stretch the imagination, a notion of an "absolutely perfect 'crooked line.'" The moral implications for the non-ontological status of "evil" should be apparent here. Much of Plato's project, in the Republic, for example, was devoted to clarifying this point.

Crucial here is the somewhat psychological content of the thinking quest or impulse. Socratic eros is a yearning for self-fulfillment, completion, wholeness—in a word, meaning: "ugliness and evil are almost by definition excluded from the thinking concern." Heidegger looks at this notion of thinking's "need" as though it were some sort of gravitational "draw": "Whenever man is properly drawing that way, he is thinking...All through his life and right into his death, Socrates did nothing else than place himself in this draft, this current, and maintain himself in it."24

3. The quality of *wholeness* mentioned above is intrinsic to the moral concept we are examining. Consider the Socratic injunction: "Better to be wronged than to do wrong." The truth of this doctrine rests not so much on rational analysis as it does on the elementary psychological/philosophical grasp indicated earlier in our discussion of the dialectical nature of thinking. Arendt put it well:

> If you want to think you must see to it that the two [i.e., the conscious ego and the conscience] who carry on the dialogue be in good shape, that the partners be *friends*. The partner that comes to life when you are alert and alone is the only one from whom you can never get away—except by ceasing to think. It is better to suffer wrong than to do wrong, because you can remain the friend of the suffered; but who would want to be the friend of and have to live together with a murderer? Not even another murderer.25

The "wholeness" here involves a unity or conviviality between the self's ego and the self's conscience.

4. Thinking is "thanking." In the etymology of "to think" we see a reference to "to thank." While I am by no means sure of my understanding of this odd connection, the following reflections may be

suggestive: Is it possible that when one thinks one is simultaneously expressing gratitude, or an acknowledgment, as one experiences, say, in some Socratic way, the joy or exhilaration of "erotic" self-unification? Heidegger expressed something similar:

> How can we give thanks for this endowment, the gift of being able to think what is most thought-provoking, more fittingly than by giving thought to the most thought-provoking? The supreme thanks, then, would be thinking? And the pro-foundest thanklessness, thoughtlessness?...Pure thanks is...that we simply think—think what is really and solely given, what is there to be thought.[26]

Conclusion

If my position is right, then those of us involved in the "Critical Thinking" movement must take care to distinguish between two radi-cally different mental activities: reasoning and thinking. I have argued that almost all of the material currently being taught under the heading of "critical thinking" should, more authentically, be deliberately conceived as "critical reasoning," "informal logic," "right reasoning," or the like. I have urged that the activity of thinking is a qualitatively different (than reasoning) mental experience, particularly in its unique connection to moral consciousness.[27]

With respect to critical reasoning, while I certainly do support the establishment of "CT" courses "across the curricula," a somewhat digressionary note of caution seems appropriate: It seems to me that the CT movement, this great wave of rational analysis that is sweeping the country, may be in large measure—consciously on the part of the public, and not-so-consciously on the part of the educators—a response to a world of ever-increasing technological, quantitative, and physical com-plexity and sophistication. Indeed, if the general scientific thrust of education beginning in the 1960s was a response to the advent of "Sputnik," then similarly may we not see the Critical Thinking movement as a response to a growing (primarily) Japanese technological superiority?

One needs only, for example, to review a recent *U.S. News & World Report's* feature article, "The Brain Battle," for evidence of my claim.[28] The article is a description of how "America's standing as the world's top economic power is in peril," and how the "schools are catching much of the blame." While the article does not directly refer to a need for greater critical reasoning abilities in our students, it is implied. One educational "expert" captured the spirit of the "battle" (and the gist of the article): "Fifty-five percent of America's jobs involve information processing. If we don't have good solid skills in language, geography, math and science, we'll be at a severe disadvantage."

My concern is simply this: To whatever extent the CT movement, as understood and funded by the general public, is primarily a drive to help America regain the "cutting edge" in the world economic market, then American education is rapidly losing its moral nerve and thereby defaults not only on its responsibility to engender true critical thinking but debases the ideal of critical thinking as well.

Alternatively, we must, if this essay's argument is correct, deliberately re-prepare the grounds for *thinking* in our classrooms and communities. We must construct the conditions for genuine thinking if we as educators are truly intent on developing moral character in our students.

We need *practica* in the virtue of thinking (as well as reasoning). Of course, "teaching" thinking, that is igniting the kind of meaning-wonderment, contemplation, and self-transcendence described above, is exceedingly difficult. It is extraordinarily difficult (if possible at all) in the classroom to make good on the claim that "the unexamined life is not worth living." Yet, does not Socrates' challenge *remain* as our most fundamental challenge?

Notes

1. This title was inspired by John McPeck's article titled "Critical Thinking Without Logic: Restoring Dignity to Information," in *Philosophy of Education 1981*, ed. Daniel DeNicola (Normal, Ill.: Philosophy of Education Society, 1982).

2. Hannah Arendt, *The Life of the Mind: Thinking* (New York: Harcourt Brace Jovanovich, 1977).

3. Ibid., p. 14.

4. Ibid., p. 15.

5. Ibid., p. 57.

6. I am referring to the *Republic*, trans. R. M. Cornford. For a useful additional comparison of the two terms, see F. E. Peters, *Greek Philosophical Terms* (New York: New York University Press, 1967).

7. Arendt, p. 88.

8. Ibid., p. 169.

9. Ibid., p. xiii.

10. See Robert H. Ennis, "Goals for a Critical-Thinking/Reasoning Curriculum," a paper handed out at the Fourth International Conference on Critical Thinking and Education Reform, Sonoma State University, Rohnert Park, California, August, 1986.

11. McPeck, p. 220.

12. Ibid., p. 223. The concept of "open texture" (which I believe McPeck is recommending) is set forth in Friedrich Waismann's "Verifiability," in *Logic and Language*, ed. Anthony Flew (Garden City, N.Y.: Doubleday and Company, 1965), p. 122.

13. Quoted in Richard Paul's "Critical Thinking and the Critical Person," p. 10, a paper presented at the Fourth International Critical Thinking Conference on Critical Thinking and Education Reform, Sonoma State University, Rohnert Park, California, August, 1986.

14. Plato, Meno, 80c.

15. Arendt, pp. 78–79.

16. Ibid., p. 185.

17. Ibid., p. 189.

18. Ibid., p. 179.

19. Paul.

20. Hannah Arendt, *Eichmann in Jerusalem* (New York: Penguin Books, 1965).

21. Arendt, *Thinking*, p. 4.

22. Ibid., p. 5.

23. Ibid., p. 179.

24. Martin Heidegger, *What Is Called Thinking?*, trans. J. Glenn Gray (New York: Harper & Row, 1968), p. 17.

25. Arendt, *Thinking*, p. 188.

26. Heidegger, p. 143.

27. Two contemporary moral philosophers have expressed views that share my doubts of a rationalistic and analytical basis for moral thought. See Alasdair MacIntyre, *After Virtue*, 2nd ed. (Notre Dame, Ind.: University of Notre

Dame Press, 1984); and, Bernard Williams, *Ethics and the Limits of Philosophy* (Cambridge, Mass.: Harvard University Press, 1985).

28. Lewis Lord et al., "The Brain Battle, " *U.S. News & World Report*, 19 Jan. 1987.

14

Is Critical Thinking a Technique,
or a Means of Enlightenment?

Lenore Langsdorf

Introduction

This paper proposes a theoretical basis for practicing and teaching
critical thinking as *both* "technique" and "means for enlightenment."
Since the current state of the art (as reflected in journal articles as well as
textbooks) seems to me more advanced in developing techniques, the
stress here is on "enlightenment." Thus, the ideas I explore are offered
as a contribution on the "basic theoretical underpinnings," which
Richard Paul recognizes are needed for "critical thinking in the 'strong'
sense."[1] This is to say that I will be proposing a theoretical basis for
understanding that conception of critical thinking as a means for
enlightenment. In order to do so, I will offer some thoughts on what
enlightenment might be, why certain features in our cultural history
have resulted in its atrophy, and how we might make a start toward
changing that situation.

The present paper has three parts. Part One presents the notion of
"instrumental reason" as a mode of reasoning quite different from
"judgment." The former is concerned with developing techniques for
achieving already-stipulated ends by utilizing already-given means. The
latter is concerned with an extended sense of reasoning, which examines
those means and ends in the light of human needs and goals. In
presenting this concept, I'll be relying on the work of Ian Angus, which is
situated at the juncture of phenomenology (as developed by Edmund
Husserl) and the Critical Theory developed by the Frankfurt School.[2] The
inadequacies of "instrumental reason" and the prospects of "judgment"
seem to me illustrated in Richard Paul's critique of any teaching of critical
thinking that would be the mere application of techniques, rather than the
cultivation of a "dialectical mode of analysis."

What I'm doing in Part One, then, is associating Angus's "instrumental reason" with Paul's "critical thinking in the 'weak' sense," and Angus's "judgment" with Paul's "critical thinking in the 'strong' sense." I hope that relating Paul's proposals to the phenomenological and Frankfurt School traditions in this way provides us with the beginnings of a theoretical basis for "strong sense" critical thinking.

In Part Two, I consider a question that seems to me comparatively neglected in Paul's work: why is it so difficult to reach the nonegocentric standpoint that is the starting point for the "dialectical mode of analysis" he advocates? Here and in Part Three, I rely on Paul Ricoeur's conception of "ego" as contrasted with "self" in proposing that we might be more successful in cultivating a non-egocentric standpoint if we have some understanding of egocentricity as an inevitable, but transcendable, starting point.[3] In Part Two, I suggest that an insistently pervasive technology—television—suppresses a capacity—imagination—that is crucial to any attempt to move beyond "ego" to "self." A form-and-content distinction is crucial to this suggestion: if the portrayal given here is accurate, suppression of imagination occurs by virtue of television's very form, not only or even primarily because of its programming content.

In Part Three, I propose that another technology—the printed word, which does not share television's form—stimulates rather than suppresses imagination. Ricoeur's thesis that "ego" becomes "self" through involvement with "text," I suggest, provides "theoretical underpinnings" for a critical thinking that responds to Paul's critique, as well as to Angus's call for an undoing of the "reversal of enlightenment" brought about by universalized instrumental reason.

Part One: Instrumental Reason and Judgment

The expansion of techniques which is legitimized by instrumental reason turns the *objects* of the life-world into mere residues...while it reduces the *subject* to an untheorized plurality of ends— instrumental reason results in world alienation and self-alienation. This systematic crisis involves a new situation for philosophy.[5]

I take it to be self-evident that virtually all teachers of critical thinking want their teaching to have a global 'Socratic' effect, making some significant inroads into the everyday reasoning of the student, enhancing to some degree that healthy, practical, and skilled skepticism one naturally and rightly associates with the rational person.[6]

In this section, I propose that the prevalence of "instrumental reason," as identified in Ian Angus's critique, is one of the powerful factors in our culture that work against our efforts at having, in our teaching of critical thinking, the "global 'Socratic' effect" on our students that Richard Paul identifies. This is to say that our students come equipped with instrumental reason, since it is endemic to our culture, and that this form of reason is inimical to critical thinking.

Angus's critique identifies instrumental reason as the type of reasoning that is limited to determining appropriate means for achieving a particular end. What it does not do is consider the appropriateness of either means or ends to larger contexts, such as an individual's or society's everyday or major life decisions.[6] His term for the type of reasoning that would take up that larger—indeed, "global"—task is "judgment." In exploring both these conceptions of reasoning, Angus is expanding upon work on the nature of reason done from the very perspective of the Critical Theory developed by the Frankfurt School, in that he adds the "self-reflective and critical character of phenomenology," and, in particular, Husserl's emphasis upon the "constitution of theoretical objectivities" (such as the elements of a logical system), in order to develop a theoretical basis that would enable us to "renew the promise of enlightenment."[7]

This renewal is needed, according to Angus's account, because of an historical paradox: the science and technology that earlier philosophers and scientists expected would liberate humanity from the arbitrariness and harshness of nature, now appear to many as replacements for the domination practiced prior to the rise of science in the Enlightenment by the "mythico-religious tradition."[8] This has occurred, he argues, as the science develped by Bacon, Descartes, and Galileo required a "transformation from the Classical question 'why' things are to the modern 'how'."[9] Angus retains both questions within his own analysis, although my focus here is on just one: how does this "reversal of enlightenment" occur?[10] For considering Angus's analysis together with Paul's suggests that the critical thinking courses that many philosophy departments now find are their most popular offerings are training students in instrumental reason (at most), rather than cultivating that "Socratic" and "global" form of reasoning that Angus calls judgment.

We are teaching instrumental reason rather than judgment, I suggest, insofar as we use what Paul calls the "standard modes of teaching critical thinking," based on "a fundamental and questionable assumption": that it can be taught as a "battery of technical skills" to be "mastered" and applied (as means to an end) without asking any "why" questions concerning the context in which the student (subject) or issue (object) is embedded.[11] On this model, Paul goes on to say, arguments are encountered "atomically," rather than as "networks" delineating "world views." In effect, what we are doing in this mode of teaching critical thinking is taking the student, who comes to us more-or-less well equipped by our culture with instrumental reason, and working to instill techniques that exercise that equipment.

Paul calls this "critical thinking in the 'weak' sense," and gives us a succinct summary of its usual results. One likelihood is "'sophistry'": the student "learns to use technical concepts and techniques to maintain his most deep-seated prejudices and irrational habits of thought." The alternative is "'dismissal'"—outright rejection of rational modes of thought "in favor of some suggested alternative—"feeling,' 'intuition,' 'faith,' or 'higher consciousness.'"[12] Both of these are a long way from the goals of teaching critical thinking that are cited at the start of this section, and there are a variety of responses we can give to this disjuncture between goals and results. I will sketch Angus's response, and then Paul's, and then suggest two inadequacies in the latter that may be remedied by incorporating elements of the former.

Angus finds that instrumental reason's restriction to the application of given means—such as logical systems—to given ends is a contribution to what Husserl called "the crisis of Western humanity [which] rests on a conception of reason in which formalization held sway such that the genuine advances by special sciences and formal logic are severed from philosophical enlightenment."[13] Husserl's own response to that situation was to show that formalizations derive from (in his words, are "founded in") material conditions (in his words, again, the "lifeworld").[14]

This phenomenological description of the relation between intellectual and everyday life (e.g., logic and the lifeworld) is incorporated into Angus's theory of "judgment" when he argues that using logical structures in a normative manner within the whole of our experience does not depend upon any "cosmological intuition," or transcendent "organizing principle," or "traditional authority" of the sort associated with "mythico-religious worldviews" that have been rather discredited, since the onset of the Age of Science, as sources of epistemological justification or ontological validation.[15] Rather, the justification for using logic normatively has its source in evidence that results from a phenomenological analysis of the lifeworld:

> Husserl's transcendental logic sets itself the task of delineating the range and legitimate objects of traditional logic through a regressive analysis into the 'sense' of the formalizing abstraction that is at its [logic's] root, and teleological inquiry into the 'truth' with which formalizing abstractions can judge about individuals.[16]

For Angus as well as Husserl, the "'sense'" found in this regressive analysis is that the formal is manifest, as inherent modes of structure and order, in the material. In other words: Husserl's work on logic and the lifeworld shows that the latter displays the former; that the form of our reasoning is implicit in that content. Thus, his "redirection of philosophy [which] take[s] the whole of the experienced lifeworld into thought" is a redescription of practice as always already informed by theory.[17]

If we accept Husserl's demonstration that "formalism is not self-enclosed, but rests on presuppositions of sense and teleology of truth in the lifeworld," we need not accept the "reduction of human action to technique."[18] Angus takes Husserl's demonstration of logic as embedded within experience as the basis for his claim that insofar as logic is justifiably (rather than arbitrarily or dogmatically) applicable to theorizing in general, we are justified in extending our reasoning beyond the limitations of instrumental reason; he calls this expanded conception "judgment." He goes on to develop this broader notion of reasoning as including rational consideration of the *contexts* from which issues and arguments arise and to which techniques apply.

Identifying contextualized objects as the recipients of technical action implies two further differences between instrumental reason and judgment. First, *ends* can now be thematized as distinct from, and perhaps problematically related to, *objects*. Also, judgment, in reflecting upon objects within their contexts, discovers that "it is the context from which technical ends stand out that establishes the *possibility* of a *plurality* of ends" that are "formulated from" their contexts and "cannot be conceived as existing prior to the formation process."[19]

Reasoning, understood as judgment, is thus revealed as an activity with two intrinsic and usually unnoticed dimensions. It thematizes objects in the lifeworld as *presentations* of a particular individual's "immediate experience," and it thematizes them also as *representations*, informed by theory. In other words, this conception of reasoning understands our reasoning as intrinsically incorporating both presupposed logical systems (formalization) and means-ends correlations that are supplied by cultural and individual goals, needs, and values—which is to say that they are inevitably egocentric and sociocentric. In contrast to instrumental reason, judgment thematizes those unnoticed presupposi- tions *within* its own activity, as well as reasoning *about* the objects that are instrumental reason's sole interest. In Angus's words,

> Both sides of this theory/life-world relationship are involved in judgment. In order to overcome the crisis of reason judgment must be both representative and presentational....The tradition of thought cannot be taken to be exhaustive; we must return to the generating experiences from which thought emerges. Judgment is an inter-relationship of immediacy andcritique...[20]

The contrast between instrumental reason and judgment deepens when we notice that judgment is intrinsically bound to a judging process, carried out by a judging *self* who is capable of actualizing a spectrum of possible perspectives on judged subject matter, and is also capable of reflecting upon that process. Cultivating or developing these capacities is then a force for undoing the "reversal of enlightenment" brought about by instrumental reason's limitation to formalizations, uncon- nected to the lifeworld, and technique, connected only to means-end deliberations.

A last, rather lengthy quotation from Angus stresses the integra- tion of self, process, object, and reflection in his notion of judgment, in a way that enables us to see the explicit connection between his proposal and Paul's:

> Judgment makes the absent present....The compatibility or con- tradictoriness of representations which are gathered from varying perspectives must be considered; what is at issue is not the accuracy of each one in isolation but the degree to which they can be combined into a comprehensive judgment. This involves a dual reflection: on the object as it emerges and...on the subject which must harmonize, or comprehend the dissonance of, represen- tations....These considerations culminate in an individual judg- ment, a universalizing claim embedded in a singular statement about the public object. This claim can be contested—its journey around the object is not the only possible one...similarly...the entirety of the self...is open to constitution in judgment....The constitution of self and world by judgments is never exhausted by existing judgments. It remains a particularlization of an unlimited possibility of constituting judgments....*Judgment is critical thinking;*

it proceeds as critique...both inside and outside received representations. Actual judgments hand down the public realm, yet critical thought measures its limitations by incorporating new elements derived from the present and forming a new individual judgment....There is no method for critique...[it] does not proceed arbitrarily, but it cannot be fixed into a method.[21]

This reconception of our reasoning ability offers a theoretical basis for Richard Paul's "alternative view" of critical thinking.

The "'strong' sense" of critical thinking that Paul has been developing abandons atomic skills, arguments, and issues in favor of comprehending any technique as only one among "a more complex set of actual or possible moves" that enable us to "organize or conceptualize the world, and our place in it, in somewhat different terms than others do."[22] Rather than remaining within the limitation of any *actual* argument or issue, then, Paul would relocate the reasoning process to a realm of *possible* personal and social worldviews, actions, and judgments. He stresses that it is only when we (both students and teachers) come to recognize that any

given argument reflects, or if justified would serve, a *given* interest that we can, by *imaginatively* entertaining a competing interest, construct an opposing pointof view and so an opposing argument or set of arguments. It is by developing both arguments dialectically that we come to recognize their strengths and weaknesses.[23]

"Arguments," as he goes on to say, "are not things-in-themselves"; rather, they are actual or possible presentations of factual or imagined contexts, from actual or imagined perspectives (worldviews).

The example Paul provides of how to teach "critical thinking in the 'strong' sense" seems to me to respond, in some ways, to the need to move from the actual to the possible; from a "given" situation or arguments to "imagined" alternatives. Two films that present radically different sets of "facts" in portraying one situation—U.S. involvement in Central America—do provide a demonstration of Paul's recognition that "the media" typically present "a profoundly nationalistic bias," and that any "'ego' is identified in part with the national 'ego.'"[24] Exploration of that situation can be the first step toward recognizing that our usual means of reasoning—i.e., instrumental reason—do not go beyond the "given interest" represented in any "given argument." We can then go on to make that interest itself explicit, to "imaginatively construct" others, and to develop our considerations of these alternatives in a dialectical manner.

There are two aspects of the notion of judgment that are not paralleled in Paul's proposal, however. My suggestion that they be added is offered on the basis of agreeing with the problems and dangers (e.g., "sophistry" and "dismissal") he identifies and so proposing additional "theoretical underpinning" for effective teaching of "critical thinking in the 'strong' sense."

The first aspect of judgment that I would add to Paul's procedure is suggested by the following remark, which occurs when he gives us "some basic theoretical underpinnings for a 'strong sense' approach":

> Reasoning is an essential and defining operation presupposed by all human acts. To reason is to make use of elements in a logical system to generate conclusions.[25]

But if we do not inquire into what appears here to be the merely "given" character of "a logical system," we limit ourselves to the question of "how" (do I apply these "elements") and exclude the question of "why" (they should be applied). This allows a powerful feature of instrumental reason to remain within our reasoning.

We need, therefore, to do some phenomenological analysis in order to discover just what logical elements are implicit in our reasoning. Although Husserl's analysis of formal systems can serve as a model for this activity, I suggest that actually carrying out this analysis in classroom practice is preferable for theoretical and pedagogical, as well as ethical, reasons. The theoretical and pedagogical advantages derive from our ability to justify the "use of elements of a logical system" on the basis of identifying them as intrinsic structures of actual arguments— rather than as independent, abstract rules, which the critical thinking teacher prescribes in much the same way that the medical doctor prescribes drugs for an illness. The ethical aspect involves our ability to show *why* "elements in a logical system" *should* apply to our arguments and actions. For neglecting to justify our prescriptions places us in the rather paradoxical position of saying to our students: "If you want to be a critical thinker, do exactly as I say."

The second aspect of judgment that I would add to Paul's proposal is suggested by this mention of his own context:

> I teach in the United States....[T]he media here as everywhere reflects, and the students have typically internalized, a profoundly

'nationalistic' bias.…[T]heir 'ego' is identified in part with the national 'ego,' nevertheless they are not…incapable of beginning the process of systematically questioning it.26

Despite the phrase "as everywhere" in this remark, Paul's proposal is often read as critical of our media in particular; and even, as claiming that American students and American culture in general are more nationalistic than others. This seems to me a misreading of his proposal, which may be encouraged by a lack of explicit attention to the question of whether he is talking about reasoning in general or as it is present in his particular situation. The principle of charity seems appropriate here, for the overall context of his work suggests that he is talking about the nature of reasoning itself, and how to cultivate improvements to it, rather than about any particular manifestation.

Presentation (as contrasted to representation) is the aspect of Angus's conception of judgment, which would be helpful here in two ways. First, it provides us with a theoretical (i.e., ideal) point from which to recognize that the "constitution of self and world by judgment is never exhausted by *existing* judgments."27 Exploring the evidence for this feature of judgment (as provided by our own biographies and in fiction) allows us to recognize that *any* worldview is intrinsically—by virtue of the very nature of human reasoning—a "particularization [an *actual* instance] of an unlimited *possibility* of constituting judgments."28 We can thereby avoid getting sidetracked into any implication that our own reasoning is being singled out as particularly or especially deficient; e.g., that the media in our society is especially biased, or that a particular individual has a psychological deficiency or social disadvantage that interferes with reasoning.

The second way in which the shift from a focus on individual cases to a concern with general structures is helpful involves understanding how it is that we can "internalize" bias without becoming "incapable of the process of systematically questioning." The feature of human being which allows this to occur, I suggest, is the theoretical reciprocity of perspectives that phenomenological analysis of the life world confirms. In practice, this is often limited; one way to understand what critical thinking teaching is about, I suggest, is as the cultivation of that capacity for reciprocity. Paul refers to this as the necessity of moving from an egocentric and sociocentric worldview to a dialectical one and notes that he is "beginning" on the "development of 'strong sense' approaches" to teaching critical thinking on the dialectical mode.29

One of the "theoretical underpinnings" for those approaches (which also need development, I suggest) is the effect of the media on our capacity to move from the egocentric standpoints from which human beings inevitably begin. In the following two sections, then, I will consider the ways in which two of the media—television and the printed word—may influence our capacity for moving from egocentricity toward a more public—dialogical or dialectical—position in which we are more capable of "systematic questioning."

Part Two: Television and Imagination

> Critical thinking is possible only where the standpoints of all others are open to inspection. Hence, critical thinking while still a solitary business has not cut itself off from 'all others.'...[By] force of *imagination*, it makes the others present and thus moves potentially into a space which is public, open to all sides....To think with the enlarged mentality —that means you *train your imagination to go visiting*...[30]

> If you decide to watch television, then there's no choice but to accept the stream of electronic images as it comes. The first effect of this is to create a passive mental attitude....Thinking only gets in the way.   There is a second difficulty.   Television information seems to be received more in the unconscious than the conscious regions of the mind....The *image doesn't exist in the world*, and so cannot be observed as you would another person....Perhaps this quality of nonexistence, at least in concrete worldly form, disqualifies this image information from being subject to conscious processes: *thinking, discernment, analysis*.[31]

My theme in this section can perhaps be best stated in hypothetical form: if, as Hannah Arendt claims, the 'force of imagination" is crucial to moving us from egocentricity; and if, as Jerry Mander asserts, television as a technology—i.e., in its very form, rather than by virtue of its *contents* (the programming)—suppresses our "power of forming a mental image of something not present to the senses or never before wholly perceived in reality" (which is a dictionary definition of "imagination"), *then* we have a situation in which the most pervasive technology in most of our lives, television, works against the capacities for "imagination, discernment, [and] analysis" that are basic to thinking critically.

The "four arguments for the elimination of television" developed (albeit in a speculative and "nonscholarly" fashion) by Mander focus primarily on the "technology being used upon viewers" so that they—which is to say, we—can separate "technique from content" and examine the

> erroneous assumption that technologies are 'netural.' We have not learned to think of technology as having ideology built into its very form.[32]

By virtue of its *form*, Mander argues, television is

> less a communications or educational medium, as we wished to think of it, than an *instrument* that *plants images*—and does so in a way that allows for no cognition, no discernment, no notations upon the experience one is having.[33]

Before going on to consider Mander's claims, I want to discuss the role that imagination plays in Angus's and Paul's critiques. We can then consider Mander's claim that the *form* of television—television by virtue of its very technology—suppresses the development of imagination, and thus, suppresses our capacity to "go visiting" beyond egocentricity; i.e., exercise judgment in that "public space" where dialogical thinking occurs.[34]

In the course of discussing Hannah Arendt's remarks on imagination (quoted at the start of this section), Ian Angus indicates how imagination expands judgment beyond the limits of instrumental reason:

> The operation of representation is a function of the *imagination* in which the 'free play' of the mind is *not limited* by a definite concept. Kant describes the imagination as 'gathering together the manifold of intuition': it is not limited to *actual* presentations but consists in the combination and rearrangement of previous, present, and *anticipated* presentations. This imaginative reconstruction does not take place with reference to a pre-defined purpose but rather involves a relationship to an anticipated singular judgment of a particular which itself implies a universalization.[35]

There are three ways that imagination functions, then, which makes it essential to judgment: it "gathers" the contributions of our different senses; it gives us access to presentations that are actually absent, but potentially—as "anticipated"—present; and it enables us to transcend "reference" (delimited, "predefined" ends) by anticipating alternative possibilities. If we consider how the mind would function *without* these abilities, we have a close approximation to Angus's characterization of instrumental reason that limits us to actual techniques for means-end deliberation.

Richard Paul's discussion of the differences between critical thinking in the "strong" and "weak" senses suggests that these same three functions of imagination are necessary if the ego is to move beyond "atomic arguments" that are presented without any concern for context—i.e. either the individual subjects or the specific situations that give rise to those argument. "Strong sense critical thinking" recognizes that these arguments "are in fact a limited set of moves within a more complex set of actual or possible moves reflecting a variety of logically significant engagements in the world."[36] Since we can only evaluate the "strengths and weaknesses of the [particular case of] reasoning in relation to alternate *possibilities*," "critical thinking in the 'strong' sense" simply cannot be practiced within the limits of *actual* egocentric and sociocentric positions:

> It is only when we recognize…that a given argument reflects…a given interest that we can, by *imaginatively* entertaining a competing interest, construct an opposing point of view….[37]

Paul's "sample assignment" certainly uses the imagination in this way. For it is designed to go beyond the ego's all-too-comfortable starting point and resting place, by requiring the student to "view and analyze critically…two incompatible world views" and then "construct a dialogue between two of the most intelligent defenders of each of the points of view."[38] Rather than *apply* a technique to an *actual* argument, the student must *generate* and reflect upon *possible* arguments in a dialogical manner, and so transcend the egocentric worldview from which we all begin to reason.

However, the technology of television, as Mander portrays it, is one which encourages the ego to develop quite an opposite set of reactions. "Instead of training active attention," one of the researchers he cites says, "television seems to suppress it."[39] Instead of requiring the ego to *use* its experience and imagination to transcend egocentricity, this technology requires the ego to stay put—quite literally, as well as figuratively.

In contrast to imagination's function in "gathering" the contributions of all five senses, television engages only two, and even these are often sundered in a way quite alien to the presentations of pretechnological life.   For example: the visual and aural stimuli are often nonsynchronized, as when we see people walking on a distant hillside but hear their conversation as though they were next to us.

> The natural informational balance between aural and visual has been shattered. Now, information that you take in with visual sense cannot be used to modify or help process the information from the aural sense because they have been isolated from each other and reconstructed.[40]

This "isolation" and "reconstruction," moreover, are not a product of our own imagination, and so the process that accomplished them is not available to our reflection. If it were, we might train our imagination to thematize other ways in which it might have been done, other products that might have resulted. Instead, we have a hidden process, instigated by an unknown author, and resulting in a product quite isolated from our own actual lived experience. The "two semi-operative senses cannot benefit from the usual mix of information that human beings employ to deduce meaning from their surroundings."[41] The ego is instead reinforced in its isolation, supplied with "implanted images," all of which "arrive in sequence with equal validity."[42] It has passively received the product of a "process of...dissociation and restructuring...which automatically confines reality to itself."[43]

What this isolated ego has *not* done is interact, both actually and imaginatively, with pretechnologically processed lived experience— which is the real context of both logic and logic-users. In that interaction (and in situations such as Paul's sample assignment) the ego has opportunities to choose and develop alternative possibilities, and then, to discover and develop logical practices in order to judge competing claims to validity. "Knowledge is gained," as Mander points out, "by discerning change, by noting the event that is different from all others, by making distinctions and establishing patterns."[44] Our everyday lived experience provides opportunities for these activities, but they are absent in the processed experience (so to speak) provided by television.

Although I have limited this consideration of television to the effect of its form upon the development of imagination, and thus on the cultivation of our capacity to become critical thinkers, one remark by Mander about content is so directly relevant to critical thinking as to demand inclusion. In a study reporting on what sorts of knowledge viewers believe they gain from television programs, "practical knowledge and methods of problem-solving lead the list of knowledge reported acquired through these programs."[45]

Regardless of programming content, however, the very form of television deprives the ego of the conditions for attaining knowledge that are offered by actual and imagined experience. Nor will additional technology—e.g., recorders that allow us to replay fleeting images, or pause when we wish to reflect on them—repair this lack. For we have no part in the supply and mix of its perspectives, no contribution to the internal temporal structure of the finished product, and no ability to supplement it with alternative images of the same kind.

My consideration of television as a form has focused on its technology as one that intrinsically suppresses the conditions needed for an ego to develop the "imaginative force" needed to relocate from egocentricity to that dialogical "space" identified by Hannah Arendt as "public, open to all sides."[46] This should not be construed as any sort of generalized rejection of technology or even as agreement with Mander's assertion that television should be "eliminated." Rather, my interest in the effects of cultural factors on reasoning capacity is instigated by the conviction that our attempts to teach "strong sense" critical thinking stand a better chance of surviving those "moments of frustration and cynicism" that Paul mentions if we are aware of factors in the culture that operate at cross purposes to ours.[47] Correlatively, I believe that we are more apt to teach "strong sense" critical thinking effectively if we make use of factors in our culture that support the development of imagination, and thus, aid in cultivating our capacity to be critical thinkers. If Paul Ricoeur's thesis is correct, another technology—the printed word—provides such aid. We can now consider his proposal: the ego becomes the self—i.e., transcends its egocentricity—through encounter with text.

Part Three: Ego, Text, and Self

Fiction is not an instance of reproductive imagination, but of *productive imagination*...all symbolic systems have a cognitive value: they make reality appear in such and such a way...they *generate* new grids for reading experience or for producing it.[48]

Appropriation is the process by which the revelation of new modes of being...gives the subject new capacities for knowing himself.... Thus appropriation ceases to appear as a new kind of possession....It implies instead a moment of dispossession of the narcissistic ego....I should like to contrast the self which emerges from the understanding of the text to the ego which claims to precede this understanding. It is the text, with its universal power of unveiling, which gives a self to the ego.[49]

My theme in this concluding section is that at this point in human history, the ability to think critically, as nonegocentric selves, is dependent upon the encounter with texts that portray an imagined world—i.e., with literary texts.

A crucial distinction must be stressed at the outset. Just as the previous section proposed that the *form* of television suppresses imagination, and thus opposes the very possibility of critical thinking, my argument here is that the *form* of literary texts supports, and perhaps even fosters, the development of imagination and (therefore) critical thinking. Since this claim is directly dependent upon Paul Ricoeur's theory of text, I offer a summary of that theory and conclude with a brief mention of one endeavor to teach critical thinking from the theoretical basis I propose here, and which derives from his work. Before considering Ricoeur's work, however, I begin with Mander's remarks on the technology of text, in contrast to television.

The persistent theme in Mander's critique of television as a technology is that its very form "implants images" that rule out depth, subtlety, and comparison with actual experience, and it does this all in a manner that "dissociates" and "restructures" those images. Thus, he argues, "discerning" their variation from sequences in the lifeworld, "making distinctions" among them, or "establishing patterns" that transfer reliably to the lifeworld that they purport to represent—in short, all of the actitivies that critical thinking seeks to develop—are discouraged. Instead, "passive" reception of these technologically produced images is encouraged.[50]

One reason for discounting Mander's portrayal, I suspect, is our recognition that *all* of our experience is "artifically reconstructed" by technology. Mander holds that our only choice is between "accepting this interpretation of reality as our own" and rejecting it in favor of "trying to understand the world solely through [our] own isolated mental processes."[51] A third alternative, however, would be to seek, within our technologically formed environment, means that provide *some* assistance in transcending our sociocentric and egocentric context. Mander does note that the printed word, by virtue of its form, offers that possibility:

> print can express much greater depth, complexity, change of mood, subtlety, detail....Books...can be written in much slower rhythms, encouraging a perception that builds, stage by stage, over the length of a long reading process....[52]

As one of Mander's sources noted: "The response to print may be fairly described as active...while the response to television may be fairly described as passive."[53]

Ricoeur's analysis of "response" as the "appropriation" moment of our interaction with printed discourse—text—identifies it as a culminating moment that displaces "narcissistic ego" in favor of an emerging "self." Both the author's and the reader's egos are transcended in this moment:

> The relation to the world of the text takes the place of the relation to the subjectivity of the author, and at the same time the problem of the subjectivity of the reader is *displaced*. To understand is not to project oneself onto the text but to expose oneself to it; it is to receive a self enlarged by the appropriation of proposed worlds which interpretation unfolds.   ...fiction is...a fundamental dimension of the subjectivity of the reader: in reading, I 'unrealize myself.' Reading introduces me to *imaginative variations of the ego.*[54]

In the public space of the proposed (i.e., possible or potential) world "in front of the text," then, we have "a recourse against any given reality and thereby the possibility of a critique of the real."[55] To interact with the possible world of the text is to enlarge "reality" by including "ideality"—i.e., possibilities that transcend time, or are omni-temporally available. When the ego encounters text, then, there is a displacement from a given, actually existing egocentric situation, to a domain of meaning that is always potentially available to anyone who takes up the text, reads, and may thereby become enlightened.[56]

Appropriation of the text's meanings is a process that contrasts quite dramatically to reception of television's images (as in Mander's account), or projection of the ego's worldview (as in Paul's portrayal), or assimilation of the culture's values (as in Angus's critique). In Ricoeur's analysis of the nature of our interaction with text, "appropriation is the dialectical counterpart of distanciation," which is, in turn, "the condition of possibility of understanding oneself in front of the text."[57] This latter feature of the form of text is unique in our present historical situation: neither television's images nor our culture's values are distanciated; i.e., they do not appear to us as objects that are alien to us as subjects. In the case of television, they quite literally come to be within our perceptual processes: "the image doesn't exist in the world."[58] In the case of cultural values, they are incorporated into ends that are assumed (by instrumental reason) to lie outside of reason's proper sphere.

The evidence for Ricoeur's dialectic of appropriation and distanciation is phenomenological: i.e., it is derived from his observations of lived experience. Distanciation as an essential feature (moment) of the reader's encounter with text is documented quite vividly in reports by poetry and literature teachers. They despair, at least at times, of making the *content* of the "great books" accessible to their students. In terms of Ricoeur's analysis: the spatiotemporal distance between the world of those texts and the situations of contemporary students is such that appropriation of the text's world appears to be impossible. Students insist that requiring them to defend their interpretations amounts to denying those "feelings," "intuitions," and "higher consciousness" mentioned by Paul as common alternatives to critical thinking. Or, they refuse to encounter the texts on any level past that of plot synopsis, and that only for purposes of passing an examination. Accepting either result, if we continue to use Paul's terms, would be teaching literature in a "weak sense"; i.e., as an aid to "sophistry" or incentive for "dismissal"—despite the teacher's hope that a "global 'Socratic' effect" (even, enlightenment) would occur.

Ricoeur proposes that distanciation, as a moment (essential feature) of the *form* of text, determines that distance of *content* evidenced by this classroom experience. Both types of distancing can now be understood positively, as part of the "condition of possibility of understanding" both self and world.[59] We have already looked at the nature of appropriation in that way; a correlative look at the nature of distanciation will enable us to focus on a common feature in both moments and—by means of that feature—on the value of literary texts for teaching critical thinking.

Distanciation is Ricoeur's term for the text's presence as a perennially distant and autonomous force—an "atemporal object" that solicits temporal responses.[60] This is not the sort of object that can be possessed; Ricoeur specifically warns us that "appropriation" is not "a new kind of possession."[61] The atemporality of the text—also called omnitemporality and ideality—reinforces its character as alien to us. It has an essentially distant nature that

is the ruin of the ego's pretension to constitute itself as ultimate origin. The ego must assume for itself the 'imaginative variations' by which it could respond to the 'imaginative variations' on reality that literature and poetry, more than any other form of discourse, engender.[62]

In other words: faced with an object that presents alternatives to the "false evidences of everyday reality"—especially its implicit claim to be the *only* possible reality—the reader is pushed to respond to the force of the text from a standpoint other than that reader's everyday reality; i.e., from a standpoint that remains centered upon, but is no longer limited to, the actual ego.[63]

Given the mode of inquiry inculcated by our "scientific age" (operating with instrumental reason), the inevitable question that greets this analysis is: "how"? Ricoeur's response is to direct us toward a capacity, rather than to impose a method (technique):

> Are we not ready to recognize in the power of imagination, no longer the faculty for deriving 'images' from our sensory experience, but the capacity for letting new worlds shape our understanding of ourselves? This power would not be conveyed by images, but by the emergent meanings in our language.[64]

The less-asked question, and the one that moves us beyond instrumental reason, is: "why"? Paul's and Angus's critiques suggest the teleological response to that question: the goal of encountering text is that 'global 'Socratic' effect" called "enlightenment."

The power of the text resides, then, in *ideal* (omni-temporal) meanings that originate beyond the *real* (temporally restricted) situation of the reader. Actualizing or realizing those meanings requires exercise of the "power of imagination," if they are to have significance within the reader's particular situation.[65] Correlatively, readers "unrealize" (so to speak) those particular meanings in their encounter with the text's meanings. Through this process, the egocentricity of both reader and author are transcended.[66] The "ego divests itself of itself," freeing the reader for relocation "beyond the limited horizon of his own existential situation."[67] And this is precisely where he needs to be, Richard Paul argues, if "critical thinking in the 'strong sense'" is to occur.

Not coincidentally, the college within which I teach is developing a conception of teaching literature, critical thinking, and writing in an integrated manner, so that our students and we ourselves can reflect upon our egocentric situations from within the public space—the world—constituted by the text.[68] We would like to reverse the culturally implanted presupposition that books, logic, and composition are things that have a quasi-existence in the classroom, at best.

Our hypothesis is that the way to accomplish that reversal is to thematize the origins of these "things" in, and their applicability to, the

lifeworld of readers, writers, and thinkers. The aim is to integrate philosophy, literature, and composition within the context of the students'
lives, rather than present them as abstract entities to be applied as
techniques or seen as conducive to some form of "higher consciousness"—and thus limited to an inner, egological situation. The multiplicity of interpretations arising from reading texts can be used, in that
integrated context, to thematize the appropriateness of a "logic of
probability" for validation (in contrast to verification) of conflicting
claims as to the nature of reality in the imaginatively constituted world
of the self and the text.[69]

When students enter the writing process, then, we expect them to
do so as selves, rather than as egos (using both of these terms in
Ricoeur's sense). The enlightened position we hope to encourage is
described by Ricoeur as one in which, when "arguing about the meaning
of an action [or a text,] I put my wants and beliefs at a distance and
submit then to a concrete dialectic of confrontation with opposite points
of view."[70] That dialogue of selves within the public sphere established
by text is critical thinking as a force for enlightenment.[71]

Notes

1. Richard Paul, "Teaching Critical Thinking in the 'Strong' Sense: A Focus
on Self-Deception, World Views, and a Dialectical Mode of Analysis," *Informal
Logic Newsletter* 4: 2–7 (May 1982). Hereafter, cited as "Paul."

2.   The most relevant texts would be: for Angus, *Technique and
Enlightenment: Limits of Instrumental Reason* (Washington DC: Center for
Advanced Research in Phenomenology and University Press of America, 1984).
Hereafter, cited as "Angus." For Husserl, *The Crisis of European Sciences and
Transcendental Phenomenology*, trans. D. Carr (Evanston, Ill.: Northwestern
University Press, 1970) and *Formal and Transcendental Logic*, trans. D. Cairns (The
Hague: Nijhoff, 1969). For Critical Theory, Max Horkheimer and Theodor W.
Adorno, *Dialectic of Enlightenment*, trans. J. Cumming (New York: Herder and
Herder, 1972) and Max Horkheimer, "Traditional and Critical Theory," in
Critical Theory, trans. M. O'Connell et al. (New York: Herder and Herder, 1972).

3. The most relevant text would be: Paul Ricoeur, *Hermeneutics and the
Human Sciences: Essays on Language, Action, and Interpretation*, trans. J. B.
Thompson (Cambridge, Eng.: Cambridge University Press, 1981). Hereafter,
cited as "Ricoeur." For a discussion of egocentricity as inevitable but
transcendable, see my "Egocentricity: What it is and Why it Matters," presented
at the Fourth International Conference on Critical Thinking and Educational
Reform, Sonoma State University, August 1986.

4. Angus, 94 (my emphasis).

5. Paul, 3.

6. As he notes (in his footnote 24, p. 12), "while it is legitimate to attribute the term 'instrumental reason' to Horkheimer, it is by no means his favored one." The term is quite generally in the Frankfurt School tradition; Angus's correlative term, "judgment," is equally common in the Kantian and Husserlian traditions.

7. Angus, 17.

8. Angus, 56, 67, 121, 135–37, 140–41. Although Angus's analysis denies the possibility of any such grounding, Husserl's places any such claim "under the epoche." That is, the possibility is not denied, but it is rigorously removed from consideration.

9. Angus, 4; cf. 12, 48, 51, 85.

10. This phrase is used throughout Angus's book to refer to the historical effect of "universalized instrumental reason."

11. Paul, 3.

12. Paul, 2.

13. Angus, 19.

14. These "translations" between Marxian and Husserlian vocabularies are accurate, I would argue; but that argument cannot be given here. I use them *as if* they were unproblematic, for heuristic purposes: i.e., to stress the convergence between some strands of neo-marxist analysis (such as Critical Theory) and Husserlian phenomenological analysis. Also, I use them to reinforce the reciprocity of evidence Angus finds in Husserl's analysis of lived experience as the origin and telos of ideal structures (theoretical entities), and neo-marxian (even, perhaps, Marx's) analysis of economic base and ideological superstructure.

15. Angus, 56; cf. footnote 8.

16. Angus, 33.

17. Angus, 20.

18. Angus, 93.

19. Angus, 126–27 (my emphasis).

20. Angus, 125. This accessibility of objects as both presented in individual, immediate experience and represented in systems is a major difference between Husserl's analysis and those semiotic and hermeneutic traditions that hold that we have access only to objects as constituted by system. For these latter traditions, our reflection can only capture experience as already limited by

systems (and so, informed by theory and history); it cannot also encounter immediately present facets of a pretheoretical lifeworld.

21. Angus, 142–43 (my emphasis).

22. Paul, 3–4 (my emphasis).

23. Paul, 5 (my emphasis).

24. Paul, 5. In keeping with the persistently self-critical character stressed in the notion of judgment, I would note that the instructions (given to the students who are to analyze the "incompatible world views" represented in these films) are heavy with cultural assumptions. Paul characterizes the two positions as "a right-wing think-tank alleging..." and a "World Council of Church's [sic] film in defense..." (Paul, 6).

25. Paul, 4.

26. Paul, 5.

27. Angus, 143 (quoted in context in the quotation identified in footnote 21). In Husserlian terms, this step would be the "transcendental reduction"; i.e., the focus on "any subjectivity whatever" or on the very possibility of reasoning—rather than on any particular, individual reasoning process.

28. Angus, 143.

29. Paul, 7.

30. Hannah Arendt, *The Life of the Mind*, Vol. 2 (New York: Harcourt, 1978), 257 (my emphasis). Quoted by Angus (p. 107).

31. Jerry Mander, *Four Arguments for the Elimination of Television* (New York: Quill, 1978), 200-201 (my emphasis). Hereafter cited as "Mander."

32. Mander, 310, 350.

33. Mander, 204 (my emphasis).

34. Angus, 105; see footnote 20 and accompanying text for "representation." The enclosed quotation is from Immanuel Kant, *Critique of Judgment*, trans. J. H. Barnard (New York: Collier Macmillan, 1974), 15. The suggestion arising even from this very brief treatment of the connection between the subject's use of imagination to transcend "ego" in a movement toward "self"— as prerequisite for the practice of critical thinking/judgment—is that "pure reason" may be dependent upon "judgment." (That is: the First Critique may be grounded in the Third.) Obviously, this is a proposition requiring consideration in a very different essay, which must also consider the connections and discrepancies between Kant's use of "imagination" and the term as used by Angus, Arendt, Mander, Paul, and Ricoeur.

36. Paul, 3.

37. Paul, 4–5 (my emphasis).

38. Paul, 6. Although the two films are the primary sources of information for these imaginative constructions, Paul notes that they are supplemented by a variety of sensory stimulation and include the reading of texts. Furthermore, Mander argues that film technology, although it makes use of some of the same surface techniques as television (e.g., high-contrast scenes and a predominance of close-ups) is not as restricted to them; nor does the film rely on the same neurophysiological techniques (e.g., projection of "non-existent" images).

39. Mander, 209.

40. Mander, 276 (my emphasis).

41. Mander, 168 (my emphasis).

42. Mander, 291.

43. Mander, 198.

44. Mander, 300.

45. Mander, 254. He identifies the report as *Television and Social Behavior*, Vol. 4, "prepared by the National Institute of Mental Health for the Department of Health, Education, and Welfare."

46. These phrases from Arendt are quoted in context at the start of this section.

47. Paul, 3.

48. Ricoeur, 292–93 (my emphasis). Ricoeur notes that he is using Nelson Goodman's term, "symbolic systems," interchangeably with "fiction."

49. Ricoeur, 192–93 (author's emphasis).

50. The terms in quotation marks are from Mander, 132–33, 197–98, 200–201, 300; all are quoted in context elsewhere in the text.

51. Mander, 87.

52. Mander, 336; cf. 202–3.

53. Mander, 208; quoting Herbert Krugman.

54. Ricoeur, 94 (my emphasis); cf. 188 and footnote 35.

55. Ricoeur, 93 (my emphasis); cf. 142–43.

56. Ricoeur, 192. My allusion is to St. Augustine's account of his conversion (*Confessions*, Books Eight and Nine). Translated into the vocabulary of this paper: after years of wandering in civilization as an ego, he encounters a text that instigates the replacement of ego with self and retires to the countryside to integrate this transformation. The public manifestation of this private enlightenment is a change of occupation: he resigns his rhetoric professorship and takes Holy Orders.

57. Ricoeur, 92.

58. Mander, 201; quoted in context at the start of Part Two.

59. Ricoeur, 94.

60. Ricoeur, 185.

61. Ricoeur, 192; quoted in context at the start of Part Three.

62. Ricoeur, 113–14 (author's emphasis).

63. Ricoeur, 113.

64. Ricoeur, 181.

65. I follow E. D. Hirsch, Jr. in using "meaning" and "significance" in this way, to differentiate the world-of-the-text from the enlarged world-of-the-subject who appropriates that text. See, e.g., *Validity in Interpretation* (New Haven, Conn.: Yale University Press, 1967), and *The Aims of Interpretation* (Chicago: The University of Chicago Press, 1976), 1–6.

66. Ricoeur, 94. The *dialectical* nature of this process must be stressed. In Hegelian terms: the ego externalizes itself in an objective moment (the text) that originates beyond ego and resists ego's attempt to reduce the text to its own projection. Yet in being understood, sublation (*die Aufhebung*) occurs: self, as the unification of subject (reader) and object (text) comes into being.

This essential persistence of the text as a perennially available moment of objectivity is crucial to Ricoeur's text theory, and thus, to the conception of enlightenment I propose with that theory as basis. As a structural feature that insists upon the availability of objective meaning, it provides a sharp contrast to that variant of the "power of imagination," which I would call the "power of deconstruction," as originated by Jacques Derrida.

By discouraging passivity toward the text, deconstruction provides a force against the ingestion of any system that would limit an ego to instrumental reason, i.e., render it incapable of judging beyond established, "given," means-ends complexes. Thus, deconstruction seems to use the distanciation moment (or move) in Ricoeur's dialectic, perhaps even to the point of the disappearance of the subject(s) (the author and/or reader) as well as the object (the text) into an all-encompassing process: the technique called deconstruction.

However, insofar as deconstruction as a technique does reach that point, it is incapable of practicing the appropriation moment in Ricoeur's dialectic. For it has brought about the destruction of the text as an objective resource, i.e., as an omni-temporal meaning, potentially available for an infinitude of actualizations by subjects who read it. In other words, the ego, in *explaining* the text as a humanly created *process*, had *explained away* the text as objective *ideality*. As a result, there is no nonegocentric world to appropriate in understanding as the new, imaginatively constructed locus for constituting a self. The ultimate result is then limitation to technique (the deconstructive process) and the reversal of enlightenment (by eliminating the conditions for the possibility of constituting self and world).

There is another way to look at the deconstructing process that also results in the frustration of Ricoeur's dialectic. This occurs if the process is understood as originating in the ego, rather than in the encounter with the text. Ricoeur's critique of the subjectivizing tendency, which he finds beginning in Descartes and continuing into Gadamer, then becomes relevant. (See Ricoeur, 190–92, 66–68) The process begins and ends with ego; deprived of object (text) as the external moment to be encountered, self cannot emerge: there is no opportunity to "exchange the me, master of itself, for the self, disciple of the text." (Ricoeur, 113; cf. G. W. F. Hegel, *The Phenomenology of Spirit*, Section B.4.A.)

67. Ricoeur, 191.

68. The project, titled "CACTIP: Composition, Analysis of Text, Critical Thinking Integrated Program," has been funded by the Division of Educational Programs, National Endowment for the Humanities, for implementation June 1985–May 1987.

69. Ricoeur, 211–13; cf. 175. Ricoeur mentions his reliance upon Hirsch's theory of text here; see footnote 65.

70. Ricoeur, 214.

71. This paper was presented at the Third International Conference on Critical Thinking and Educational Reform, Sonoma State University, July 1985. An earlier version was read at the APA Pacific Division meeting in San Francisco, March 1985. I would like to thank Harold Alderman for his thoughtful and detailed comments on that paper. Briefer versions of this paper (which present Section Two in a self-contained form) were read at the AILACT session, APA Eastern Division meeting in Washington, D.C., December 1985; Christopher Newport College Conference on Critical Thinking, April 1986; and the International Conference on Argumentation in Amsterdam, June 1986. I would like to acknowledge an especially extensive debt to these colleagues, students, and teachers with whom I've discussed various parts of the paper in its several versions: Ian Angus, Ron Bloomquist, Dennis Danvers, Jacques Derrida, Ralph Johnson, Robert E. Longacre, Tom McCormick, Nancy McKenzie, Richard Paul, Susan Lynn Peterson, Kenneth L. Pike, Thomas E. Porter, Harry Reeder, and Paul Ricoeur.

Contributors

Peter Elbow is Professor of English at the University of Massachusetts at Amherst. He has written three books about writing: *Writing Without Teachers, Writing With Power: Techniques for Mastering the Writing Process*, and *A Community of Writers* (a textbook). He is author of a book of essays about learning and teaching: *Embracing Contraries*. He has also written *Oppositions in Chaucer*, as well as numerous essays about writing and teaching. His most recent book, *What is English?*, explores current issues in the profession of English.

He won the Richard Braddock award in 1986 for his essay "The Shifting Relationships Between Speech and Writing" (in Conference on College Composition and Communication 36.2 [October 1985]).

He has taught at M.I.T., Franconia College, Evergreen State College, and SUNY Stony Brook, where for five years he directed the Writing Program. He served for four years on the Executive Council of the Modern Language Association. He has given talks and workshops at many colleges and universities.

His current interest is in the concept of voice in writing and the role of the body in learning and thinking and writing.

Blythe McVicker Clincy is Professor of Psychology at Wellesley College, where she holds the Class of 1949 Chair in Ethics and teaches courses in research methodology and in child and adult development. She received her A.B. from Smith College, her M.A. from the New School for Social Research, and her Ph.D. from Harvard University. She is coauthor, with Mary Belenky, Nancy Goldberger, and Jill Tarule, of *Women's Ways of Knowing*, published by Basic Books in 1986. She has also published papers on the evolution of conceptions of knowledge, truth, and value in males and females from early childhood through adulthood and the implications of this development for the practice of education from nursery school through college.

Delores Gallo is Associate Professor in the Critical and Creative Thinking Graduate Program (which she codesigned and cofounded in 1976) at the University of Massachusetts at Boston. Prior to receiving her Ph.D. from the Harvard Graduate School of Education, she was an

English teacher in the Brooklyn inner city high school she herself had attended. It was there that she became interested in teacher education and its impact on urban schools. Upon taking a position at the University of Massachusetts after her graduate studies, she designed and directed for ten years an innovative, undergraduate elementary school preservice teacher education program that anticipated many of the recommendations of current education reports such as the Carnegie and Holmes ones. She currently oversees the Literature and Arts Specialty Area in UMass' interdisciplinary Master of Arts Program in Critical and Creative Thinking. She also serves on doctoral committees in the Creative Studies Doctoral Program at University of Massachusetts–Amherst Graduate School of Education and is a consultant to schools on ways to integrate critical thinking and creative problem solving into subject matter instruction.

Two of her articles have been anthologized in prior collections: "Educating for Creativity" appeared in *Thinking: The Expanding Frontier* (Franklin Institute Press, 1983), and the invited chapter "Think Metric" appeared in *Thinking Skills Instruction* (NEA, 1987).

Kerry S. Walters is Associate Professor of Philosophy at Gettysburg College. He received his graduate degrees from Marquette University and the University of Cincinnati. The author of four books and over forty articles and reviews, his interests besides critical thinking include American intellectual history and philosophy of religion.

Anne M. Phelan is Assistant Professor in the Department of Curriculum and Instruction at the University of Hawaii at Manoa. She writes and conducts research in the areas of curriculum and teacher education. Currently, her research explores how students and teachers of different social and cultural backgrounds construct a sense of themselves in relation to school cultures. She is a full-time faculty member in a school-based, inquiry-oriented teacher education program, the result of a joint venture of the Hawaii School–University Partnership. HSUP is a member of the National Network for Educational Renewal, which was founded under the direction of Dr. John I. Goodlad.

James W. Garrison holds undergraduate degrees in psychology and physics, a masters in humanities, and a doctorate in philosophy, all from Florida State University. He spent two years of postgraduate work as a junior investigator on a National Science Foundation grant to study erotetic logic, the logic of questions and answers. He joined the faculty of Virgina Polytechnic and State University's College of Education in 1985, where he now holds the rank of professor. His specialties are the philosophy of education, history of science, the philosophy of science, and mathematical logic. He has published over seventy academic papers and a book on topics within his specialization, and is currently working on a book-length manuscript on John Dewey's social behaviorism and theory of meaning.

John E. McPeck is Professor of Education at the University of Western Ontario, and specializes in philosophy of education. He is the author of *Critical Thinking and Education* (St. Martin's Press, 1981), and *Teaching Critical Thinking: Dialogue and Dialectic* (Routledge, 1990).

Connie Missimer is the author of *Good Arguments: An Introduction to Critical Thinking* (Prentice-Hall), now in its second edition. She was chair of the Philosophy Department at Los Medanos College from 1974–1985. Besides the article that appears in this book, she has published on the danger of accusing another person of stereotyping rather than requesting evidence for that person's assertion (*Proceedings of the Second International Conference on Argumentation*, Amsterdam, 1990). She also has argued, based on historical evidence about acknowledged great thinkers, that one does not need a specific character to do critical thinking (*Informal Logic*, Fall, 1990). She is working on theoretical assumptions underlying current theories of critical thinking. Besides workshops in critical thinking for college faculties, she conducts seminars in thinking strategies at corporations. Professor Missimer holds an M.A. in philosophical piterature from University of California at Berkeley. She lives in Seattle with her husband and daughter.

Karl Hostetler is Assistant Professor in Teachers College, University of Nebraska–Lincoln. He received an undergraduate degree in chemistry from Dartmouth College in 1976 before going on to earn a Master of Arts in Teaching from Northwestern University. After completing work at Northwestern, he taught third grade and mathematics in grades 6 through 8 in the Chicago area, thereby entering a profession he'd sworn never to enter, having observed firsthand his father's frustrations as a career teacher.

From 1981 to 1983, he taught mathematics in an English-language school in Venezuela. At the end of this time, he entered the doctoral program in philosophy of education at Teachers College, Columbia University. He completed his Ph.D. in 1987 and joined the faculty of University of Nebraska–Lincoln that same year.

Karen J. Warren is Associate Professor of Philosophy at Macalester College in St. Paul, Minnesota. She has published articles in ethics, environmental ethics, feminism (particularly ecological feminism), and critical thinking. Over the past twenty years she has taught, conducted workshops, and developed curricular materials on philosophy, critical thinking, and environmental ethics for teachers and students in a variety of settings: colleges and universities, continuing education programs, grades K–12, and a federal prison. She guest edited the first anthology on ecofeminist philosophy, a Special Issue of *Hypatia: A Feminist Journal of Philosophy* (6.1: 1991), is editing a second anthology on ecofeminist philosophy for Routledge Press as part of their Environmental Philosophies Series, and is completing a book coauthored with philosopher Jim Cheney titled *Ecological Feminism: A Philosophical Perspective on What It Is and Why It Matters* (Westview). She is the special editor of the ecofeminism section of an environmental philosophies textbook published in 1992 by Prentice-Hall and has guest edited three special issues of the American Philosophical Association *Newsletter on Feminism and Philosophy*: an issue on "Gender, Reason, and Rationality" (88.2: 1989) and two issues on "Feminism and the Environment" (Fall, 1991 and Spring, 1992). Other works-in-progress include special issues on feminism and peace, which she and philosopher Duane Cady are guest editing, one for *Hypatia* (1994) and the other for the APA *Newsletter on Feminism and Philosophy* (1994).

Richard W. Paul, Director of the Center for Critical Thinking, and Chair of the National Council for Excellence in Critical Thinking Instruction, is widely recognized as a major leader in the national and international critical thinking movements. He has published over forty articles and five books on critical thinking in the last five years. He has written books on how to foster critical thinking at every grade level (K–3, 4–6, 6–9, high school, and university). He has regularly taught courses in critical thinking, advanced critical thinking, and theory of critical thinking, for the last 14 years. He has given hundreds of workshops at the K–12 level and made a series of eight critical thinking video programs for PBS. His views on critical thinking have been canvassed in The *New York Times, Education Week, The Chronicle of Higher Education, American Teacher, Educational Leadership, Newsweek, U.S. News & World Report*, and *Reader's Digest*. Besides publishing extensively in the field, he has organized two national and nine international conferences on critical thinking. He has given invited lectures at many universities and colleges, including Harvard, University of Chicago, University of Illinois, the University of Amsterdam, and the Universities of Puerto Rico and Costa Rica, as well as workshops and lectures on critical thinking in every region of the United States. He has been active in helping to develop the concept of critical thinking used to design tests in critical thinking (K–12) by the State Department of Education in California and is working with Edward M. Glaser in revising the Watson-Glaser Critical Thinking test. Working with Gerald Nosich, he has developed a model for the national assessment of critical thinking at the postsecondary level for the U.S. Department of Education.

Professor Paul has been the recipient of numerous honors and awards, including "Distinguished Philosopher" (by the Council for Philosophical Studies, 1987), O. C. Tanner Lecturer in Humanities (by Utah State University, 1986), Lansdowne Visiting Scholar (by the University of Victoria, 1987), and the Alfred Korsybski Memorial Lecturer (by the Institute for General Semantics, 1987). He is actively sought as a keynote speaker and staff development leader.

Henry A. Giroux holds the Waterbury Chair in Secondary Education at the Pennsylvania State University. He is a former high school teacher from Rhode Island, and his work on critical pedagogy is internationally renowned. He is the winner of numerous awards for his writings on liberatory education and is an active international speaker. His most recent book is Border Crossings.

Laura Duhan Kaplan is Assistant Professor of Philosophy and Adjunct Assistant Professor of Women's Studies at the University of North Carolina at Charlotte. She graduated from Brandeis University with a major in philosophy in 1980 and received an M.Ed. from Cambridge College in 1983 and a Ph.D. in philosophy and education from the Claremont Graduate School in 1991. Her first teaching experiences were at California community colleges. Of the articles she has published, her favorites are "Teaching Intellectual Autonomy: The Failure of the Critical Thinking Movement," in this volume, and "The Philosopher as Hero," *Teaching Philosophy*, 1990. She is currently coediting a volume titled *In the Eye of the Storm: Philosophers Examine Nationalism and Militarism in Regional Conflicts*. Her philosophical specialties are Philosophy of Education and Philosophy of Feminism, although she is also interested in continental philosophy, especially hermeneutics. She often wonders why she did not choose a career as an artist instead of an intellectual, as she enjoys dancing, painting, and writing poetry. Of the poetic pieces she's written, her favorites are "Truth and Experience or the Beagle's Tail," American Atheist, 1986, and "I Wouldn't Hurt a Flea," *Concerned Philosophers for Peace Newsletter*, 1992.

Thomas H. Warren received his B.A. from University of Californai at Berkeley (1961), and his Ph.D. from University of California at Santa

Barbara (1973). Both were in political science, with an emphasis in political theory and philosophy. He now teaches philosophy at Solano College in California. His principal interests are in moral and political philosophy and the philosophy of mind. His most recent publications are in the *Journal of the History of Philosophy* and *Philosophy of Education: Proceedings*. He currently is exploring the connections between thinking and moral understanding.

Lenore Langsdorf received a Ph.D. from SUNY Stony Brook in 1977 and is now Associate Professor in the Speech Communication Department at Southern Illinois University. Her research is centered in argumentation, cultural, and rhetorical theory. The orientation is hermeneutic phenomenology, strongly influenced by American pragmatic and process philosophy.

Professor Langsdorf is coeditor of two forthcoming volumes: *The Critical Turn: Philosophy and Rhetoric in Postmodern Discourse* (with Ian H. Angus) and *Recovering Pragmatism's Voice: The Classical Tradition, Rorty, and the Philosophy of Communication* (with Andrew R. Smith). She has written numerous essays on phenomenological issues and on the philosophy of communication in everyday life and is completing a book titled *Media as Embodiment of Rationality: An Essay in the Praxiology of Communication*.

Index